Dear Reader:

Some crime cases continue to haunt us long after the jury has returned its verdict. Violent in the extreme, the St. Pierre case is one of the most powerful of all.

Domineerindited ex-Marine Paul S hington, where he ran r er, Chris, and lived a life e. Paul's best friend, An ociopath from a dysfunct molestation were tragic aspects of family history. Young Chris St. Pierre watched in horror as Andrew and Paul committed cold-blooded murder, and kept the severed head of one of their victims in a bucket on the back porch.

When Chris finally revealed all to Detective Yerbury of the Tacoma Police Department, all three were charged with first degree murder. What began as a story of murder and madness became a legal thriller so shocking that one judge declared a mistrial, and another became so outraged at the prosecutor that he stormed out of the courtroom.

In this newly updated edition of *Head Shot*, Edgar-award-winning author Burl Barer provides new information and insights on this case and the two surviving convicted killers—who, released from prison, recently attended their high school reunion.

Already hailed by experts, reviewers, and readers, *Head Shot* will enthrall and amaze you. Sit back and enjoy a fascinating story, told by one of American's finest investigative journalists.

If you would like to comment on *Head Shot*, we'd love to hear from you at marketing@kensingtonbooks.com.

Don't miss Burl Barer's other real-life crime thrillers, available from Pinnacle!

With my best wishes,

Michaela Hamilton

Michaela Hamilton
Executive Editor, Pinnacle True Crime

HEAD SHOT

Burl Barer

PINNACLE BOOKS
Kensington Publishing Corp.

http://www.pinnaclebooks.com

Some names have been changed to protect the privacy of individuals connected to this story.

PINNACLE BOOKS are published by

Kensington Publishing Corp.
119 West 40th Street
New York, NY 10018

All Kensington Titles, Imprints, and Distributed Lines are available at special quantity discounts for bulk purchases for sales promotion, premiums, fund-raising, and educational or institutional use. Special book excerpts or customized printings can also be created to fit specific needs. For details, write or phone the office of the Kensington special sales manager: Kensington Publishing Corp., 119 West 40th Street, New York, NY 10018, attn: Special Sales Department, Phone: 1-800-221-2647.

Pinnacle and the P logo Reg. U.S. Pat. & TM Off.

ISBN-13: 978-0-7860-2924-2
ISBN-10: 0-7860-2924-2

First Printing: October 2001
10 9 8 7 6 5 4

Printed in the United States of America

Whensoever a mother seeth that her child hath done well, let her praise and applaud him and cheer his heart; and if the slightest undesirable trait should manifest itself, let her counsel the child and punish him, and use means based on reason, even a slight verbal chastisement should this be necessary. It is not, however, permissible to strike a child, or vilify him, for the child's character will be totally perverted if he be subjected to blows or verbal abuse.

—'Abdu'l-Bahá, *Selections from the Writings of 'Abdu'l-Bahá*

As the breeze blows, the slender trees yield.
Today, you will see two souls
apparently in close friendship;
Tomorrow, all this may be changed.

—'Abdu'l-Bahá, *Paris Talks*

Prologue

The headless corpse of twenty-two-year-old John Achord and the faceless remains of twenty-year-old Damon Wells were recovered from shallow graves near Elbe, Washington, on June 19, 1984. Christopher St. Pierre, twenty-one, directed authorities to the severely decomposed bodies after telling Tacoma Police shocking details of their violent deaths, subsequent secret burials, and the ghoulish premeditated decapitation. Prior to these disclosures by St. Pierre, no one even knew that Achord and Wells were dead.

Most important, Christopher St. Pierre identified the killers. He named names and revealed all. The first shared name was that of mentally diminished and alcoholic Paul St. Pierre, his own brother; the second was a longtime friend and neighbor—tall, handsome, brain-damaged, and violent twenty-four-year-old Andrew Webb.

"Andrew Webb was my high school sweetheart, and I spent, or wasted, more than fifteen years married to him," said his ex-wife, Anne. "At first, I thought I was the luckiest girl in the world. That didn't last long. If you want an example of typical Andrew Webb behavior, ask Nellie Sanford and her children about their 1983 night of living hell."

PART ONE

One

July 5, 1983

Nellie Sanford, forty-five, and her son Shane Sanford, eighteen, were awakened at 3:50 A.M. by incessant pounding on their back door. Mrs. Sanford was first to reach the rear vestibule; Shane stood behind her as she nervously inquired through the locked door, "Who is it?"

"Joe," was the mumbled reply. Curious, Mrs. Sanford cautiously unlocked the door, eased it open only an inch or two, and peered through the crack. "Who's there?"

This time, the reply was loud and clear. Two drunken men violently pushed open the door and forced their way into the house. One was twenty-three-year-old Andrew Webb; the other, his longtime friend and neighbor, Randy Nolan. Both men were armed with rifles and shotguns, which they now pointed directly at Nellie and Shane Sanford. Mrs. Sanford, by motherly instinct or raw nerve, immediately went on the attack. She grabbed Nolan's shotgun, furiously trying to wrestle it from him. Shane jumped to his mother's aid, but Webb beat him with the rifle butt, striking him repeatedly on the arms and shoulders.

The chaotic melee's screaming, swearing, and shouting was soon punctuated by an explosive gunshot. A bullet accidentally discharged from Webb's rifle blasted through the ceiling, pierced a bedroom door on the second floor, and buried itself somewhere in an adjoining bedroom. Sleeping in those bedrooms were Mrs. Sanford's fourteen-year-old daughter, sixteen-year-old son, and a fourteen-year-old houseguest, Dennie Mason. Woken by the screams, they were terrified by the gunshot. It also drew the attention of Tacoma Police patrol officers Bahr and Troxel.

Originally dispatched to that part of town to respond to an excessive noise complaint—someone's car stereo was disturbing the peace—the officers encountered what sounded like an explosion on the 2200 block of South Railroad Street. Officer Bahr, driving the patrol car in the opposite direction, pulled an immediate U-turn.

The officers didn't see smoke, flames, or airborne debris. A hysterical fourteen-year-old girl was screaming on a rooftop, "They've got guns! They're going to kill us all!" While she screamed, a teenage boy crawled out a second-story bedroom window. "He dropped about twenty feet to the pavement and then ran directly to our vehicle," Officer Bahr later reported. "He was very upset, and he was repeating over and over, 'They're in the house; they're going to shoot us; they have guns.' " Bahr and Troxel called for backup just as an angry blast of profanities erupted in a male voice from that same bedroom window. "Officer Bahr took a position of cover on the west side of the home, where he could see into the room where the subjects were located," Troxel later reported. "I took cover at the southwest corner of the house, where the front and west side of the home could be seen."

From behind a tree about twenty feet west of the open upstairs window, Bahr watched as Andrew Webb repeatedly struck Shane Sanford and then shoved a rifle barrel into the defenseless teen's mouth. "You motherfucker," Webb yelled, his voice a drunken slur, "tell me where the guns are or I'll blow your fucking head off!"

The terrified Sanford begged for his life. "Please, please don't kill me! Don't shoot me! Don't shoot me!"

Officer Bahr decided that the situation necessitated shooting Andrew Webb.

"I had my revolver drawn and I was taking careful aim," Bahr reported. "Then Nolan entered the room, Webb slapped Sanford across the face, and Nolan pressed his shotgun against the terrified teenager's chest and said, 'Tell me where the guns are, or I'll kill you.' "

Officer Bahr aimed directly at Webb—his target perfectly framed in the bedroom window. As Bahr applied pressure to the trigger, the window shade suddenly fell across his line of sight. With a clear shot no longer possible, Bahr holstered his revolver, quickly returned to his vehicle, grabbed a shotgun, and dashed back to cover. "Then I heard noise at the back of the house. The suspects were making a run for it." Additional police officers arrived at the exact moment the two heavily armed intruders ran out the back door, attempting their getaway.

"Police! Freeze! Drop your guns!" Nolan dropped his shotgun and flopped to the ground, docile and compliant. Webb ran off, discarding his weapons and shoulder holster as he burrowed into nearby blackberry bushes. After twenty feet, he crouched down and awaited the inevitable. He didn't have to wait long.

Both intruders now detained, Tacoma Police confiscated an impressive collection of deadly weapons, including a shotgun, .44-caliber handgun, .22-caliber long rifle with chrome-plated wood stock, and Webb's .357 Ruger.

"Andrew Keith Webb cheated death on the first day after the Fourth of July, 1983," Detective Robert Yerbury of the Tacoma Police Department commented several years later. "If the upstairs window shade hadn't dropped, it would have been curtains for sure. That wasn't the first time Andrew Webb cheated death, and it wasn't the last."

It also wasn't the first time Andrew Webb, loving husband, father, and employee of Royal Donuts, had attacked the Sanford residence. This was Webb's third armed assault since January. In March, Webb and unknown accomplices, armed with guns and a baseball bat, had stormed into the Tacoma home of Thomas Shannon and Richard Daylo. "Again, they were yelling about missing guns," explained Yerbury. "Webb's accomplices hit Mr. Shannon across the knuckles ten or twelve times with the baseball bat, and then Andrew Webb grabbed Mr. Shannon by the hair and punched him in the head. Webb, and whoever was with him, left that house and immediately went to the Sanford residence, crashed in with the same method—pistol and baseball bats—and ransacked that house again looking for missing guns."

"We were at a loss as to who committed those two assaults on the same day in March, and we didn't have any lead as to the identity of the assailants. Mr. Webb took care of that when Nolan and he were arrested at the Sanfords'. We had three incidents—two on March third, and one on July fifth—where an armed Andrew Webb entered a house claiming things have been stolen from him. He admitted to all three assaults, but refused to say who was with him on those first two."

Many of the boys who grew up in the same neighborhood with Webb and Nolan could have named the men most likely to have accompanied Webb on a mission of that nature. Andrew Webb had friends he could count on—Cory Cunningham and Paul St. Pierre. "Paul St. Pierre and Andrew were good buddies, although Cory and Andrew were superclose since childhood, all of them had known each other for years," recalled Webb's former wife, Anne. "Andrew even lived with Paul St. Pierre for a while after I kicked him out. But the kind of friendship shared by Paul and Andrew was based mostly on drinking, taking drugs, and playing tough with guns—not a very firm foundation for true emotional intimacy. Anyway, almost a year after the Sanford incident, Paul hauled off and shot Andrew point-blank with a forty-five automatic. Andrew survived, but their relationship never recovered."

Neither, some say, did the city of Tacoma. The fallout of Webb and St. Pierre precipitated an avalanche of disturbing accusations, conflicting confessions, and shocking revelations of death and dismemberment.

"Everything started crashing down," recalled Detective Yerbury, "at precisely eight fifty-two, Saturday morning, June 9, 1984, with a single gunshot followed by a frantic phone call."

June 9, 1984, 8:52 A.M.

Helen Lorentzon, morning waitress at Ray and Gene's Tavern on Tacoma's Pacific Avenue, looked up when she heard the front door open. Standing in the doorway was an agitated and obviously inebriated young man in his early twenties. His light brown hair was badly disheveled, and his blue jeans and plaid shirt were liberally blotched with blood.

"Call the cops," he blurted out. "Someone's been shot!" He pointed down the street toward Ericson's Auto Body. "There! The house across the alley from Ericson's. He's bleeding real bad."

Lorentzon dialed 911 and summoned the police. The bloodstained man took the phone from Lorentzon, identified himself as Jim Mullins, and insisted that the cops "step on it." Then, with the same speed as he had entered, Mullins ran away.

"Officer Boik and I arrived at the tavern almost immediately," said Officer Lowry in his official report. "We had no information other than that someone called from Ray and Gene's and that there had been a shooting."

As the squad car pulled up, Lorentzon ran out. By 8:55 A.M., the responding officers and several others dispatched as backup had arrived at Ericson's. "Between the body shop and the first house south, I saw three men apparently attempting to enter a parked Dodge Challenger," Boik reported. "These men were later identified as the suspect Paul St. Pierre, the witness Kevin Wiggins, and the victim Andrew Webb. It appeared as if St. Pierre and Wiggins were trying to help Webb inside the vehicle. I could see that Webb was in pain, and his clothes were covered with blood."

Police approached with guns drawn, ordering the men to freeze and put their hands above their heads. St. Pierre let go of Webb and tossed his car keys toward the police. Kevin Wiggins obediently placed his hands above his head and stepped aside from his blood-drenched companion. Released from all support, the seriously wounded Andrew Webb fell backward into the dirt. Detective Yerbury later commented. "Andrew Webb, despite being shot at close range with a forty-five automatic, cheated death."

Lowry ran over to Webb and immediately noticed

the wound's seriousness. "It was a bullet entrance wound in the right side of the chest, and an exit wound on the left back side of his abdomen. He didn't say anything to me. The fire department arrived on the scene and immediately began to treat Mr. Webb."

Boik repeatedly told the apparently drunken Wiggins and St. Pierre to keep their hands up and away from their bodies. Paul St. Pierre repeatedly brought his hands down. "I finally told him to place his hands on the hood of the car," recalled Boik. "I attempted to do a pat-down search but he was very uncooperative. I noticed a long, hard object in St. Pierre's left rear pants pocket. It was a black magazine for a forty-five-caliber gun, loaded with at least five fully jacketed forty-five-caliber ball ammunition."

Paul St. Pierre resisted and tried to pull away. Officer Lowry, coming over to assist, saw that St. Pierre was continually pulling his black T-shirt over the front of his jeans.

"I lifted up the shirt," reported Lowry, "and saw the brown leather holster clipped to his jeans. We took it into evidence, and Boik handcuffed St. Pierre, who refused to tell us anything." He also refused to provide his true name—he told them he was Chris St. Pierre, his brother.

Kevin Wiggins was no more helpful and kept violently throwing his arms around. The officers calmed Wiggins's windmill-like extremities by handcuffing him and stuffing him in the back of a squad car.

"We still had no idea what had happened," said Lowry. "We didn't know who, or how many, were involved. Officer Langford positioned himself at the back of the residence while I entered through the front. I wanted to make sure that there were no other victims or assailants." Lowry noted several blood splatters on the porch and an exceptionally large pool of fresh blood on the kitchen floor. "There was also a fresh bullet hole in the refrigerator door," he noted in his official report, "and on the floor, away from the blood, was a forty-five shell casing."

While the ambulance transported the near-death Webb to the hospital, the drunken Paul St. Pierre and Kevin Wiggins were retained in separate squad cars for individual questioning. Tacoma detective Robert Yerbury, who handled the inquiry, arrived within twenty minutes of the initial call.

"I already knew both Paul St. Pierre and Andrew Webb," Yerbury said years later. "The first time I met them was several months earlier. Andrew Webb was with Paul St. Pierre when there was a violent altercation at a grocery store during which Paul St. Pierre shot and wounded a man named Kevin Robinson. We investigated the matter and determined that Paul St. Pierre acted in self-defense, and no charges were pressed. Andrew Webb and I, of course, saw each other again when he was arrested after his assault on the Sanfords."

Detective Yerbury was also aware that Paul St. Pierre shared the house on Pacific Avenue with several roommates: Donald Marshall, Mark Perez, Tony Youso, and Paul's younger brother, Christopher St. Pierre. Andrew Webb, recently separated from his wife and child, had also lived there for a while.

"It was Chris who rented the house in the first place," said Yerbury. "He worked next door at Ericson's, and it was Mark Ericson's dad who owned the rental house. When I got the call telling me the address, I knew exactly whose house we were going to."

A two-story brown wood-frame dwelling almost completely obscured by large bushes, the essentially good quality rental didn't look its best under the St. Pierres' care. The unkempt lawn, perhaps mirroring the na-

ture of its recalcitrant caretakers, was high, weed in-
fested, unruly, and full of broken beer bottles. The
home's interior reflected a sense of decor best described as contemporary disheveled, with beer bottles
and clothing randomly strewn about. There was also
an authentic 1984 industrial-strength bong—a large
marijuana pipe.

Yerbury attempted questioning one of the suspects,
but communication proved impossible. Unable to
penetrate St. Pierre's drug- and drink-induced fog, Yerbury focused his inquiry on the moderately more rational Kevin Wiggins.

Wiggins told the detective that Paul St. Pierre, Tony
Youso, Jim Mullins, Andrew Webb, and Chris St. Pierre
had all been drinking, and some of them had also
taken Valium. "When I decided to go home," explained Wiggins, " I couldn't find my car keys. I kept
asking Paul if he'd seen them and Paul was getting
pissed. Well, we got into a big beef and then Paul St.
Pierre got even more mad and shot Andrew Webb with
a forty-five, and stashed the gun somewhere before the
cops showed up."

"Apparently, St. Pierre started picking a fight with
Wiggins," Yerbury later explained. "Not wanting any
trouble, Wiggins attempted talking his way out of the
situation, out of the kitchen, and away from Paul St.
Pierre. Then, for reasons that are unclear, St. Pierre
turned his attention to Andrew Webb. St. Pierre then
insisted that Webb owed him seven dollars, and demanded instant payment if Webb didn't want to die."

"I told Paul that I had already paid him back that
money," Webb later explained. Much taller than the
five-foot-seven, 155-pound St. Pierre, Webb responded
to his adversary's aggressive posture by easily pushing
him to the floor using only an index finger. St. Pierre
scrambled back up; again, Webb used his finger. St.

Pierre, for the second time in thirty seconds, landed unceremoniously on the kitchen's stained linoleum. Tony Youso, a remaining spectator, began losing interest. The argument could and would continue without him. As he left the kitchen for the living room, where Christopher St. Pierre was sleeping on the couch, the angry and humiliated Paul St. Pierre struggled to his feet, then directed dire threats toward his former childhood playmate, Andrew Webb. He could, he insisted, do whatever he wanted to whomever he wanted, and Andrew Webb couldn't stop him.

"What are you going to do, Paul, shoot me?" asked Webb. Paul St. Pierre yanked out his .45, pointed it directly at Webb, and jerked the trigger.

"The bullet went right through me," Webb recalled, "and I just stood there in shock. Then I fell on the floor and blacked out. I do remember Kevin Wiggins saying he was going to take me to the hospital. He really saved my life."

"I heard the gunshot," stated Tony Youso, "I turned back around to see what happened. Andrew was all bent over, and down, and leaning against the refrigerator."

"Why, Paul? Why?" Webb asked before he collapsed, according to Youso. Paul St. Pierre hastily apologized. "I'm sorry, I'm sorry," he said, then ran off to hide the gun. Tony Youso rushed to Webb's side, saw the damage, and ran to awaken St. Pierre's younger brother, Chris.

"Paul shot Andrew," he shouted, "We've got to call an ambulance!" Chris St. Pierre got up and quickly looked in the kitchen. Tony wasn't kidding.

While the two ran from the house to summon aid, Kevin Wiggins helped Webb up off the floor, out to the alley, and toward the parked cars. It was in the alley that Paul St. Pierre, having stashed his weapon, caught up with them.

Seeing his assailant, the wounded Webb feared for his life. "I was afraid that he was going to kill me and bury me out in the woods. He looked like he was going to shoot me again." To convince St. Pierre that another bullet was unnecessary, Webb utilized his best reasoning and oratory skills. "I'm dead, Paul," he shouted, "I'm dead!" Before Paul St. Pierre could agree or differ, Officers Boik and Lowry arrived. As their investigation began, Jim Mullins, distinctive in his tattered, bloodstained blue plaid shirt, came careening around the corner, his arms flailing wildly.

Authorities were never quite able to fit Mullins into the chronology of the morning's events. "We know he's the one who summoned the police by running over to the tavern," said Yerbury, "but he was so highly intoxicated and combative that he was impossible to communicate with. I tried to interview him, and at times he would tell me that Paul St. Pierre shot Andrew; then in the next breath he would say that he didn't want to tell us anything because he was afraid of what Paul St. Pierre would do to him if he talked."

Because Mullins, a transient with no permanent address, continually insisted that he was leaving for Oregon the minute police were done talking to him, police booked him into the Pierce County Jail on a RCW charge—witness to a violent crime.

Paul St. Pierre became even more violent when placed under arrest. Boik and Lowry forcibly restrained him, and Sergeant Justice of the Tacoma Police took a residue test. "We then set up the breathalyzer machine," recalled Boik, "but St. Pierre refused several times, and we were never able to get a reading."

While talking to Officer Boik, Paul St. Pierre mentioned that "maybe it was self-defense." When asked

if he really did shoot Webb in self-defense, St. Pierre
didn't give a direct answer. "Maybe he had a gun,
too," he said, as if it were a remote possibility.

Andrew Webb's older brother, Wesley, unaware of
the current crisis, arrived on the scene just as the ambulance sped away. Simply intending a friendly morning visit, Wesley discovered the 4000 block of Pacific
Avenue transformed into a Saturday circus of aid cars,
squad cars, fire trucks, ambulances, glaze-eyed witnesses, gawking neighbors, uniformed police officers,
and plainclothes detectives.

"Wesley went out to get a haircut," recalled his former wife of seventeen years, Margaret "Marty" Webb.
"He was just going to stop by and see what was going
on. By that, I mean he sort of wanted an update on
Andrew's latest 'project'—another one of his proposed
acts of retributive violence against someone he
thought had 'done him wrong.' He always thought
someone had done him wrong, ripping him off, stuff
like that. Paul was sitting in the back of the cop car
when Wesley showed up." Noticing Andrew's brother,
Paul St. Pierre victoriously gave Wesley "the finger."
Wesley, however, insists Paul St. Pierre gave him "the
high sign." Detective Yerbury insisted that Paul St.
Pierre, and everyone else, be hauled down to Central
Station for questioning by Detective Mike Lynch.

While Lynch attempted to penetrate the Valium and
alcohol clouding Paul St. Pierre's limited thought pro-
cesses, Sergeant Parkhurst drafted a search warrant for
presentation to Judge Stone. "The purpose of the warrant was to search for evidence, and for Paul St.
Pierre's forty-five," recalled Yerbury. "We didn't find
the weapon, and the residence was released back into
the care of Christopher St. Pierre, who was one of the
fellows living there at the time."

Based on available information and evidence, the

case didn't look the least bit complicated. "Especially once we got Webb's version," concurred Yerbury. "Basically, Paul St. Pierre hauled off and shot him. The information and evidence were presented to the prosecutor's office, and it was determined that a charge of Assault First Degree would be filed against Paul St. Pierre in superior court."

Detective Robert Yerbury wrote his final follow-up report concerning the case on June 11, 1984. "At this point," stated the detective with confidence, "there will be no further investigation. This case was cleared by the arrest of Paul St. Pierre."

More than a decade afterward, veteran broadcast journalist and award-winning newscaster Chet Rogers commented on that Saturday morning wounding of Andrew Webb, "The cops thought they were dealing with one drunk shooting another drunk over a seven-dollar debt. An anonymous tip to Crime Stoppers changed everything. The next thing they knew, Tacoma Police were digging up a corpse without a face, and another one without a head. This whole Andrew Webb/St. Pierre brothers' thing unearthed the most gruesome and bizarre double homicide in the city's history."

Two

On June 13, 1984, an anonymous female informant called Tacoma Police Crime Stoppers. She told Officer Rod Cook that Paul St. Pierre, in custody for shooting Andrew Webb, was connected to the unexplained disappearance several months earlier of a young man named Damon Wells.

The anonymous caller said that Wells, reported missing on February 27, had been beaten to death by Paul St. Pierre. She told Cook that "Paul St. Pierre broke Wells's neck, and then they put his body in the trunk of a car and drove off for about four hours. They reportedly put the body in a Dumpster." That same anonymous source indicated that other people who had lived in the residence as roommates of Paul St. Pierre also had information and knowledge of that incident, reported Officer Cook, "those being Donald Marshall and Mark Perez. According to the caller, Donald Marshall and Mark Perez were going to come to the station and tell what happened, but decided not to when Paul St. Pierre threatened to kill them."

Based upon the phone call, Detectives Yerbury and Price reviewed the Missing Persons file on Damon

Wells. "He was twenty years old, about five feet tall, maybe one hundred ten pounds," recalled Yerbury. "According to the original report, he lived with his great-grandmother Ann Robertson on South C. Street. The last time she saw him was Friday night, February 24, 1984, at about ten-thirty."

Mrs. Robertson described Damon as an exceptionally kind and thoughtful young man who was always willing to help others, especially his aged great-grandparents. Damon didn't complete high school, she said. He tried enlisting in the navy but was rejected because of his height, and because he suffered a severe spleen injury in an auto accident when he was ten years old.

The last time Mrs. Robertson saw Damon Wells, they were having coffee in the kitchen at about 10:15 P.M. when they heard the doorbell ring. Damon got up to answer the door. "It was a kid he knew," Robertson said. The kid to whom she referred was eighteen-year-old Steve Wood. "Damon went upstairs and got dressed. Then he came down and said, 'Grandma, I'm going to be right back,' and that was the end of it. I thought he was going down to Pacific Avenue to buy a pack of cigarettes or something, but he never came back."

"Apparently, Damon Wells always kept his grandmother informed of his whereabouts, and never gave her reason to worry about him," said Detective Yerbury. "Naturally, when he didn't come home and he didn't call, she became very concerned and called the Tacoma Police asking them to help look for her grandson."

"They wouldn't look for him," lamented Robertson. "The detectives said, 'All kids run away.' I told them he had a life here, that he was happy. I was afraid that maybe he was robbed, even though he left his billfold and Social Security card upstairs. He was wearing a very expensive genuine topaz ring, and he had an expensive watch."

Saturday, February 25, passed with no contact from Damon. Understandably concerned, his mother, Patricia Wells, called Steve Wood. He told her he and Damon had stopped by a party at a house on Pacific Avenue, and that he got into a fight with a fellow named Andrew Webb. Damon wasn't involved in the altercation, and when Wood decided to make a hasty exit, Damon stayed behind. He assured Mrs. Wells that Damon was fine when he last saw him, and perhaps her son had had too many beers and was sleeping it off somewhere.

As the day wore on, nerves wore thin, and Damon's extended family experienced increasing anxiety. Excuses, rationalizations, and hopeful optimism gradually gave way to desperation. On Monday, February 27, his mother filed an official Missing Persons report with Officer Meeks of the Tacoma Police Department.

"Damon Wells has shown absolutely no history of unexplained absences, according to his mother," noted Meeks. "He was last seen wearing a blue nylon jacket, blue jeans, and white Nike shoes. He has a 'T' tattoo on his left forearm, 'DW' tattooed on right upper arm, and a six-inch abdominal scar. Patricia Wells said that her son has no history of drugs or alcohol abuse, and was not currently seeing a female."

Informed of the beer bust attended Friday night by Damon Wells, Meeks drove to the house on Pacific Avenue. He intended to question the residents, but no one was home. Two days later, Detective Price was assigned to the case.

"On March second, I contacted Steve Wood at his father's barbershop," reported Price. "He said that they had been at the party for a short time when a guy named Andrew Webb arrived. Shortly after, Webb and Wood got into a fight. They were told to move it outside, at which time Wood ran. He said that the last time he saw Damon, he was in the house."

Wood also told Price that Damon didn't know the other guests at the party, that they originally went to the party to see someone named Mark, and that both Wood and Wells drank some beer. Wood drank ten to fifteen beers; Damon consumed six. "He had a good buzz on," remarked Wood.

"According to the report," recounted Yerbury, "Detective Price returned to the house on Pacific Avenue and spoke to residents Christopher and Paul St. Pierre. The brothers confirmed Wood's account. Chris St. Pierre said he didn't know Damon Wells, and wasn't paying attention to who was at the party. His older brother, Paul, said the same thing."

Looking for any possible clue, police searched Damon's room at Robertson's home on March 22, 1984. Per Detective Price's report, all they found were his wallet, one unidentified phone number, and his clothing. He also continued his investigation by calling the mystery phone number. Judy Kraft of Sumner, Washington, answered the call. She told Price that her husband, Jerry, knew Damon, but neither she nor her spouse had heard from him recently.

Detective Price kept working the case, and all trails brought him back to the house on Pacific Avenue, the venue for the Friday night fight of Steve Wood and Andrew Webb. On May 7, Price located Webb in an apartment on South M Street.

Separated from his wife and child, Andrew Webb said that when he arrived at the party, Steve Wood and Damon Wells were already there. He admitted having words with Steve Wood, and that their verbal exchange escalated into a fistfight.

"Webb said that after the fight he cleaned up in

the bathroom and left," said Price. "He didn't know
what happened to the victim, and he has no additional
information." The original investigation into Wells's
disappearance was unable to establish Damon Wells at
any location other than the Pacific Avenue party.

"The circumstances surrounding the anonymous
phone call were very unusual," Yerbury later commented. "We don't often receive detailed descriptions
of alleged homicides. We took it very seriously."

Based on the call to Crime Stoppers, and Yerbury's
prior knowledge of Paul St. Pierre's potential for violence, the detectives decided to conduct interviews
with the two men mentioned by the anonymous
caller—Mark Perez and Donald Marshall. "We wanted
to establish if the information received from the
woman who called Crime Stoppers was correct," explained Yerbury. "If we were to request a search warrant for the house on Pacific Avenue, we would need
more justification than a phone call. We would need
some corroborating indications of reliability."

Mark Perez, twenty-two, was contacted on June 14,
1984, and readily agreed to the interview. "I moved
into [address] in September of 1983 with Don Marshall, my brother Steve Perez, and Chris St. Pierre,"
he explained. "We were all doing OK in the house,
and my brother had a girlfriend there for a short time.
They moved out, and we had Chris's brother Paul
move in. Sometime after Paul moved in, there was an
incident at the IGA grocery store where Paul shot
someone at the store in self-defense. After that, Paul
was on sort of a 'power trip' and none of us could
disagree with him in any way, so things got kind of
tense around the house."

Perez told detectives that Steve Wood was a friend
of his, that Wood brought Damon Wells to the party,
and described the fight between Steve Wood and An-

drew Webb. "I told Steve I didn't know what had started the fight, but that he'd better leave. The last I saw of Damon," Perez said, "he was standing between the kitchen door and the hallway door. Steve jumped off the porch and ran down the street. Andrew held his nose and went straight into the bathroom. I assumed Paul was also in the bathroom because he came out and asked Don, Chris, and I where Steve's friend Damon had gone. We looked around outside and came back into the living room, looked in the basement, and didn't see him anywhere. When I attempted to get into the bathroom to check on the condition of Webb's nose, I was denied access by Paul St. Pierre."

"As a final note to that interview," stated Yerbury, "Perez indicated that the subjects were in the bathroom approximately a half hour, and then they left stating that they were taking Webb to the hospital for examination of his injuries."

"They returned about forty-five minutes later," stated Perez, "and Andrew had a creamy stuff that he was putting on his nose—it had no bandages. I was drinking beer and watching TV in the living room when they returned, and I got up to use the bathroom. Paul and Don Marshall were in there wiping down some blood. The blood was on the sink, above the toilet, and below the windowsill."

After Perez finished his statement, Yerbury attempted to contact Donald Marshall. "I left word with his employer that we wished to speak with him. Then, at about one that afternoon, we got word that Marshall wished to speak with *us*. We met him at Friday's Unfinished Furniture, where he worked as a salesman."

"When I first lived at [house number] Pacific Avenue, I lived with Steve Perez and his girlfriend, Vicky, Mark Perez, and Chris St. Pierre. I moved in with them and it was nice living with them. Everything was normal," said Marshall, "just like regular roommates. Then, after about two months, Chris's brother Paul moved in. Then, after that, Andrew Webb moved in about two weeks later. Then things started to change. Everyone seemed more aggressive, a lot more drinking, and things were more rowdy."

Once again, the shoot-out with Kevin Robinson at the IGA store was perceived as a significant turning point. "Paul seemed to change. He seemed like he was more of a macho man, and he talked a lot about killing. Basically, everyone was afraid of him in our household, with the exception of his brother Chris."

Don Marshall's version of the Friday-night party, the Webb/Wood rumble, and Steve Wood's hasty exit was almost identical to that of Mark Perez. His memories of the postparty bathroom incident, however, were significantly more upsetting.

"As I came out of my bedroom," he told the detectives, "and was going by the bathroom, I heard a scuffle, pounding on the walls, someone fell into the toilet seat and hit the floor. I heard, like, legs kicking up and down off the floor like someone was in pain.

"Paul said, 'Andrew, that drunk motherfucker, got blood all over the place'; then he asked Mark Perez to help me clean up the blood in the bathroom while they took Andrew to the hospital. At this point, I noticed the toilet seat was broken, blood around the washup sink, the left wall, and the right wall when you first come into the bathroom. It was mostly spotty, but the blood on the wall looked deep and dark."

When Andrew Webb and the St. Pierres returned from their supposed visit to the hospital, Marshall found it peculiar that they built a fire and began burning their clothes. "I then confronted them on exactly what was going on, or if they were hiding something from me. Andrew put his hand on my chest and stated that I don't need to know nothing, and that we Marshalls used to be something but we ain't nothing now, and he also said to me that I don't need to know shit."

If Don Marshall harbored doubts concerning the appropriate time to consider future residence options, they evaporated in the heat of Andrew Webb's scathing remarks. "I decided that I was going to move from that point on, and I told Mark Perez that he should move, too. I never returned to the house by myself from that day on because I was afraid of what might happen."

Marshall had good reason for concern, according to Andrew Webb. "Paul and Chris were angry with Don for moving out so quickly. They said he had chicken shitted out on them, and they talked about wasting him because they feared he would tell what he knew."

On Monday June 11, Chris St. Pierre showed up at Friday's Unfinished Furniture. He wasn't there to buy a bookcase. "He said that everyone was talking too much. He told me that I better shut my mouth and don't worry about anything. Then he showed me a handful of bullets he had in his pocket, shook his head, and walked away."

Two days later, said Marshall, he heard secondhand that Paul St. Pierre had "picked up some kid on the way to the Rush concert and took him to the house on Pacific Avenue to buy some drugs. Somehow, an argument broke out between Paul and the kid in which Paul just pulled his gun out and blew the guy's head off. At this point," admitted Marshall, "I really feared for my life, and when a friend advised me to come forward, that's exactly what I did."

"The friend who advised Don Marshall to come forward was a gentleman named Roy Kissler," recalled

Detective Yerbury. "Don Marshall told us that Mr. Kissler would be very valuable to our investigation, and that Paul St. Pierre allegedly confessed to Kissler, giving him graphic details of a homicide. Naturally, we got hold of Mr. Kissler, and he was eager to meet with us and give a sworn statement."

"It was June 15, 1984, that I showed up at Detective Yerbury's office," Roy Kissler recalled, "and I was more than happy to tell them everything I knew, everything I suspected, and everything I feared. I think fear probably being the primary word. Not so much fear for myself, but fear for other members of my family.

"After Paul came back from the marines," continued Kissler, "I started hearing all sorts of strange stuff from the other guys in the neighborhood. The first thing I heard was that Paul St. Pierre shot Kevin Robinson, a black man, at the IGA supermarket—shot him in the stomach with a forty-five, and got away with it. From the things I heard, it was obvious that things were getting out of hand. Some of the stories were insane, but believable. Like the St. Pierre brothers driving by the Drift Inn Tavern down on Fifty-sixth and Portland in Chris's Pontiac Firebird. They had an M-one carbine, and they started shooting into a group of blacks.

"Then another time," added Kissler, "Paul supposedly started shooting at a guy in a Corvette for some reason. I mean, they were just getting more and more out of control, and I could see that their lives were going nowhere fast. My old friends from the neighborhood would talk to me about it because I was completely out of all that stuff by then. I'd changed my lifestyle one hundred percent, and they knew they could trust me. I'd known these fellows all my life, and deep down I cared for them. I thought maybe I could reach them, have a heart-to-heart talk or something like that. Most people were too scared of Paul St. Pierre to talk to him about anything, but I was never scared of him in the least. I could kick his butt any day of the week, and he knew it. He may have been in the marines, but I'd had six years of intensive martial arts training. Paul respected that big time. I was bigger, faster, stronger, and Paul would never dare to pick a fight with me. Anyway, I said to myself, 'I'm not afraid of them. I'll go down and talk to them. See if I can talk some sense to them.' "

This well-meaning attempt to pull the St. Pierre brothers from the slough of self-destructive behavior was neither an expression of naivete nor the ill-informed effort of a self-righteous prig. Kissler's personal résumé of unrighteous acts and illegal activities easily eclipsed the then-known behavior of Paul and Chris St. Pierre. While Kissler is now a respected family man and successful builder of custom homes, he was once a hard-drinking, drug-dealing madman on a motorcycle.

"I rode a Harley-Davidson, and so did Paul St. Pierre and his brother, James. Paul and I would go riding together quite a bit. Back in the 1960s and 1970s," admitted Kissler, "I was real involved in drug-trafficking out of California with the Hell's Angels. I was full tilt into drugs.

"One Friday night back in 1976, I was driving up Thirty-eight Street by the Tacoma Mall at three-thirty in the morning. I'd been smoking angel dust and drinking whiskey," he recalled, "and I was talking to myself out loud. I said, 'God, there's got to be more to life than this.' The next thing I know, I'm sitting in a church parking lot on Thirty-eighth Street. I just sort of sat there for a while. I mean, I'd said, 'God this' and 'God that,' but I never had God talk back—I was really impressed. I made that one comment, and all of a sudden, I'm staring at a church.''

Kissler finally decided to get out of the car, and was halfway to the church's front door when he realized that he not only reeked of whiskey and pot, but also was carrying deadly weapons. "I had two guns, so I went back and stashed them in the car. Then I walked up and rang the doorbell, and the pastor of the church actually answered. He'd been there all night, and told me he just felt he was supposed to be there. We sat there talking until the sun came up, and that's when my life started getting turned around.''

By the time Roy Kissler walked on over to Paul St. Pierre's house, he was clean, sober, respectably employed, and perfectly willing to reach out to his old buddy. "I went down to their house, where they're living next to Ericson's Auto Body. Paul was there, and I invited him to come with me up to my cabin and check it out for hunting season.''

"Let's go up to my cabin for the night,'' Kissler said to St. Pierre. "We can talk.'' Paul St. Pierre wasn't doing anything anyway, so he grabbed a sleeping bag, strapped on his .45, and joined Roy Kissler for a leisurely drive to the little cabin in the big woods on the Cowlitz River. "On the way to my cabin, he told me about the shooting incident at the IGA store when he shot Kevin Robinson, and how he got away with it. I didn't tell him that I'd already heard the story; I just let him go on about it like it was all news to me. Then he was quiet for a while until we crossed the bridge at Alder Lake. Right in the middle of that bridge, Paul turned to me and said, 'Yeah, we've been killing these guys.' ''

There was no mistaking the plurality in St. Pierre's impromptu confession. "He said 'we' and 'guys,' and it was like someone dropped a chunk of dry ice in my gut. I continued driving, trying to process what I just heard. Paul didn't say another word; he just sat there staring out the window."

It was four o'clock in the afternoon when Roy Kissler and Paul St. Pierre arrived at Kissler's remote cabin. "We were way back in the woods, and there was nobody around for miles and miles. My cabin is about twenty by sixteen—one big room. There we were, just the two of us. Well, three of us if you count my dog. As soon as we got inside, Paul just starts spilling his guts. He gave me graphic details on how this one guy was killed. He didn't give me the name of the victim, and he didn't tell me the names of the people he was with, but I could tell for a fact he was telling me the truth. I mean, it was very obvious. I told him straight out, 'Paul, you owe society a price for what you did, but you can get your life right with God because of what Christ has done on the cross for you.' "

Paul St. Pierre told Kissler that he didn't care, and he didn't want to hear about it. "Then he starts telling me how he cut this poor guy's throat and watched him as he tried to breathe. He just started getting into some real graphic, brutal stuff about how one of them stabbed the guy in the back, and that was when Paul St. Pierre said that he cut the guy's throat. He talked about how they put him in a sleeping bag, put him in the trunk of Paul's white Cougar, and took him up toward Mt. Rainier, dug a grave, and buried him. He told me that the guy wouldn't fit in the grave, so he put the guy's legs on the side of the grave and jumped on him until they could fold him up and put him in the grave. He said it took place outside, and that they buried him up toward where we were."

"You need to get your life right with God," insisted Kissler, "and you're going to have to pay for [what] you did." St. Pierre, increasingly aggravated by Roy's religious attitude, became hostile and threatening. "How about if I do something like that to you, Roy?" he hissed. "Whatcha gonna do then?" Kissler offered an immediate and honest response: "Just try it, Paul, and I'll break your fucking legs."

"It kind of shocked him when I said that," Kissler later recalled, "after all, he was supposed to be the bad guy, but I confronted him. My language in those days hadn't quite been cleaned up yet." In response to Kissler's remark, Paul St. Pierre peeled off his shirt and began growling like an animal. "The whole countenance of his face was angry, mad, and vicious. I don't know if he's trying to intimidate me, [or] if he was just totally nuts. He was just standing there shirtless, snarling like a puma. I was thinking that maybe the best thing to do was to put a bullet in him."

When growling failed to either impress or intimidate his host, Paul St. Pierre relaxed and, as if nothing upsetting had transpired, shifted into a more conversational mode. "He started telling me about a girl they had tied up in the house at [address] for at least a week. He said that they were raping her, and all sorts of different things. He didn't say how old she was, and he didn't say that he or they killed her, but you know that she's not going to walk out of there afterward and let him get away with that. Later I learned that Wesley and Marty Webb, and her best friend, Christie Castle, saw that girl at Paul's house. She was in the bedroom with Mark Perez. I think it was Christie who heard her crying that she wanted to go home. I don't know all the details, but Andrew Webb's wife said she heard from Andrew about that girl being kept against her will."

Wesley and Marty Webb remembered that unpleasant and unsettling incident. Most specifically, they remember the little pink tennis shoes they saw on the floor. "I knew none of those guys wore little pink tennis shoes," said Marty. "We caught a glimpse of the girl—she looked really young, hardly teenage. She was very unhappy."

"I could hear her through a crack in the door," recalled Wesley Webb. "The poor little thing sounded miserable. I could hear her whimpering little voice say, 'I just wanna go home.' That isn't something you listen to and feel comfortable about."

Roy Kissler listened uncomfortably as Paul St. Pierre continued on about the repeatedly violated female captive and the throat-slash killing of an unknown victim. "He also said that he would like to kill people for money," stated Kissler.

The hours crept by; each filled with morbid details of beatings, murder, and burial. As the night wore on, St. Pierre wore out. "He rolled out his sleeping bag and got in it. My dog gets up, walks over, and lays right on top of him. He didn't say a word to the dog. He said to me, 'Your dog's laying on me.' I said, 'That's OK. He likes to sleep that way.' I think the dog had a sense of everything that was going on. It was a good-sized Lab, too, so that was a little bit of comfort. Of course, I didn't sleep a wink. I was up all night trying to figure out what I'm gonna do. We drove back into town first thing in the morning, and neither of us said a word. It was dead quiet."

When Kissler pulled into the alley next to the house, Paul St. Pierre invited him to see his Mercury Cougar's bloodstained taillights, and then made a friendly offer of hospitality. "Come on inside," said St. Pierre, "let's go see what the rest of the guys are doing."

Begging off, Roy Kissler drove directly to the home of his older brother, Joe. "I told him everything, and made sure he knew this was all for real. I wanted him to know what was going on if something should happen to me.

"Shortly after Paul St. Pierre confessed to me, my younger brother, Boyd, went over to his house for a party. The two of them—Paul and Boyd—had somewhat of a falling-out previously, but not severe enough to keep Boyd from going over. The St. Pierres sort of chased everybody out of the place, and took Boyd out back by the garage and started beating the hell out of him. I firmly believe that my little brother would have been murdered, had it not been for a guy named Rick Hunt. Rick showed up for the party, couldn't find anyone in the house, and went out back to see if the action was out there. Well, it only took Hunt about two seconds to size up the situation. He immediately rushed to Boyd's aid, knocked those jerks back, grabbed my brother, and got him out of there as fast as he could. I really think that Boyd could have got murdered that night if it wasn't for what Rick Hunt did, and I really appreciated that.

"At that point," admits Kissler, "I was in the consummate quandary. I was worried that someone else was going to get either hurt real bad or killed, maybe one of my own family. I figured that I couldn't go to the cops because I didn't know who he murdered, and I didn't know who he was involved with. So I took a risk and started sort of asking around, talking to some of the guys, leading them into conversations.

"One of the guys I talked to was Don Marshall. Turns out that Paul and Chris St. Pierre ran Marshall out of the house, so he knew there was something up, but he didn't know exactly what. It was about the second week of June that I decided to drive over and have a chat with him. We had a nice long talk. I strongly suggested that he go to the cops, and that I'd back him up if he did."

"It was June twelfth that Roy Kissler approached me," Marshall confirmed. "He asked me out to his nice car and we sat down and discussed a lot of things. Roy told me that Paul told him in detail that they had really, actually killed that kid. Roy said Paul showed Andrew how to really kill the guy by cutting his throat after Andrew had already stuck him in the kidney. They wrapped him in a sleeping bag and threw him into the trunk of the car. Andrew, Chris, and Paul took him out to some secret place where Paul buries people. Roy said that they dug a hole to bury him in, but the kid wouldn't fit in with the sleeping bag. They took him and Paul proceeded to break his arms and his legs so that he would fit in the hole."

In this close-knit neighborhood, there were soon enough whisperings and violated confidences that it was only a matter of time until someone called the cops. When Paul St. Pierre shot Andrew Webb, that was all anyone needed—it gave a good excuse for someone to pick up the phone and call the Tacoma Police. "Sure enough," said Kissler, "one of the neighborhood moms, I think, at the prompting of her kids, called Crime Stoppers. The next thing you know, there I am with Yerbury, Price, and a stenographer giving them my statement."

At police headquarters, the sworn statement of Roy Evan Kissler, twenty-eight, lasted exactly sixteen minutes. In part, Kissler's official deposition, reads: "He said they started beating a guy up just for fun, and he said the guy was going to 'get them back' for what they had done. That's when one of them stabbed him in the back. Paul St. Pierre said that's when he cut the guy's throat. The guy lay there for quite a while and didn't die right away. After cutting his throat and he was dead, they put him in a sleeping bag, put him in the trunk of Paul's white Cougar, then took him towards the Mt. [mountains] to bury him out there. Paul said that by the time they were ready to bury him, rigor mortis had set in and the hole they had dug wasn't big enough. So Paul had to jump on the guys [*sic*] legs to break them to get the body to fit in the hole. By the time they had finished, the sun was coming up. At that point I told him he was crazy, and he got rather upset with me at this, and during the next part of the evening (for the remainder) he just kept going over certain things which he had already told me. I just waited for him to go to sleep and as soon as morning came around, I headed back into town with Paul as soon as possible. He just kept talking about the incident and I finally told him I didn't want to hear anymore. We got back to town and I dropped him off at his house, and at that point, he pointed out to me where he had blood left on the Cougar around the taillights. I didn't check that, I just left."

Because Kissler's narrative meshed with the basics related by the anonymous caller, and the previous statements of Perez and Marshall, the detectives brought Mark Perez back for a second interview. They were especially interested if he knew anything about the alleged shooting the night Rush played the Tacoma Dome. Mark Perez remembered the date perfectly—May 18, 1984—because it was three days after his birthday. Perez didn't attend the concert, but Paul St. Pierre and Andrew Webb did.

"I was sick and missed work on the eighteenth," Perez told Yerbury, "because of an ear infection and high fever. I was awakened at three A.M. by a loud noise that sounded like somebody kicked in my front door. The noise was loud, and I heard Chris say, 'Fuck! Goddamn it, Paul, what the fuck did you do?' Paul said, 'I had to; he was going to stab me with a knife, so I had to shoot him.' Then Chris came into my bedroom and asked, 'Were you sleeping?' I said I was and he said, 'Oh, well, never mind.' Andrew came in and asked me if I heard anything; then Paul came in and said, 'Come on, Mark, get out of bed and come see this.' Andrew said, 'Are you crazy? Come on, get out of here.' He pushed Paul out of the room and said to me, 'No, no, stay here, don't move; the less you see and the less you know, the better off you'll be.' He stressed this several times. He told me to just go back to sleep like nothing had happened."

The next morning, Perez noticed that the living room carpet had been cut up, and the carpet mat had two large, round bloodstains approximately 3 1/2 feet from each other. According to Perez, Paul St. Pierre told him that he and Andrew Webb picked up a guy hitchhiking, invited him to party at the house, and then, later, Paul shot the man in the head. According to Mark Perez, Chris St. Pierre told him, "This guy's body was over here and part of his head was here, and his brain could be seen, and there was a bullet hole in his head, and it looked like half his face was blown off."

"He also told me," related Perez, "that they just rolled up his body in the carpet and dumped it way up by the mountains—they drove about three hours. He said, 'We hid the body so good, it'll take 'em ten years to find the body, if they ever do.' No one mentioned the incident again. Within a few days, I moved out of the house. My personal belongings were still there, but I didn't spend any nights there."

Detective Price remembered a Missing Persons case of a young man who inexplicably vanished after his mother dropped him off not far from the Tacoma Dome. A quick check of police files confirmed the date of his disappearance as May 18, the night of the

Rush concert. The young man's name was John Achord.

According to a Tacoma Police incident report, Mrs. Opal Bitney, mother of John Lynn Achord, contacted the Tacoma Police Department on Monday, May 21. "I spoke to her personally," said David McNutt, communications officer with the Law Enforcement Support Agency. "We live in a rather enclosed environment down there, so our conversation was purely by phone. She called to file a Missing Persons report on her son, John Achord."

Born in 1961, John Achord was a student at Tacoma's Bates Vocational School. He stood six feet two, weighed 165 pounds, and had short, curly dark brown hair, a mustache, hazel eyes, a one-inch scar above his right eyebrow, and a severely scarred right shoulder.

Mrs. Bitney explained to police that John Achord was in an automobile accident in 1980. His injuries were of such severity that Achord had to learn to walk and talk all over again. Achord not only made the best of his situation, he improved upon it. Inspirational in accomplishment, and cheerful by attitude, the residual moderate brain damage primarily affected his memory. He was not dangerous or troublesome in any way. Able to care for himself, and in good physical health, he did not drink or use drugs. Open and friendly, John Achord would readily accept rides from strangers.

On May 18, his mother dropped him off at South Twenty-seventh Street and Pacific Avenue, not far from the Tacoma Dome. From there, he would walk to the Rush concert. Achord was carrying perhaps $50 and a concert ticket, which he had bought in advance from the Bon Marche outlet of Ticketmaster. He was last seen wearing a green fatigue jacket, white knit shirt, and blue jeans.

"The family did everything possible to create public

awareness of his disappearance," said Yerbury. "Virtually every business and building in Tacoma had the 'Missing' poster of John Achord." One such business was a Mt. Tahoma 7-Eleven store.

"Andrew and I stopped to buy some cigarettes at that Seven-Eleven," recounted Andrew Webb's former wife, Anne, "and as I was leaving the store, I noticed a flyer on the window. It was all about John Achord being missing. I was standing there reading it, and when Andrew saw what I was looking at, he suddenly got all upset and angry and insisted we leave immediately. I told him I wanted to finish reading the poster, but he was so uptight I just stopped reading and we left."

"They also had one of those posters up at Gene and Ray's Tavern," said Mark Ericson. "That really gives me chills. I would maybe have a beer after work with Chris, Andrew, or Paul because Chris worked for me and they lived right next door to the shop. I mean, we would be there right in front of that poster about John Achord and the whole time they knew what had happened to him. I don't know how they could have done that."

"Based on the Missing Persons report," Detective Yerbury said, "it certainly seemed as if John Achord could be the unfortunate gentleman reportedly shot by Paul St. Pierre. At that point, Detective Price and I figured we had enough cause to seek a search warrant."

Judge James Healy signed a search warrant on June 18, 1984. The warrant commanded "a diligent search of [house number] Pacific Avenue to retrieve a broken toilet lid, blood, hair, tissue trace evidence, a black handled, two edged hunting knife, bullet fragments, carpet samples, a large caliber handgun (possibly a .45 cal. automatic), evidence of burned shoes and trousers, and papers and documents attesting to persons living at the residence."

"Also included in the search warrant," noted Sergeant Parkhurst, "were two vehicles—a 1957 Ford station wagon, green and white in color, and a white 1967 Mercury." Parkhurst and Lieutenant Moorhead decided the warrant would be served on June 19. Prior to heading over to Pacific Avenue, they called a conference in the County-City Building with Detectives Price and Yerbury, and Officers Brame, Cook, and Getz. "During the conference," Parkhurst later explained, "a plan was devised on how the residence should be approached and searched."

It was ten minutes before 9:00 A.M. when Tacoma Police arrived. There was no one home, but police knew that Chris St. Pierre worked next door for Ericson's, and had done so since high school.

Chris St. Pierre had been nearly in tears ever since he arrived for work. Mark Ericson later commented, "I kept trying to reassure him that everything was going to be OK. I asked, 'Chris, what is your problem?' He said, 'We're just all going to go to jail. Paul just fucked it up for everybody.' No matter how much I attempted to reassure him that everything would turn out OK, Chris just kept saying, 'You don't understand, you don't understand.'

"It was bright and early when the cops showed up," Ericson said. "It was such a nice day that I had the back door to the alley open. I just happened to walk to the ramp, look over, and there were all kinds of cops and plainclothes police. I figured maybe they were doing some follow-up on the shooting of Andrew Webb, maybe they needed to ask Chris some more questions since he was the one who called the cops in the first place.

"I said, 'Chris, you got company over there.' He

had his white coveralls on, and he stopped what he was working on, hung his head down for a second; then, without saying a word, he just walked out that door. He had that kind of faraway look in his eyes. I never saw Chris St. Pierre face-to-face again. He walked out that door as if he were walking right out of this life."

As Chris St. Pierre approached the house, Detective Yerbury greeted him. "I read him the search warrant and advised him of his rights," the detective recalled, "and then Officers Cook and Brame secured Chris St. Pierre in an unused bedroom while the evidence search was conducted."

Parkhurst, Moorhead, Price, Yerbury, and Identification Technician Doug Walker began an extensive search of the living room area. "Several blood spots were noticed on the stereo and speakers," said Parkhurst. "We photographed them in detail, and the stereo and one large speaker were taken into evidence."

The search temporarily ceased when Chris St. Pierre volunteered the location of the .45-caliber pistol listed on the search warrant. "After Paul St. Pierre shot Andrew Webb," Yerbury explained, "he hid the gun. It was no secret that he stashed it somewhere; the secret was where he stashed it. Chris St. Pierre told us that his brother called him on the phone at work earlier that morning and told him where to find the forty-five."

Officer Brame stayed with Chris St. Pierre while Parkhurst and Cook looked for the weapon. "Chris, who was seated on the floor, looked up at me," said Brame, "then dropped his head and stated something to the effect, 'I just don't want to see anybody else hurt with it.'"

The .45, according to Chris, was hidden in a pile of bricks in a neighbor's yard just south of the house.

Sergeant Parkhurst knew that Bill Ericson, father of
Mark Ericson, owned that property as well. "I contacted Bill Ericson," reported Sergeant Parkhurst,
"and presented him with the consent-to-search warrant, and explained the details concerning what officers were looking for and what they had been told.
He was informed that he did not have to allow us to
search if he didn't want us to."

Bill Ericson authorized the search and Officer Cook
located the weapon. "Sergeant Parkhurst and I went
to the adjacent yard and observed a pile of stacked
tile roofing," reported Cook. "As I walked along the
side of the tile, I observed a forty-five-caliber semiautomatic handgun on the ground between two stacks."
The gun was cocked when Cook found it, with one
cartridge in the chamber. "I unloaded it," Cook recalled, "by grasping the handle grips and the grooved
area at the side. There was no clip. Identification Manager Walker photographed the weapon before taking
it into evidence."

Returning to the living room, officers noticed that
the carpet and pad had been cut, new carpet installed,
and the covering around the baseboards had been removed. "There was a sticker on the pad that appeared
to be new," said Parkhurst. "After rolling the pad and
the carpet, we could see the oak hardwood floor,
which looked like it had been recently sanded."

"The sanding was so severe," commented Yerbury,
"that it was to the point that it almost caused a depression in the wood, and the wood was definitely
lighter in these areas. Walker then checked these areas
with a Hemo Stik Test, and it proved positive in all
five areas. The bloodstains on the living room floor
certainly corroborated the statements we'd received;
so at that point, we arrested Christopher St. Pierre
and charged him with rendering criminal assistance."

Meanwhile, Mark Ericson wondered what in the world was going on next door that required Chris St. Pierre to be gone so long. "He was in there for hours, and then the detectives come over to me and asked if I'd come out and answer some questions. I said, 'Sure. 'Where's Chris?' They said he was inside, and that he was cooperating with them now. Cooperating with them? I mean, I had no idea what was happening. Then they did let me know that this is serious—'We're investigating a homicide,' or something like that. He said, 'You ever noticed that the carpet had been cut out underneath from the table in the living room?' I didn't go in there very often and I didn't notice the carpet.

"By this time, I'm thinking, Paul must have done something stupid," recalled Ericson. "Chris should have gone to the cops earlier. He's an accessory now, but at least he's cooperating. He should've got himself a lawyer."

According to Yerbury, Christopher St. Pierre was advised off all his rights, including his right to a lawyer, and was repeatedly told that he need not speak to the detectives or answer any questions. When they arrived at Tacoma Police Central Station, Yerbury and Price again advised him of his rights, and St. Pierre signed the form indicating he fully understood.

Christopher St. Pierre, with full knowledge of exactly what he was doing, addressed the following words to Detective Robert Yerbury of the Tacoma Police: "I might as well tell you everything. I'm dead or I'm going to prison." Yerbury asked St. Pierre to reveal everything, beginning with the night Andrew Webb and Steve Wood got into a fistfight at the house on Pacific Avenue. The recently arrested St. Pierre stared at the floor, took a breath, and began his bone-chilling narrative.

Three

"Paul St. Pierre wielded a toilet seat lid as a weapon, repeatedly striking Damon Wells over the head. The blows eventually rendered him unconscious or semi-unconscious," said Christopher St. Pierre. He readily admitted that he and Andrew Webb joined the beating, each striking Wells several times.

"When Chris made the admission that he assisted in the beating of Damon Wells," recalled Detective Yerbury, "he stopped speaking, and while continuing to stare at the floor, he stated in a reflective thinking-out-loud manner, 'Maybe I should have an attorney.' I advised him that if he was asking for an attorney that we would not talk to him any farther. He then asked, of no one in particular, 'Can I get protective custody?' "

When St. Pierre inquired about protective custody, Yerbury left the room to seek advice from the chief deputy prosecutor. "St. Pierre was not advised of my intention to contact the prosecutor's office," said the detective. "Upon my return, Chris St. Pierre voluntarily started up the conversation again. I again warned him that if he was asking for an attorney, we would not talk to him unless he chose to do so."

Christopher St. Pierre did not request an attorney.

Instead, he related the tragic fate of young Damon
Wells. "We were going to take Damon Wells to the
other side of town, just to drop him off somewhere,"
he told them. "Andrew came up with the idea to drop
him off at Salmon Beach. We arrived at Salmon Beach
and drove into a road about a half a mile. We all got
out of the car."

According to Christopher St. Pierre, Damon Wells's
shoes were removed and thrown away—the idea, coming from Paul St. Pierre, being for him to have to walk
home shoeless. "Damon was yelling that he was going
to get revenge," said St. Pierre. "He started running,
yelling for help. We ran after him, and Andrew caught
him and knocked him to the ground. We were yelling
at him to shut up. Andrew took out a Gerber knife
that he had obtained from my brother earlier in the
evening. I'm not sure what time Andrew had obtained
the knife, but he did have it. While we were yelling at
Damon to shut up, Andrew pulled out the knife and
slit Damon's throat. He had him facing down on the
ground, pulled back his head by his hair, and drew
the knife across the throat about three times."

"Chris St. Pierre further adds," wrote Detective Yerbury in his Official Supplementary Report filed June
16, 1984, "that he, Paul St. Pierre, and Andrew Webb
then stood there for a period of time and watched as
Damon Wells bled to death. He states that Damon
Wells had no opportunity to fight back, and further
states that Paul St. Pierre did not participate in that
actual homicide event. Andrew Webb committed the
actual act of slitting Wells' throat."

From Chris St. Pierre, Yerbury further learned: "At
some point after Damon Wells's throat had been cut,
Andrew Webb stood over the victim and threw a knife
at him on at least two occasions, both times sticking
it into the back of the victim. After Damon Wells was

dead, Andrew Webb and Paul St. Pierre removed his jacket and pants and threw them into the bushes."

"As far as I know," St. Pierre said, "the clothes are still out there. Paul and Andrew picked up Damon's body and dragged him off about twenty-five feet into the brush. Paul was driving his '67 Mercury Cougar. We went back to our house, took our clothes off that had blood on them, and threw them in the washing machine. . . . I took a pair of my boots that had blood on them—the blood was on my boots from being in the bathroom earlier—I threw them into the fireplace, along with the broken toilet seat lid. Don [Marshall] watched me throw my boots into the fireplace. Then we took showers to wash away the blood. After taking a shower, Paul gave Don the knife that was used to cut Damon's throat, and told Don to hold on to it for him. About this time, I went to bed. The next morning, we discussed what happened the night before, and decided to go back to where Damon had been killed, and take his body and bury it."

The St. Pierres returned to Salmon Beach and brought with them one of Paul St. Pierre's old sleeping bags, noted Yerbury. "Chris said they put Wells's body in the sleeping bag, and then placed it in the trunk of Paul St. Pierre's 1967 Mercury Cougar. From that point, it was transported to the eventual burial site."

"We drove up by Alder Lake," explained Chris St. Pierre. "Paul knew a secluded spot from a friend of his, Bill, who was at the house the night Damon was killed. We picked a spot and buried Damon's body. We had obtained two shovels, one was in our garage, I think it was Don Marshall's. The other shovel we had obtained from my father's toolshed. We camouflaged the grave, and we left."

When Chris St. Pierre finished describing the death

and burial of Damon Wells, the detectives asked him about John Achord. Once again, Chris St. Pierre did not hesitate giving them a full disclosure.

"[Chris] told us that his friend Tony Youso got drunk and was in some sort of auto accident. Andrew Webb and he took Youso over to Webb's apartment to calm him down and sober him up. Then the two of them went over to [house number]. As they walked in, they saw John Achord facedown in the dining room, and Paul St. Pierre standing over him with a gun. Paul told Chris that he had to shoot Mr. Achord in self-defense because Achord attacked him with a knife. Chris told us that he saw a rather small pocket-knife on the floor, and they threw it out in the garbage. He went on to describe how they cut up the carpet, rolled Achord's dead body up in it, obtained tools for burying Achord from Mr. and Mrs. St. Pierre's garage, and then transported the body in Andrew Webb's car. Chris St. Pierre followed in his station wagon."

St. Pierre omitted a slight detail—prior to transporting the body, the men had a beer party and invited friends and relatives, including Wesley and Marty Webb. John Achord's corpse, wrapped in carpet, was stashed away in the back bedroom. Marty was advised not to wander around the house alone, for Paul "wanted to do her."

"We were almost all the way there," said Chris St. Pierre, relating to Yerbury about taking Achord's body to the proposed burial site, "when Andrew lost control of his car and put it into a ditch." Perhaps that was when the carpet containing Achord's body became unwrapped, exposing the lifeless corpse. Andrew Webb, looking in the rearview mirror, saw John Achord's sightless eyes staring back at him. That image burned itself into Webb's brain. Not a day or night goes by,

Webb admits, that he does not see John Achord staring at him.

"Paul and Andrew then put the body into the back of the station wagon that I was driving," continued St. Pierre, "and I drove to where we were going to place the body. Paul and Andrew came up the trail. I was waiting for them. Paul dragged the body to near where we were going to bury him. Andrew and I left Paul there to dig the grave with the tools we obtained from my father's shed. Andrew and I got into my station wagon to drive back down to the gas station to locate a tow truck to pull Andrew's car out of the ditch."

They found a wrecker at the nearest Chevron station, and had the truck's driver follow them to the vehicle. "The tower pulled Andrew's car out of the ditch," he recalled, "and he told us that the charge was twenty-five dollars. We didn't have any change, so between the two of us we paid him thirty dollars and told him to keep the change. I left Andrew and Paul, went home, took a shower, and tried to get some sleep."

The tow-truck driver wasn't the only one to see Andrew Webb's ditch-bound Dodge. Mark Schneider, a former resident of their old neighborhood, saw Webb, the St. Pierres, and the Dodge Challenger twice in less than twelve hours—once in Tacoma, and again near Elbe.

"On May eighteenth, I got off work at about eleven P.M.," recalled Schneider. "I went to Lively Market on Forty-fifth and Pacific to buy groceries for a baseball tournament the next day. There were people in the store who said they had just been to the Rush concert. While at the store, I saw Paul St. Pierre and Andrew Webb buying beer. When they left, they got into a 1971 light gold Dodge Challenger, and I noticed someone else in the car—a guy in the backseat. Then I went to spend the night at Silver Lake with some friends. I got up about seven A.M. to go to the baseball tournament. I was driving up with Paul Barabe and his girlfriend, Cheryl. We drove up to Elbe and took a right at the bridge, and on the right side of the road, I saw the same car that I had seen the night before—it was the gold Challenger—in the ditch. There was also another car parked on the side of the road, and there were several people standing outside of it. Two of the people appeared to be Paul St. Pierre and Andrew Webb; we didn't stop, we just kept going." Another person in a separate car, Jack McQuade, also noticed Andrew Webb's Challenger. "Alongside the Challenger," confirmed McQuade, "was an old white station wagon."

"We continued questioning Chris St. Pierre," Yerbury later explained, "and I asked him what happened in the days following the burial of John Achord. Well, once again Chris St. Pierre told us everything, and—" He stopped, drummed his fingers on the desk, and shook his head as if trying to clear away a lingering, unwanted, image. "OK," he said, "this is the part where they go out there in the middle of the night, dig up the body, chop off the head, and bring it home in a bucket."

"They had that head in a bucket, set in concrete, sitting right over there," Mark Ericson later recalled, pointing toward the back wall. "There was a five-gallon orange bucket, filled with cement. I didn't really notice it much, but I finally asked Chris, 'What's with this bucket of cement right here?' He says, 'Oh, my dad was doing some work on this porch, some cement, and he had some extra left over, so I just grabbed that bucket and filled it up.' Well, then the next day or so, the bucket was gone. I never thought of it at all, until . . .'' Mark Ericson stopped speaking as an involuntary shudder made its way through his body. "Stuff like that just makes the hair on the back of your neck stand up, you know what I mean?''

"They actually had a reason—or excuse—for removing his head," stated Yerbury. "Paul St. Pierre was concerned that somehow we—the police—would make a connection between the bullet recovered from the black fellow he shot at the grocery store and the bullet recovered from the head of John Achord, if he was ever found. I guess the same concern might have prompted Paul St. Pierre to throw away the gun, but he kept the gun and attempted throwing away Mr. Achord's head. The way Chris St. Pierre described things, it sounded rather ghoulish.''

"Paul and I decided to put the head in a five-gallon bucket and fill it with cement," confirmed Chris St. Pierre. "Paul and I went back up to where we had buried the second guy that Paul had shot, and then dug up the body. I made Paul do the digging up of the body with the shovels we got earlier from my father, the same tools that we used to bury him a couple days earlier.''

While digging, Paul St. Pierre accidentally broke one of the shovels. His younger brother used the broken handle to mix and stir the concrete while Paul went to the car, got the ax, and chopped off John Achord's head.

"After placing the head in the bucket," said Chris St. Pierre, "we put the lid on it, put it in my car along with the tools, and then reburied the body. Before leaving, we dumped the leftover bag of concrete and the carpet the body was wrapped in about twenty yards away. When we got home and opened up the bucket, [we] saw that the concrete had set up. We placed the five-gallon bucket containing the head in the garage.

The next night, Tony [Youso] and I drove in my station wagon to a bridge over the Puyallup River; Tony got out of the passenger side with the bucket and threw it over the side of the bridge. Tony knew what was in the bucket because Paul and I told him."

The ax used to decapitate John Achord was, Chris told Yerbury, hidden under a woodpile at the home of Youso's brother. "The brother knew nothing about any of this," recalled the detective. "The knife used in the assault on Damon Wells was discarded near the freeway entrance between McKinley and Pacific Avenue at the Thirty-eighth Street on-ramp."

Detectives Price and Yerbury were continually impressed by Christopher St. Pierre's eagerness to assist them. "He told us that he wanted to cooperate in this investigation so he could attempt to prove that he was not the person responsible for the two deaths, and that he wanted to get the whole situation off his conscience. In fact, Christopher St. Pierre also stated that he wanted to take us to the burial site so the bodies could be recovered."

Price and Yerbury transported Chris St. Pierre to a meeting at the Pierce County Coroner's Office with Sergeant Parkhurst, other assisting officers, and Dr. Emanual Lacsina, medical examiner. "I explained the situation," recalled Yerbury, "and preparations were made to go to the burial site. Due to conflicting jurisdictional problems, Sergeant Parkhurst made arrangements with the Lewis County Sheriff's Office for support of that agency."

"When Yerbury told us that Chris St. Pierre volunteered to take officers to the scene where the bodies were buried, I contacted Detective Glade Austin of the Lewis County Sheriff's Office," said Sergeant Parkhurst. "Detective Austin said that if we were positive the homicide occurred in Tacoma, and that the burial

of the victims was the only incident that occurred in
Lewis County, they would be willing to release juris-
diction of the bodies to our medical examiner in
Pierce County."

Parkhurst contacted Dr. Lacsina, Pierce County's
medical examiner, and he agreed to perform the
pathological and forensic examinations on the singular condition that Lewis County provided an official
written release. A few telephone calls, capped by verbal
assurances of complete cooperation, resolved Lacsina's
professional concerns. The required permission obtained, all significant participants convened in the little town of Elbe, Washington.

"Going to the crime scene from Tacoma were Lieutenant Moorhead, Detectives Price and Yerbury, Officer Brame, Identification Technician John Penton, Dr.
Lacsina, Deputy Coroner Dean Patterson, and myself,"
recalled Sergeant Parkhurst. Once in Elbe, the investigating officers met with Detective Austin, Sergeant
Joe Frace, and Lewis County evidence officer Rick
Harrington. "It may also be noted," wrote Parkhurst
in his official report, "that arrested suspect Chris St.
Pierre accompanied arresting officers Price and Yerbury on a voluntary basis to point out where the victims were buried."

The caravan passed over the Nisqually Bridge into
Lewis County, took a right turn at Lubkin Road, and
continued about a mile before turning off onto an
old logging road. "Officers traveled one thousand
fifty-six measured feet down this road," reported Parkhurst, "and again Chris St. Pierre instructed Price and
Yerbury to stop their vehicle, and the bodies would
be found off to the right of the road."

"Walking toward the grave sites," Yerbury recalled,
"Chris St. Pierre pointed out various important pieces
of evidence. He showed us portions of carpet rem-

nants, the ripped and discarded bag of cement, and a pile of dried and hardened concrete, which had been left in the bag and discarded by the side of the road. Once he pointed out the grave sites, he was placed in a police vehicle and kept there."

⬩ Parkhurst, Price, Yerbury, and Penton approached the first grave site from a common pathway. "This is an area of sandy soil covered with dry ferns," commented Parkhurst. "Just in front of the grave site was an area where a circle of cement was found. This circle represented a five-gallon bucket that was utilized after decapitating Achord's head. Once the dried ferns were removed, officers could observe a pronounced area of raised dirt, probably an inch or two in height."

"Once the burial sites were confirmed, and before they actually removed the bodies, Detective Price and I drove Christopher St. Pierre back to Central Station," recalled Yerbury. The ride back was neither uneventful nor nonproductive. First they made an unscheduled stop to chat with Mr. Gayle W. Adams of Elbe, Washington.

"We were driving back to Tacoma," Yerbury explained, "when I saw a tow truck leaving a gas station. We stopped him and introduced ourselves. We asked him if he was the person that towed Andrew Webb's Dodge out of the ditch. He clearly remembered the incident, and although he didn't have the license plate number, he did recall that it was a brown or gold Dodge. He also remembered that the fellows didn't have exact change, and he didn't have any either, so he was paid thirty dollars instead of twenty-five."

The two detectives and Chris St. Pierre were heading toward Central Station when St. Pierre offered another helpful bit of evidentiary advice. "He pointed out the area where the Gerber knife used to murder Damon Wells had been thrown out of the car, and he also pointed out the area where the head had been discarded—approximately midspan of the Lincoln Avenue Bridge."

During the initial interview, Christopher St. Pierre told Yerbury and Price the reasons why he fully cooperated. "I told you 'cause there was so much evidence, and I didn't want to get caught up in anything else," said Chris St. Pierre. "It's been on my conscience. I wanted to point out the facts and evidence, and clean everything up because if I told you the truth, I wouldn't be charged with a homicide. I didn't kill anyone. I was just an accessory. I just wanted to be charged with what I did and nothing else.

"I may be cutting my own throat for a big term, but I don't want to be charged with a murder. Now I'll probably talk to an attorney and he'll say that I shouldn't have talked and they are charging me with murder. I'm trying to help you guys just to get this shit over and done with. I decided while I was in the bedroom to tell you everything I know."

Upon arrival at Central Station, Christopher St. Pierre confirmed again that he was willing to provide a sworn, notarized, formal statement of everything he knew, and everything he did. "We took his statement, and after he had the opportunity to read and review it, he signed it in the presence of Detective Price and myself," said Yerbury. "At that point, he was booked into the Pierce County Jail on charges of rendering criminal assistance."

Officers Peterson and Washburn were dispatched to St. Joseph's Hospital to place Andrew Webb under arrest for first-degree murder. A steady stream of visitors had kept Webb's spirits up, including his estranged wife, Anne, who had raced to his bedside the day Paul St. Pierre shot him in the stomach.

"I ran right to him, comforted him, cried over him,

and worst of all—once he was charged with murder—I believed him. At first I felt sorry for him; I guess I still loved him. Or at least I was neurotically attached to him. The whole incident made me crazy," she said.

When the police arrived at Webb's hospital room, they found him chatting with his brother Wesley about how eager he was to get out of the hospital. Wesley was asked to leave, and when he requested an explanation, he was informed that Andrew Webb was now under arrest for murder and was not allowed visitors or phone calls until thoroughly interviewed by detectives.

"He was released from the hospital the next morning and arrived at Central Station about nine-fifteen A.M. He was advised of his rights, but refused to sign anything and didn't want to talk to me," said Yerbury. "He was then taken to the Pierce County Jail. I was hoping, of course, that Webb would be as forthcoming and cooperative as Chris St. Pierre, who was actually eager to provide a full sworn statement."

While St. Pierre was giving that sworn statement, officers assisting Sergeant Parkhurst and Lieutenant Moorhead were carefully removing the headless corpse of John Achord from its shallow grave. "The body was on its right side and fully clothed," said Parkhurst. "A body bag was placed on the foot of the grave, and the body was then slid out directly into the body bag. It was then secured and left at the grave site pending removal after the recovery of the second victim."

The grave from which the remains of Damon Wells were removed was much deeper than the first. "The body was enclosed in a sleeping bag of the mummy type," Parkhurst later reported. "The body contained in the sleeping bag was not removed, nor examined prior to being encased in the body bag. Both bodies were removed from the wooded area and released to

Medical Examiner Lacsina and Deputy Coroner Dean Patterson."

A thorough examination of the surroundings revealed a large area of cement, more carpet, and a broken shovel handle. "The shovel was adjacent to the second grave site behind some trees," Parkhurst noted, "but in retrospect, if one went back to where the pile of cement was, this shovel handle could have been thrown from this area and landed where it was found. This is only speculation."

As the approaching darkness would affect the investigation's accuracy, the area was quickly and completely photographed. Detective Austin and Evidence Officer Harrington, assisted by Officer Brame, diagramed the entire crime scene in intricate detail.

Homicidal depravity, clandestine burials, and recovering decomposed bodies from remote crime scenes are not for the faint of heart. Even experienced homicide detectives are often shocked by what they encounter. "There's certainly been incidences or crime scenes that were appalling to me," confirmed Yerbury. "I can't believe that people would do these things. But you kind of get this emotional detachment. You got a job to do; you do your job."

Yerbury's pride in, and dedication to, the Tacoma Police Department is accompanied by one seldom-considered drawback of his chosen profession. "Whatever you do for a living, people will come to you because you have something they want. You may not have to lock your door to keep them out, but people will come to you. But in my business, nobody wants to talk to us—it's not uncommon that families or victims don't want to talk to us, and certainly witnesses don't want to talk to us. So it's one constant struggle, just to keep the case on track. People do care, but they are afraid."

Tony Youso was more afraid of Paul St. Pierre than

he was of the Tacoma Police. Fear for his life, and the lives of family members, compelled him to clean up Achord's blood, help Paul St. Pierre get the cement, and throw the bucket containing John Achord's head into the Puyallup River.

When news of the grisly discoveries near Elbe, Washington, hit the news media on June 20, Youso knew he'd better go to the police before the police came for him. That morning, Dean Phillips, director of Police Services, issued a formal press release detailing the recovery of two bodies from Lewis County. "They appear to have been shot and stabbed; one was decapitated. Names of the victims will not be released until positive identification has been made by the Pierce County medical examiner, and their next of kin is notified," said Phillips. "Tacoma Police have arrested three Tacoma men in connection with the homicides. Two men have been arrested for murder, and the third for rendering criminal assistance. The investigation has revealed that both victims were killed in Tacoma; one in the suspects' south-end home, and one in an isolated area of Tacoma. The bodies were then transported to Lewis County, where they were buried in a shallow grave."

"Immediately following that news announcement," recalled Detective Yerbury, "I was contacted at Central Station by Anthony Youso, who stated that he wished to discuss the investigation and all knowledge he had of it. According to what we heard from Christopher St. Pierre, Anthony Youso played a significant role in the assistance of the destruction of evidence that would be of importance to this investigation."

Born in Fort Leonardwood, Missouri, on February 14, 1961, Anthony Youso was twenty-three, single, and had recently completed four years in the United States Marine Corps Reserve. He was working as a laborer for Sherwood Products when he moved into the house on Pacific Avenue in March 1984, immediately following the disappearance of Damon Wells. "There was a rumor," acknowledged Youso, "that a young man had disappeared from the house before I moved in. All I know is that this is a rumor."

Once ensconced amid the inebriated revelry of the St. Pierres' self-named "Animal House," Youso adopted his fellow roommates' all-consuming interest in brewed and fermented beverages.

On May 19, 1984, at 2:00 A.M., while driving under the influence, Tony Youso was involved in an auto accident. Bloody, intoxicated, and panicked, Youso ran away from the accident scene. According to Andrew Webb, Youso kept running until he ran through the front door of their Pacific Avenue home.

"Youso ran into the house screaming and yelling hysterically," Webb later recalled, "and he was searching for a knife, saying he was going to kill himself. Paul and I tackled him. He said he was in an accident and thought he had killed some people. His head was bleeding and [so was] his knee, and he didn't have a shirt on. We asked him where the accident was, but we couldn't get any sense out of him because he was too drunk."

"Andrew Webb took me to his house and left me there overnight," confirmed Youso. "The next morning, Andrew came and picked me up from his house. He said Paul St. Pierre had shot somebody." Chris St. Pierre later accorded Youso further explanation. "Chris told me that this guy had pulled some kind of weapon out on Paul. He said it was a very big steel blade, that's what Chris had told me."

"When I arrived home, there were two holes in the carpet that had been cut out, and there was no padding where the holes were—it was all the way down

to the wood. It appeared to me that there was blood
on the wood. Chris St. Pierre and I removed the rest
of the carpet with the holes in it," admitted Youso.
"Chris St. Pierre had poured lacquer thinner over one
of the spots where the hole was, and had sanded the
spot he had put the lacquer thinner on. I believe the
spot was blood."

As for dumping John Achord's head into the river,
Youso acknowledged removing the bucket from Chris
St. Pierre's station wagon, walking to the bridge's midspan, and pushing the bucket off into the water below.
He also helped dispose of the Gerber knife used to
kill Damon Wells. "Chris St. Pierre and I had taken
the knife in Chris's car and threw it out on a freeway
on-ramp. I threw out the Gerber knife," Youso explained, "because Chris St. Pierre did not want anything of Paul St. Pierre's around." Advised of his
rights, and following his sworn statement, Anthony
Youso was arrested by detectives.

While Youso was being booked into the Pierce
County Jail, Sergeant Parkhurst attended an autopsy
performed by Dr. Lacsina on "two unknown males
found on 6-19-84 in Lewis County, Washington."

Dr. Lacsina carefully examined the severely decomposed body of Damon Wells, stuffed in a mummy-style
sleeping bag, while Sergeant Parkhurst looked on and
took notes. "The victim's body is soiled, and there are
sticks and brush protruding—especially from the neck
area. There is an obvious throat wound, and the victim's mouth has extremely protruding and crooked
front incisors. There are no facial features on the victim."

Identification Technician Christian was able to fin-
gerprint a portion of the right thumb after Dr. Lacsina
removed the thumb's skin, and Christian soon con-

firmed an exact match to the known thumbprint of Damon Wells.

As the autopsy continued, Lacsina found two stab wounds on the left side of Wells's back, and two puncture wounds to the left lobe of his left lung. In the final analysis, Damon Wells died exactly as Christopher St. Pierre had described. Someone cut open Wells's throat and stabbed him twice in the back. He died from severe blood loss. "The cause of death is attributed to each multiple stab wound," Dr. Lacsina reported, "as well as slashing wounds to the neck."

As for the other recovered body, Sergeant Parkhurst reported that "prior to the autopsy and external examination, the body of the subject was fully X-rayed. I notice that the victim has been decapitated and his head is missing."

Lacsina and Parkhurst tried taking the victim's fingerprints, but the skin was so decomposed that it was sliding off the body. Dr. Lacsina removed the loose skin from the victim's left hand, washed it thoroughly, and then put the victim's skin on over his own in "an attempt to create a surface which would allow printing and possible latent comparison. This failed," said Parkhurst, "because the victim's skin was too wet and the ink would not cover adequately the victim's finger." They agreed to try this technique again when the skin was dry.

Piece by piece and item by item, clothing and personal items were taken away from the body. "Dr. Lacsina removed the shirt of the victim, which can be described as a pullover polo-type shirt with a collar. It is in such a soiled condition that it is impossible to tell the original color. It is also observed that there are several cuts in the back of the shirt."

Lacsina turned the body over and scrubbed the back clean. Sergeant Parkhurst immediately noticed several knife wounds in the victim's back. Dr. Lacsina confirmed that there were at least twelve knife wounds, all caused by a double-edged blade. Opening the victim from the back, Dr. Lacsina examined the hemorrhaging resulting from these stab wounds.

"The wounds were antemortem," stated Parkhurst. "That means they occurred before death. The heart had to be beating at the time the wounds were inflicted." Further examination revealed more knife wounds in the neck area. "Dr. Lacsina removed the body organs, and stab wounds were observed in the area of the liver."

Chris St. Pierre swore that Paul St. Pierre killed John Achord by shooting him in the head with a .45 automatic. This fatal head wound, and the bullet lodged in the victim's skull, prompted the decapitation and the subsequent disposal of John Achord's cement-encased head into the Puyallup River. The autopsy performed by Dr. Lacsina revealed that John Achord did not die from a gunshot wound. John Achord was stabbed to death.

Four

Paul St. Pierre prized his Gerber Fighting Knife, Christopher St. Pierre was handy with a hatchet, and Andrew Webb's reputation included proficiency with any pointed object suitable for throwing, jabbing, or stabbing. Andrew Webb was deadly with a blade, but unlike Paul St. Pierre, Webb didn't carry a deadly weapon on his person every hour of the day.

The sixth child of nine born to Lowell Webb and Dolores Armstrong Webb, Andrew Webb was raised in a close-knit family of four brothers and five sisters, all nurtured by a loving and protective mother. His father, a dedicated Christian, was hardworking and loud hollering; he harbored a marked disdain for the show of any emotion other than anger.

Modest in income, unassuming in presentation, and reassuringly old-fashioned, the Webb family valued the Bible, honesty, loyalty, and unflinching dedication to the higher standard to which those who arise to serve the Lord are continually summoned. All nine children were uncommonly close, especially Andrew Webb and his two younger sisters.

Anne Webb later said, "He told me he tormented them just for the hell of it. He gave me the impression that he made his little sisters do things whether they wanted to or not. And he said that he wasn't the only one in the family taking advantage of the girls, either. If you aren't safe with your own brothers, who can you trust? Who can you turn to? That's abuse, and these folks were so Christian, so devout, and also so screwed up that brothers and sisters were doing that, and it was *normal* for them!"

According to Anne, her husband gave every indication that sexual, emotional, and physical abuse were intrinsic aspects of Webb family life. "Oh, yes," insisted Anne, "from what I understood from Andrew, incest was as much part of their lifestyle as grace before meals or prayers at bedtime."

"It is so sad to acknowledge that our home, our family, was very troubled," said Gail Webb, the eldest offspring of Lowell and Dolores, who is professionally educated in the study of child abuse. "The tragic truth is that we lived in a household characterized by anger and inappropriate behavior. It is even more heartbreaking when you consider how honestly sincere Mom and Dad were. They were doing the best they could, considering where they came from, and how they were raised."

"You can try to clean it up all you want," stated Marty Webb, "but the moral and emotional soil from which the Webb children drew sustenance was irrevocably polluted."

"The first polluted soil someone should dig up would be Dolores's dad, Grandpa Armstrong," insisted Anne.

Dolores Armstrong entered the world in 1932, the middle child of six born to destitute Oklahoma sharecroppers who owed more than they owned. The only way out of debt was the way out of town. Under cover of darkness, the eight indigent debtors scurried away to Arizona.

Laboring migrant workers, the Armstrongs were poor in all—save God. Their unyielding faith in the Bible, and a firm belief in prayer, softened the material world's harsh realities. Sadly, neither steadfast devotion nor prayerful supplication restrained Mrs. Armstrong from deserting her husband and youngest children, leaving ten-year-old Dolores as primary caregiver to her two younger siblings.

Within a few years, Dolores blossomed into puberty. Her physical charms were undeniably attractive, as was the intensity of her religious convictions. The local church's new family pastor found that all attempts to resist Dolores's charms, or his own desires, were of no avail.

"In other words, the pastor was screwing her," commented Marty Webb, "but the way Dolores told the story, that wasn't the first time that guy had banged a postpubescent parishioner. I guess he did the same thing at the church he was at before."

After prayerful consideration, the pastor came to believe that a power greater than himself wanted him to leave town. When his replacement arrived, he was no less tempted.

Dolores's father, a known faith healer, knew that the town's new man of the cloth was also his daughter's new lover. For impressionable teenager Dolores Armstrong, firm, upright religion was now forever coupled with unbridled, albeit secretive, sexuality. Her father didn't punish the pastor; instead, he punished his own daughter.

Dolores's runaway mother, Mary, would often make clandestine raids on her former household, kidnap the youngsters, and seemingly abandon Dolores to face her father's uncontrolled anger. Dolores, however, perceived her mother's intent differently—this was not abandonment; this was being entrusted with responsibility. Mary Armstrong knew Dolores's strength of character. Her daughter would continue to sacrifice her own dignity for the well-being of her younger siblings until they could be freed permanently from their father. Mr. Armstrong, antagonistic toward his better half, initiated forceful campaigns of paternal retaliation and child reclamation. The two traumatized youngsters were repeatedly dragged from parent to parent, and state to state. Through it all, Dolores acted as surrogate mother, doting big sister, and oft-beaten caregiver, to her devoutly religious and dangerously violent father.

At sixteen, Dolores Armstrong met Lowell Webb at church in the little town of Glendale, Arizona. She was there to pray; he was there to sing. Mr. Webb, ten years older than Dolores came from stock as plain as his face. He was the younger and less handsome of two boys growing up in Bakersfield, California.

"Sometimes he says his mother ran a dance hall," remarked Marty Webb, "other times he says it was a whorehouse." The environment's purported licentiousness created a heady atmosphere that a young boy such as Lowell Webb could find both physically stimulating and morally detrimental. Lowell Webb and his brother, Dick, were separated soon after their parents' divorce. The extended family took in better-looking Dick, but Lowell was handed over to foster care when his father ran off to join the circus.

As he grew up, Lowell Webb and his well-worn Bible were inseparable. He had neither need nor desire for modern tomfoolery. If the King James Version was good enough for Jesus, it was good enough for him. His dream profession, the career to which he aspired, was that of a licensed preacher of God's Holy Writ.

As patriotic as he was devout, Webb enlisted in the air force early in World War II. He wanted to be a paratrooper, but bad arches kept him stateside working as a clerk. After the war, he returned home to the church. Through hard work and dedication, he gained his long-coveted preacher license. His gift for sharing the gospel, and his pleasant singing voice, earned him a place in a traveling gospel group, where attractive teenager Dolores Armstrong first met him.

"Actually, Dad had a dream in which he saw the face and heard the name of the woman God wanted him to wed," stated Gail Webb. "This is true. Well, when he first saw Mom and heard her name, he absolutely knew that she was the one from God. There was no way around it. She was for him, and him alone."

Although Lowell was firmly convinced Dolores was his marital destiny, she was still firmly under the control of her father. The only time she was on her own was when she was in school, at church, or doing mission work. To date and woo her, continual travel and creativity were imperative. Lowell also had to scour the railroad yard to find the empty boxcar that often served as his sweetheart's domicile.

Dolores and Lowell became Mr. and Mrs. Webb in January 1951. The happy couple rejoiced in the marriage and their first child, Gail, was born exactly nine months later.

Several years and locales later, including Los Angeles, birthplace of their first six children, the Webbs made it to Tacoma, Washington, in 1963. Mr. Webb landed a decent job in downtown Tacoma, and Dolores, having graduated from nursing school, began working at St. Joseph Hospital. Lowell also served as an assistant pastor, and the church graciously provided housing until the family got on its feet. The family first lived in the back of the church building. Next they moved into a former Japanese internment camp converted into low-income housing, then into a more pleasant rental home, and finally, in 1966, the Webbs bought their home on D Street—a purchase realized by direct result of an honest-to-God miracle.

Lowell had an auto accident in which he was rear-ended by the other driver with such force that Lowell's car was pushed through the intersection, almost hitting three Catholic nuns. The nuns were a godsend, and excellent witnesses.

The insurance company asked Lowell Webb how much he would take to settle the matter out of court. "I'll have to pray about it," said Mr. Webb, and came up with a number that seemed to repeat itself over and over: $12,000.

Lowell Webb paid $11,000 for the house on South D Street, and it was here that the nine siblings made friends with the neighbors: the Kisslers, Marshalls, Greens, Clarks, Nolans, Chollenders, and St. Pierres.

"We grew up a block away from each other," remembered former neighbor Roy Kissler. "The Webb family lived three houses in from Forty-third Street; the Marshalls lived next door; the St. Pierres lived down around the corner on Forty-third Avenue, not far at all from Ericson's Auto Body, just three or four houses off Pacific and across the street from the Forty-third Street Tavern. My family lived down on the next block off of Fortieth Street and D. There were other families, too, and everyone knew everyone else."

How well D Street residents knew each other is subject for speculation. At a minimum, they knew names, games, and gossip just like in any other neighborhood. But awareness of, and empathy for, the interpersonal and spiritual battles waged behind closed doors was appropriately slim. Good neighbors respect boundaries; they don't pry into the personal lives of others. Everyone on the block, suggested Roy Kissler, had his or her own issues, tests, problems, and spiritual challenges to work through. At one time or another, everybody plays the good guy, the bad guy, and the innocent victim.

Gail Webb admits seeing herself as an innocent victim throughout her entire adolescence—victimized by a stern, implacable God who was represented by equally demanding and wrathful parents. By her fifth decade, Gail recognized her parents' perennial emotional martyrdom, and acknowledged the terror, trauma, abuse, exploitation, and sacrifice inherent in their haphazard upbringing.

"Mom yearned for normalcy and simplicity," said Gail sadly. "She was committed one hundred percent to having a happy family, and by God, we were going to be happy whether we were happy or not."

"No Sadness Allowed" was an unwritten rule in the home of the Webbs. It was okay to be happy, and it was okay to be mad, but you were never allowed to be sad. If a child was going to cry, he was to do it behind closed doors. "Imagine how much work it is for a kid, how much energy it takes, to act exactly the opposite of how you're really feeling," stated Gail. "You have to pretend all the time—pretend to be confident when you were scared, or happy when you were fighting back tears. I listened to Mom and Dad talk about God, and to me, God and Mom and Dad were very similar—they could never be pleased. I strained for perfection and always failed. No matter what I did, it was never good enough. I tried to do everything exactly the way God and they wanted, until I was about seventeen or eighteen; then I just gave up and went the other direction. Both extremes were hell."

"Speaking of hell," added the onetime Mrs. Anne

Webb, "the 'religion thing' was a real big deal to the Webb family's whole life and personality." Idiosyncratic extrapolations of biblical admonitions, leading to dogmatic interpretations characterized by threats of dire consequences, comprised Lowell Webb's conversational armory.

"Lowell was always coming over to the house to chat. He would sit there and say the same things over and over again while I was trying to take care of the kids and housework. Once he said I was an unfit wife because I stopped doing housework to listen to him—that was very wrong of me—I should have kept working. He always talked about the same two topics.

" 'Well, you know I was never circumcised,' he would begin, and then go into big detail about his sex organ," recalled Anne. "Lowell gave this same spiel to all his daughters-in-law. I threw a fit, however, when Grandpa Lowell brought over some cookies, sat down, and talked about his penis to my thirteen-year-old daughter! Later I told my husband that I was sick and tired of his dad's penis talk, and I never wanted to hear about that thing of his again!"

Hearing Anne's reaction, Gail Webb laughed with a tinge of sadness. "Poor Dad. She didn't understand what he was trying to say, even though he shouldn't have said it at all."

When Lowell Webb read in the Bible that circumcision was a sign of the Covenant, he felt excluded. Although circumcision was an outward symbol of inward truth, he felt his foreskin marked him to forever be seen as "outside" the Covenant. When Lowell Webb later internalized the words of the New Testament about "circumcision of the heart," he felt much better.

"That made the difference to him," said Gail, "realizing that the outward sign of being in the Covenant was the conscious decision to have a change of heart, an alteration of behavior, a revision of attitude, and a dedication to God's Covenant—even if it involved personal pain or discomfort, that dedication was as irrevocable as circumcision."

The significance of inappropriate conversation from a grandfather shrinks in comparison to the inference of incessant abuse within the family. "I might have to draw some sort of chart or diagram to explain it," asserted Marty Webb in half jest. "That doesn't necessarily mean sexual abuse. There are many forms of brother/sister hurt, mistreatment, and exploitation. I've heard some scary stories of what may have gone on behind closed doors in that house, but no matter what you did in that family, everything was OK as long as you prayed for forgiveness. I'm not just talking about Lowell and Dolores's little nuclear family, but the whole extended family of grandparents and uncles. It didn't matter what sin you were committing. If Jesus forgave you, and He always did, then you could do it again and again. . . . Yep, a combination of sex and prayer was perfect for that family—as soon they finished with one, they were already on their knees for the other."

Marty alleged Dolores Webb sexually molested her son, Wesley, when he was ten years old, and that he confronted her about it as an unpleasant Christmas surprise shortly before she died.

"I think Marty is off base with that," responded Gail Webb. "Mom, because of her own horrid experiences, was very protective of us, or tried to be. Wes, like me, doesn't show pain. For example, when he had appendicitis, by the time he mentioned that he was in pain, it had already burst and he was doubled over. Mom was a nurse, and if he said something hurt, she knew that it meant it had really been hurting him for some time, and she needed to check it out. Any touching of him in any sort of way that could be interpreted as inappropriate would have been purely in a clinical sense. Wes had problems with his genitals when he was younger: his testicles didn't drop, he had mumps, and Mom was concerned that he would be infertile. Perhaps her medical examinations of him were misinterpreted in retrospect, attributing impure motives that Mom never had."

Wesley's version is significantly different from either Marty's or Gail's. He remembers touching his mother in an improper way when he was ten, the result of a leg massage going too far up, and acknowledged bringing it up one Christmas before his mother passed away. According to him, she didn't remember the incident at all.

The event was also a breakthrough for Dolores. It was not until her father's funeral that she acknowledged the intense hate and resentment she harbored toward the man who beat her, raped her, and repeatedly abused her. As a Christian, she knew that she had to forgive him—free herself from the burden of his sins and her resentments. As they lowered him into the ground, Dolores forgave him. He was gone, but his influence lived on.

"One of my younger sisters," recalled Gail, "is exceptionally intelligent, a genius IQ, but Andrew and Wesley always told her she was stupid. I believe she was abused physically and emotionally by Andrew and Wesley, and it is really tragic."

"Wesley told me," insisted Marty, "that he had a sexual relationship with one of his older sisters. But now he says that she, who was about four years older than he, wasn't having any kind of sex; they were just 'playing around' out of normal childhood curiosity. You can call it whatever you want," she said, "but brother-sister hanky-panky makes a big impact on your life, and I'm pretty sure that it has an influence over your choices of boyfriends and husbands. The Webb girls seemed to have no more judgment when it came to picking husbands than I did," she said with obvious self-mockery. "Take a look at Gail's taste in men—all of her husbands were either self-centered jerks, murderers, molesters, rapists, crack addicts, or all of the above in various combinations."

Gail Webb didn't disagree with Marty's characterization of her record of failed romances, destructive divorce-bait matrimonial matchups, and life-threatening relationships. The men Gail Webb found inexplicably appealing were those who lived for the moment, loved themselves, preferred a crack house's paranoid chaos to the calm comfort of hearth and home, and regarded their wives and children as warm-blooded punching bags and/or spent lust depositories.

"I got married for the first time in 1971 at the age of nineteen," recalled Gail, "to a nice fellow who didn't abuse me. He also didn't work, didn't want to work, and had no interest in being a parent. I left him after six years. I married my second husband, a military man, in 1979."

Gail's second spouse was beyond abusive, and disgraced his uniform by horrendous acts of child molestation, including children of his own family. Despite her religious dedication to "stand by her man," enough was enough. In 1984, while he was stationed in South America, she notified him of her intention of divorce, the irrevocable finality of their separation, and the existence of "another man" in her life.

Exactly one week before Paul St. Pierre shot Gail's brother Andrew Webb, Gail's recently rejected husband flew back to the States and murdered Gail's boyfriend. "He stabbed him to death," Gail said tearfully.

"My mother flew down and got the kids and took them back with her to Tacoma. About a week later, Mom called and said to get the kids, Andrew had been shot, and then charged with murder. It was all too much. I was already traumatized by what I was going through. My brother—the eldest one, the one whose wife, if I remember correctly, was molested by her grandmother—they just up and took off. They didn't want to deal with any of it. Because both my situation and Andrew's were so emotion-heavy, Dad became withdrawn. The combination of crises was more than what Mom could handle. She just snapped."

Dolores Webb, who survived so much, finally confronted the limitations of her own elaborate coping strategies. If the crises had abated from that point on, perhaps Dolores Webb's final decades would have been partially tolerable. Instead, yet another son-in-law was also revealed to be a compulsive child molester who had sex with his own young children, and with virtually all his nieces, and perhaps the nephews, too.

"Not to be left out of the multigenerational incest and molestation marathon," added Anne, "Wesley was arrested and sent to prison for sexually molesting Marty's fourteen-year old daughter from a previous marriage. The poor kid ran away from home and went to the police about it. At first, Marty didn't believe her."

"I'm ashamed to admit that, but it's true," said Marty. "I didn't believe her at first, at all. I thought she was just saying that because she hated Wesley. But it was one hundred percent true. Wesley made a deal with the prosecutor for a shorter sentence, and he pleaded guilty to a lesser charge."

Wesley Webb doesn't deny a certain amount of truth to the allegations against him, admitting to one episode of easy familiarity. He maintains to this day that the primary offense alleged against him was a complete fabrication.

Sexually inappropriate behavior, promiscuity, or avoidance of sexual activity are common among incest survivors, rendering healthy relationships in adulthood almost impossible. "The Webbs either can't get it up, get it in, or they can't get enough," joked Marty. "Some of them can't bring themselves to do it in any normal way, and the others can't stop doing it with everybody in any way. One of Wesley's sexual problems," Marty said, "was that he had sex with his cousin—I believe it was the daughter of the uncle who molested Gail—and the cousin gave Wesley the clap. Face it, for the Webb clan, childhood play meant toying with the kids. Either they were kissing and fondling, or slapping and hitting."

Incestuous relationships, such as those alleged in the Webb family, also self-perpetuate over multiple generations. Among the recurring and most obvious behavioral symptoms of incest victims are sudden outbursts of extreme and violent anger. This can include willful destruction of personal property, furniture, clothing, and other household items.

Extreme violent anger was a common characteristic of both Lowell and Dolores, and their children were convenient targets. Kids were bounced off walls, whacked with broom handles, and hit repeatedly with a wide variety of household items and utensils. Any comment or happenstance with a possible negative connotation was dealt with immediately.

The Webb children would often cower outside their own home after school, peeking in the front window to see if it was safe to enter. Many times it wasn't safe at all because Dolores, on a rampage of destruction, was smashing everything in sight.

"Mom's reputation for violence didn't lessen with

age or time," acknowledged Gail. "We grew up and had kids of our own, and she would explode at them as well."

"The whole family had an issue with abuse, but Grandma Dolores had the worst reputation," said grandson Travis. "We all knew how bad she could get. I knew because she was still beating on me when I was a teenager. The last time, but not the first, was when I was fifteen. She came at me with her fists, hitting me, striking me, and pummeling me over and over. I just curled up and let her do it. What do you do when an old woman beats you? My aunt heard the ruckus, came in, pulled Grandma off of me, and threatened to call the cops. I don't know how much further it would have gone."

Such painful behavior is seldom discussed beyond household walls, and the Webb family's violent nature was not shared with the neighbors. The St. Pierres, for example, knew nothing of Dolores Webb's horrid upbringing or ongoing anger. They knew her only as a friendly neighbor, living in a spacious older home, who, like the other moms on the block, had plenty of kids: the Webbs had nine, the Kisslers fourteen, and the St. Pierres—George and Carmella—had five.

George St. Pierre is a man of many accomplishments, a schoolteacher, an avid fisherman, and a caring, if strict, father. Carmella St. Pierre is remembered with affection by the Webb boys as the type of neighborhood mom who would meet you at the door with a plate of cookies, and then put you to work.

Hard workers and attentive parents, George and Carmella St. Pierre were especially protective of their youngest son, Christopher, born with a heart defect. "He had open-heart surgery when he was three and a half months old," explained his mother years later. "They changed the pressure in the chambers of his heart. Then, when he got to be about four or five, they had to go in and close the hole in his heart. They didn't give him a fifty-fifty chance to survive. He was the youngest in Pierce County to have survived the operation."

Undaunted by his condition, and eager for acceptance, he threw himself into the rigorous demands of boyhood. Exhaustion often outpaced intention; tenacity overrode reason. Being "one of the guys" was all-important; too important. An unofficial third-grade rite of passage—a fistfight—was Chris St. Pierre's first entree into the world of American masculine stereotypes. George St. Pierre, a "ringside" spectator eager to see his son in action, tacitly approved the prearranged one-fall no-time-limit battle against eight-year-old Willie McGraw. The two third-graders went at it, their dimpled little fists flying. Chris was no match for the more mature and experienced champion, and soon he sought reprieve and turned to his father.

Little Willie suddenly felt his neck's scruff clamped by fingers larger than the white-knuckled pink ones pinned beneath his knees. The adult grip of George St. Pierre lifted and ultimately launched Willie into the air. Willie landed a few feet away, more surprised than hurt. George St. Pierre declared the fight over, grabbed his son above the elbow as dads do when they're displeased, and marched him away in disgust. Christopher St. Pierre gleaned an important insight: no matter what, never give up.

"As for Mrs. St. Pierre," said Ericson, "she was also a schoolteacher. She was always a really nice person, and a very sweet lady. Chris wasn't the only one of their boys with a problem. Paul St. Pierre was challenged as well."

Paul St. Pierre's heart was strong, but his mental and social skills were weak. Forever the outsider, the "slow" one, the brunt of jokes, and perpetual victim, Paul St. Pierre was continually teased, pelted by insults, or rendered invisible by intentional ignoring.

"Wesley told me that Paul St. Pierre was really mistreated by the other boys in the neighborhood," said Marty Webb. "They were cruel to him—and kids can be so cruel—when he was a kid." Desperately wanting friends, hungrily seeking acceptance, baffled by circumstances and overpowered by individuals, Paul St. Pierre lived in a world in which he was seldom welcome—a hostile environment where almost everyone was hell-bent on making him miserable. There were notable exceptions—those treating him kindly received courtesy in return more often than not—but exceptions are, by definition, never the norm.

"I probably made him miserable myself when we were younger," acknowledged Roy Kissler. "Then again, I can't honestly say that Paul got it that much worse than the rest of us when it came to teasing or what you would call 'kid cruelty.' That behavior was common back then, and maybe it still is. Perhaps Paul got it worse just because of the way he was—different, sort of slow on the uptake. Then again," Kissler added thoughtfully, "perhaps Paul St. Pierre was more sensitive. And I don't mean that in a negative way at all— maybe that stone-cold heart of his wasn't stone cold at all when he was younger."

Paul St. Pierre's pubescence and adolescence were long past before pediatric researchers discovered that newborn males are more sensitive than females. This male sensitivity continues until banished by the unwritten rules of "American Boyhood"—rules by which it gets trained out, beaten out, or repeatedly stuffed so far down that resurfacing is exceptionally unlikely.

For boys such as the Webbs, Kisslers, and St. Pierres, the prevalent misconception that somehow boys are biologically wired for aggressive, violent, and risky behavior was an operational reality. Andrew Webb's younger brother, Ben, who was also Christopher St. Pierre's best friend, acknowledged that they all did their best to conform to that faulty theory of maleness. By the time they were teens, the boys were acting like hoods, doing the dangerous, illegal, or absurdly stupid.

Unaccepted as a kid, Paul St. Pierre found teenage inclusion through chemistry. By beclouding his already diminished mental capacities with illegal intoxicants, and stilling any remaining shreds of sensitivity, Paul St. Pierre bought bragging rights with truancy and trouble. More aggressive than assertive, more the bully and less the victim, Paul St. Pierre reinvented himself from the inside out.

While his older brother became increasingly antisocial, Christopher St. Pierre was developing compensatory tenacity to offset his weak heart and related physical defects. An example of his evolving tenacity, but not his good judgment, was when a schoolyard bully harassed him at Lincoln High School.

The young St. Pierre took matters into his own hands. He crafted a fistfight equalizer as a wood shop and metal shop project. He made a handle from a wooden cylinder, and then formed a bar of bent metal. He fashioned this into something rather like a pair of brass knuckles. The handle fit into the palm so he could grip it while making a fist; the bar was on the outside of his fingers.

As a result of using his metal shop ingenuity, Christopher St. Pierre got in trouble. Even this event did not scale the heights of antisocial and illegal activities beyond the Tacoma norm. Then, with the advent of too much beer augmented by too much pot, the neighborhood boys experienced their first "real problem"—one that involved the cops.

"It was Paul St. Pierre and my younger brother, Boyd," recalled Roy Kissler. "They broke into a house when they were about sixteen years old. It was about three-thirty in the morning, and they were smoking some pot in an abandoned house. Boyd and Paul came out of the house just when the cops showed up. One of the officers got out and yelled for both to freeze, but they made a mad dash for the car, jumped in, and started it up to make their getaway."

The police officer knelt down, aimed a shotgun at the back windshield, and fired. This ended the car's getaway, but not *their* getaway. The blast through the back windshield fanned out the pellets, and they hit Boyd in the back of the head. He was thrown against the steering wheel and against his cohort. Paul St. Pierre panicked, jumped out of the car, and took off on foot. He ran through a yard, down the street, to an alley—where he stashed his stocking cap, gloves, jacket, and gun in a nearby garbage can—and jetted toward the front sidewalk.

As he was walking along, trying to look normal, an older police officer stopped him and told him he had better get off the street because there had been a shooting nearby, and the suspect was still at large. Paul thanked him and agreed to get off the street as soon as possible.

"I guess Paul thought he was home free when he turned the corner and ran down the block," said Kissler, "but a few seconds later, his life turned into a scene from a bad action movie—a whole bunch of squad cars came out of nowhere, skidded to a stop, and Paul was surrounded. All of these cops jumped out simultaneously with guns drawn, screaming at Paul to put up his hands, so he did as they asked. What

Paul didn't know was that Boyd's blood was all over one side of his blue jeans. When he turned away from that old policeman, the cop saw all the blood and called in the squad cars."

Boyd Kissler's parents considered instigating a lawsuit over the incident, but decided against any legal action. Paul St. Pierre pleaded guilty. Facing two to five years at Cascade Correctional Institute for juveniles, Paul St. Pierre accepted the judge's offer of a reduced sentence in exchange for enlisting in the armed forces.

Paul opted for the U.S. Marine Corps., and was quite gung ho at first, even trying to recruit all his friends. Once in the marines, Paul became obsessed with bodybuilding, and became stronger and more muscular. Most of all, Paul St. Pierre readily admitted to his buddies, he really liked learning how to kill people.

While Paul St. Pierre was in the Marine Corps, Christopher St. Pierre devoted his after-school hours to Ericson's Auto Body.

"I'd probably known Chris since 1976, when he was just a young kid in junior high," Mark Ericson recounted years later. "He's probably four or five years younger than me, and he started working here when he was high school age. I told him that I needed somebody to wash cars and stuff, and he fit in real good—good worker, good kid. He buffed out cars, and this gave him a lot more strength. As a result, Chris could arm wrestle the football players with one hand, and still slam a beer with the other. He loved this new attention and played it up to the hilt. As for his brother Paul, I just remember Chris saying he was trouble. 'Trouble follows him and he follows trouble.' "

Five

Trouble followed Paul St. Pierre into, and out of, the U.S. Marines. An injured leg from a motorcycle accident resulted in his early discharge, and he was soon back in Tacoma.

"I heard a knock on the door one day," said Marty Webb, "and there was Paul St. Pierre, back from the marines, asking Wesley and I if he could stay with us for a while. After that, he moved in with Chris."

"I remember when Chris came in and told me that Paul had come back from the marines and wanted to move in with him," Mark Ericson said. "Chris didn't like that idea at all. In fact, he said that Paul was 'going to ruin everything.' My advice to Chris was just to tell Paul straight out that he couldn't move in—that the house had enough roommates, there wasn't room for any more, and that Paul would have to find something else. The next day when he came to work, Chris had a black eye. I said, 'God, Chris, what the hell happened?' He says, 'I told my brother he couldn't move in.' I asked what happened then, and he said, 'He's moving in.' Brothers can scrap like that and still be best friends, so I didn't think much of it."

Returning from his tour of duty, Paul St. Pierre described his life as a marine as consisting primarily of "partying, and kicking the shit out of punk rockers and squids (navy guys)." An example that Paul St. Pierre shared with anyone who'd listen was the time he almost, or perhaps did, beat a squid to death with a primer chain belt made from the primer chain of a Harley, which he doubled over into a club.

According to Ben Webb, Paul said he took to beating this guy, and was even hitting him with the edge of the chain in the direction it didn't bend. He got so engrossed with "kicking the shit out of this guy" that he forgot to ask for the guy's wallet. The guy threw it at him out of desperation to get him to stop beating him. He even yelled, "What do you want?" Paul was seeing red, and if his friends didn't come pull him off, he would have beaten this poor guy to death. Paul said he didn't know "if the guy made it or not."

The essential difference between Paul and Christopher St. Pierre was that Paul St. Pierre enjoyed violence, and actually sought out physical confrontations. He admitted relishing the sensation of hitting people, of causing them pain.

Paul St. Pierre soon exercised a strong destructive influence over his younger brother. One significant incident involved Christopher St. Pierre being encouraged to gun down total strangers as some sort of rite of manhood. According to Andrew Webb, he and Paul St. Pierre were driving up Fifty-sixth from Portland Avenue. St. Pierre suddenly handed Webb his .45 automatic. "He told me to shoot these four black guys that were walking up toward McKinley," Webb later recalled. "He said they were up to no good with their canes and purple hats. I gave him his gun back and said, 'No, you're crazy,' and he just laughed and kept carrying on all the way to the house about how we should waste them."

Arriving home, Paul St. Pierre told his brother Chris and Donald Marshall that there were four black guys he wanted to waste, and Chris agreed to do it with him. The St. Pierres retrieved a .38 revolver stashed under the upstairs floorboards of Ericson's Body Shop so they wouldn't have to use Paul's .45, and they took off "to get those four black guys."

Webb and Marshall waited, wondering if the St. Pierres were really going gunning for the black strangers. "About a half hour or forty-five minutes later," said Webb, "they came running in, saying that they shot them." Paul St. Pierre supposedly sighted the men on the opposite side of the street, and immediately pulled a U-turn so his little brother would be facing the human targets. "Chris unloaded the five-shot thirty-eight on them and said that he got two of them, but that they all went down to the ground," Webb said. "Paul and Chris were bouncing all around and Paul was slapping Chris on the shoulder saying, 'Good job, bro.' Donald and I just looked at each other in amazement. We couldn't believe our ears."

Paul St. Pierre, so the story goes, wanted to celebrate his little brother's becoming a man. They all went to the store, bought some beer, and took off to share the good news. Their first celebratory destination was the home of Wesley and Marty Webb. "We woke them up," Andrew Webb later said, "and Paul told them what they had done. Wesley didn't seem very happy about it and didn't know what to say."

Marty was no more favorably impressed than her husband. "My God," said Marty Webb when recounting the incident, "can you imagine someone coming to your house, and waking you up, so they can brag about shooting people? I was furious, and I didn't trust those guys one bit." According to Andrew Webb, his older brother took him aside as he was leaving.

"Wesley told me that if what Paul said was true, he's crazy and I had better watch out for him."

This incident of racial violence was not atypical of either the St. Pierres or Andrew Webb. Paul and Chris were violently racist for no apparent reason, but Andrew Webb's racist posturing entailed more complexity. Gail Webb, the sister thirteen years his senior, was married to a black man and is the mother of five interracial children. Her brother is "Uncle Andrew" to her brood of beautiful and obviously "half-black" offspring. At no time did Andrew Webb ever show any prejudice against his nieces and nephews, nor did he display any racist attitudes or behavior toward them.

"He may have mouthed that antiblack talk to be further accepted by Paul and Chris," suggested his older sister. "Our youngest brother did have a very bad attitude toward blacks, primarily from his negative experiences of getting beat up every day at the all-black grade school he was bused to when we first moved to D Street in 1966. But even he was never mean to my kids. My mom's mother said that my kids weren't welcome to come visit her because they were black, but Mom said, 'If they can't come, none of us will ever come.' That settled that. Grandma did a complete turnaround and made my kids welcome. So the race-prejudice thing with Andrew was either fake, or his kindness to my kids was fake. The things that were very real, especially once he started drinking and drugging, were Andrew's hair-trigger temper, interest in violence, and really poor judgment."

Andrew Webb's proclivity for illegal and violent acts, unlike Paul St. Pierre's, didn't derive from being born with a diminished mental capacity. Instead, any thought disturbances or brain-function irregularities were due to one or more head injuries.

"Although Andrew had his head hurt a few times

when he was little, the first time I noticed a drastic change in his behavior," said his sister Gail, "was when he was about seven or eight years old. He got into a scuffle with another boy on the way home from school, and he fell down, banging his head on the curb. When he got home, he showed us the bump on his head. He kept saying the exact same phrases over and over to us as if he had not ever said them before. He would show us the bump every minute or so just like we hadn't seen it or heard about it. Then he also showed some memory loss. Turns out he had a concussion, but by the time the doctor diagnosed the problem, Andrew couldn't even remember how it happened. From then on, he was not the same in lots of ways, but he was still bright and did well in school, but he gradually became more and more weird. I'm sure smoking pot, drinking, and taking lots of acid were major factors. Especially because of the head injury."

Andrew Webb's successes were consistently noteworthy, both in secondary school and in romance. While attending Lincoln High, he became enraptured with an attractive senior-year dropout named Anne. Equally smitten Anne overlooked all blemishes beyond the superficial. Eager for adulthood and the pride of parenthood, the two married soon after Andrew Webb graduated from high school.

"When I married Andrew Webb in the summer of 1981, I was so captivated by him that I couldn't see the major problems, things that were obvious to my parents and my sister. Such as him being a weird and dangerous Bible-quoting alcoholic with a peculiar passion for guns—you know, things like that. But there seemed to be so much good about him, too. Sure, he was the life of the party, but he graduated from high school with honors, was a hard worker, and had that big pride thing going because he was a real man with

a wife and family. Then, one day, he broke his collarbone in a dirt bike accident during his lunch break
from work. As it wasn't a work-related accident, Labor
and Industries didn't cover it. Suddenly, he was out of
work, no income, and his pride was hurt more than
his collarbone. It healed wrong—the collarbone, I
mean—and he had to have it rebroken three months
later. I was pregnant, we had to go on welfare, and
that welfare thing totally crushed him. It seemed to
just drain all the confidence out of him. He started
drinking more and more," recalled Anne. "I kept telling him that if he kept drinking and acting like that,
he was gonna go to jail. He didn't listen to me, of
course. He just kept pouring Rainier Beers down his
throat one right after the other."

It wasn't until after their six-month anniversary that
Anne Webb glimpsed the first shadows of her husband's dark side. She rationalized them away as mere
manifestations of his stress and physical discomfort.
"By the time I recognized the dark side for what it
was, it was a total eclipse," she said years later. "His
dark side was so dark that even I couldn't miss it. I'll
never forget it. I'd never seen anything like it. It
started for me when we were enjoying a pleasant drive.
We were just chatting away and I made a negative comment—not an insult or verbal abuse or anything like
that—I was just sort of venting about stuff. All of a
sudden, he began crying uncontrollably—I mean hysterical sobbing and weeping and wailing like he had
just seen everyone he ever loved murdered or something. He went out of his mind. Scared the you-know-
what out of me. That's when I thought to myself,
'What have I got myself into?' The next event was
worse, and they all kept getting worse; he lost his temper when we were in the kitchen. He tipped over the
table, then went all over the room smashing holes in

the wall with his fists. I was terrified. He suddenly walked out of the room and didn't come back. I couldn't figure out what was going on. Everything was dead quiet. I finally found him. He was all curled up in the fetal position inside the cupboard underneath the bathroom sink! About three or four more times, I saw him do that—curl up in a ball and hide in the cupboard. Well, I knew then that I had married a first-class wacko. It was pretty obvious that I had to walk on eggshells around this guy."

Keeping peace with her volatile spouse kept Anne on her toes; maintaining a positive relationship with her Bible-thumping in-laws required remarkable flexibility.

"Our in-laws could always find a way to make themselves right and everyone else wrong by bending some biblical reference to fit their personal agenda," said Marty Webb. "A good example would be the time Andrew strangled his wife to death."

"*Almost* to death," clarified Anne, "but close enough. Picture this: Andrew is on top of me on the bed, and he's wearing his nine-millimeter in a holster around his waist. . . . That's where he threw me, we're both clothed, and he's wearing a gun. His hands are around my throat, and he's strangling me as hard as he can. I can't breathe. My own husband is murdering me, and I have no idea why—this happens without warning. What could be worse? My life flashes before my bugged-out eyes, and just when I think I'm about dead, he suddenly stops strangling me and leaves the room."

Without taking a breather, Anne Webb leaped from the bed, ran down the stairs, out the door, and to the neighbors' house. She banged on the door until a young boy opened it. "I ran right past the kid into the house and up the stairs—I didn't even really know these people—and I was screaming, 'Lock the doors! Lock the windows! Don't let him kill me!' I found a closet, dove into it, and piled a stack of blankets on top of me.''

Terrified and traumatized, she begged for divine intervention. "I bet I prayed with more intensity and sincerity in that dark closet than my father-in-law ever did in his entire life." Twenty minutes later, she decided Andrew Webb wasn't coming to strangle her in the neighbors' hall closet. Crawling out from under the blankets, she opened the closet door, slipped out, and asked the young boy home alone if she could use the phone. "I didn't know who else to call," she said, "so I called my mother-in-law, Dolores Webb. I told her what Andrew did, and that she should talk to him, or get some help, or something, anything, 'cause he's her son and she's his mom, and I was scared out of my wits. I couldn't believe it—my husband was trying to kill me."

Dolores had a motherly chat with her beloved son, listened to his version of the event in question, and decided how to soothe her hysterical daughter-in-law. Dolores knew there was no greater trump card than God—all knowing, all wise—who despite His absolute dominion over all worlds, seen and unseen, was apparently unable to exercise even the most minimal influence over "evil spirits."

By the time Dolores picked up the phone and dialed, she had devised a perfectly good 'biblical reason' for Andrew Webb's behavior. "My mother-in-law called me back at the neighbors' and told me that Andrew was doing me a favor, that what he did was to free me of demonic possession. I said, 'Huh?' And she explained to me that Andrew spiritually perceived that demons had invaded my body and were going to use it for evil purposes—whatever that means. Andrew, being exceptionally bright, outsmarted them. If the demons thought that their 'earthly abode'—that's me—was about to be destroyed, if they thought I was gonna die, they would get out of me real fast and go somewhere else. She told me all this like it was the most natural and normal thing for a good husband to do now and then—like taking out the garbage or mowing the lawn, except it was strangling your wife. What did I know? She was the mature adult, not me. I believed all that crap because I didn't know any better."

"Mom didn't really believe her own explanation," said Gail Webb. "When she talked to Andrew, she realized that he was out of his mind and on drugs—he had been up for three days without sleep, and nothing for nutrition but LSD and pot. She thought up that demonic-possession thing, which was plausible to her, to calm Anne down, to give the girl some peace and assurance. So there they were: Andrew out of his head, his wife scared and confused, and his mother at her wits' end. But Mom always had to come off as unruffled, self-assured, and with matters well in hand, even when they were completely beyond her grasp. An explanation involving God and Satan would seem a safe approach to just about any crisis."

Dolores Webb embraced a theology in which religion was more magic than mercy, more wrath than reason, and promulgated fearful superstitions about superstition itself. "It was bad luck to believe in superstition," Anne Webb said with a laugh. "For years I would never wish anyone 'good luck' because they convinced me I'd go to hell if I said that. . . . Poor Dolores had mental problems for sure."

"She tried to get help at St. Joseph's Hospital, Western State Hospital, and Puget Sound Hospital, but no one took her seriously," explained Gail. "Mom presented herself too well. She looked like she had it all together; she could express herself and was very well mannered in social situations. When she tried to explain to the doctors at the sanitarium why she wanted to be admitted and treated, they told her that she was just under too much stress, and then they suggested tranquilizers."

"I sympathize with what Dolores went through, and I guess it explains why she was so crazy and violent, but that doesn't change what she did, the way she treated people, including her grandkids. And think of what her own children went through," said Marty Webb. "The emotional abuse, the physical abuse, and of all tragic things, the sexual abuse. What kind of childhood is that? It sure isn't one any of us would wish on our kids. Yeah, they had some regular fun with the other kids in the neighborhood, but I guarantee you that whatever games they were playing in the yard or in the street, the games going on inside the house were more emotionally intense. Hide-and-seek takes on a whole new meaning when you know why someone is hiding, and what someone else is seeking."

Hide-and-seek, tag, freeze tag, red light/green light, run for your life, and kick the can were the energetic fun of a strictly traditional nature enjoyed outdoors by the Webbs and St. Pierres in their younger days. As the boys grew older, the games changed to knockout, truth or dare, stick 'em, stretch 'em, and target practice.

Target practice involved throwing a knife or hatchet at targets drawn on the Webbs' old garage door. Neighborhood consensus conferred the knife-throwing championship on Andrew Webb.

"Who do you think threw that knife into Damon Wells's back?" asked Marty Webb rhetorically. "Who was the champ at knife throwing? Andrew Webb, that's who. I bet he threw the knife into Damon's back. And here's something else to think about," added Marty. "There were several conflicting versions of what really happened to Damon Wells. Who of those three guys could possibly have a motive for killing that kid?"

The three requisites of homicide are means, opportunity, and motive. The knife was the means; deserted Salmon Beach was the opportunity. As for motive, Detective Yerbury easily offered his professional opinion. "From those three—Paul and Chris St. Pierre, and Andrew Webb—only one of them had anything to lose from Wells being alive, or to gain from Wells being dead. Paul St. Pierre and Chris St. Pierre had no adult criminal records. If they were charged and convicted with assault, it would be as first-time offenders. Andrew Webb's situation, however, was altogether different. He was just about to be sentenced for those three assault cases, including the one Randy Nolan and he committed against the Sanfords."

The Webb and Nolan assault on Shane and Nellie Sanford, while never rising to the status of a rational act, is more understandable when placed in perspective. In March 1983, Andrew and Anne Webb's house was burglarized, and two items were stolen: Andrew's 9mm Smith & Wesson, and Randy Nolan's nickel-plated .357 revolver. "Honor and pride were important to the Webbs," recalled Anne, "and it was a poor reflection on Andrew that Randy Nolan's gun was stolen while in Andrew's care."

So Andrew Webb decided to play detective. "He questioned some girls living down the street in a home for troubled runaways if they knew anybody who had been breaking into houses in the area. By amazing coincidence, those girls had just broken up with two guys who were bragging about doing exactly that. Andrew got a hold of the kind of friends that would back him up with no questions, only action—Cory Cunningham and Paul St. Pierre.

"Armed with baseball bats, they kicked in the door of one of the ex-boyfriends of these girls. One of them asked what our boys wanted, and they gave them the name of this junior high kid they were looking for. Well, they brought the kid downstairs, and Cory, Paul, or both held this kid's hands down on the coffee table while Andrew asked the question. If he didn't respond correctly, or in willing humble tone, they would whack his hands with the bat until he was begging for another chance to get the story correct. Meanwhile, this kid's brothers are trying to help get this thing over with, saying, 'You better tell these guys everything they want to know because they are not fucking around.' This pattern was repeated at the next kid's house. The kids admitted that they sold the guns, but our armed invaders forgot to ask the name of the guy they sold them to," Anne continued.

"On the Fourth of July, Randy Nolan was on shore leave from the navy. Soon enough, both Randy and Andrew are in a drunken stupor, talking about the robberies, and they decide to find out who the guy was that bought the guns. They loaded themselves up with every weapon they could get their hands on. . . . They had so many guns on them that they couldn't pull all of them out at once using both hands.

"The plan was the same as before: kick in the door and take the answer by force. On the way, they stopped by Wesley's place to see if he would go along; Marty threw a fit about it."

"I sure did," Marty Webb confirmed. "I threw a real huge fit. I was screaming at Wesley like you wouldn't believe, threatening him that if he went with Andrew and Randy that I was leaving him for good—stuff like that. We'd only been married about a year or so, and he still listened to me a little bit. Also, I think Wesley used my fit as an excuse not to go. He had gone on missions with Andrew before, but enough was enough."

"Before the assault charges, I think Wesley helped him go after a guy who ripped him off," said Anne. "Andrew brought a guy home from work one time who needed a place to stay. When we woke up the next morning, we discovered the guy had stolen all of Andrew's marijuana plants. Well, Andrew found out that the guy was from Olympia, so he got his pal Cory and maybe his brother Wesley and they got all loaded up with guns and took off for Olympia. They got all the plants back, and that just put more fuel on Andrew's delusion that he was invincible, that he could go crashing around, waving guns at people, and have it be OK. He just kept getting more and more violent, like it was all leading up to something. The three assaults he admitted to were almost the big finale, and I wish to God they had been."

Some people assumed that Andrew Webb's drunken assault on the Sanfords was the reason Anne kicked him out. Homeless, and not about to move back in with his folks, Andrew Webb took temporary sanctuary with Chris and Paul St. Pierre at the "Animal House" on Pacific Avenue.

"No, that wasn't the reason I kicked him out," insisted the former Mrs. Andrew Webb. "I worked at Tacoma Catering, and I got him a job in the doughnut factory. Well, he didn't come home one night because he was out till morning making out, or getting it on, with the company's attractive secretary. He finally came home in the morning with lipstick all over his neck. I just knew right away that it was hers. I told him that someone's moving out, and it's not me. That's when he moved in pretty much with the St.

Pierres. Besides, I may have been young and naive, but I wasn't stupid. Andrew was a drunk, plain and simple. The guns were legal, and Andrew had permits, so I just sort of let that go. It was the drinking. I would come home to bottles and bottles—empty bottles of beer. He absolutely had an alcohol problem. I began to wonder if Andrew could ever be sober."

On January 26, 1984, one month prior to the February murder of Damon Wells, a sober and somber Andrew Webb pleaded guilty to all charges in the three assault incidents. Judge Thompson delayed Webb's sentencing for several months because the presentence investigation of Andrew Webb by Probation Officer Gerri Woolf requested a complete mental evaluation of Webb. "When Andrew Webb is drunk, or when he drinks," said Woolf, "it seems to allow him to express the anger or whatever that's inside of him, and release those emotions that are otherwise not released. If there was a real problem—a mental problem—then the problem should be dealt with. If they could not find a problem other than Andrew Webb's drinking, then I felt he should be sentenced to prison."

On Woolf's recommendation, Judge Thompson specifically required that Webb obtain "both neurological screening and a psychiatric mental status exam to address the possibilities of psychiatric disorder and/or a biological disorder."

Therapist Michael Comte, former Assistant Director of the Sex Offender Program at Western State Hospital, conducted the evaluation and analysis of Andrew Webb. "His attorney at that time, Mr. Craig Adams, asked that I evaluate him," confirmed Mr. Comte. "I spoke with him actually on April 11, and then again on April 30 when psychological testing was administered by me."

Comte's testing procedure was to administer the test, then have it sent to Dr. Peterson, a consulting psychologist. "Dr. Peterson is not provided with any background information, nor the specifics of the event, and he's asked to interpret the testing, just the paperwork, and give his best professional shot. He came to the same conclusion I did."

"Andrew Webb has a low frustration tolerance," summarized Comte in his report of May 14, 1984, "an immediate need for gratification, and a hostile capacity to act out his feelings without regard for the consequences in an impulsive fashion." Dr. Peterson noted that "Mr. Webb is unlikely to experience true remorse or guilt for his behavior."

Comte described Andrew Webb as having a mixed personality disorder with antisocial and narcissistic features dominating, intense and abrupt mood swings, alcohol abuse, a lack of ability to deal with anger, and poor impulse control.

Further testing confirmed that Andrew Webb experienced his rapid and immediate mood swings, a high manic phase, characterized by excitability and explosive anger. "Then he would suddenly drop into a low phase, which looked a lot like depression," said Comte. "I suspected a couple different diagnoses: a psychothymic disorder and a bipolar disorder. The psychothymic disorder means that the person emotionally swings in a cycle from high to low, from low to high and to low. Bipolar also relates to rapid mood swings. When I spoke to him in conversation, I brought up the topic of hallucinations, and he did start talking about responding to voices, but when I started probing that area, he backed off rather quickly."

Andrew Webb backed off, his former wife theorized, "because he realized how stupid he sounded insisting that he held conversations with dead beavers. I'm not kidding. He had these dead beaver skulls which were very important to him. He told me that they communicated with him on a deep psychic level."

Andrew Webb's young nephew Travis has vivid memories of his uncle's treasured beaver skulls. "Mom and Dad and I went over to Anne and Andrew's house one day, and I saw these weird skulls on the mantel. As I walked toward them, Uncle Andrew yelled, 'Travis! Don't touch those skulls! They died a bad death!' What the hell was that about?"

"When I visited Andrew in jail," recalled Anne, "he told me to go home and give the beaver skulls a Christian burial. I went home and threw the damn things in the garbage. Who gives a Christian burial to beaver skulls?"

"Uncle Andrew also told me that he yearned to eat human flesh," remembered Travis Webb. "I just said, 'OK, sure,' as if they had it on the menu at Burger Ranch. Oh, he also told me that Vikings followed him around—invisible Vikings, of course—and they gave him advice. If the advice was good, it must have been in Norwegian and he didn't understand it. Either that or the advice sucked, 'cause the best advice would have been to not hit, hurt, or kill people."

Telepathic communication with dead beavers and an invisible advisory committee composed of disembodied Vikings were the more benign symptoms of Andrew Webb's thought disorders. Comte also suggested that there could be something physically wrong with Webb's brain.

"Maybe the fact that Mom ran over his head with the car when he was about eighteen months old has something to do with that," offered his sister Gail. "Mom was getting ready to back out of the driveway, and she saw my sister waving hysterically at her in the rearview mirror. She couldn't figure out what that was all about until she felt the car run over a bump."

The bump was Andrew Webb. The expression of horrified shock on her daughter's face was sufficient confirmation for the panic-stricken Mrs. Webb. "She ran over his head, but the tire wasn't still on him. She jumped out of the car, scooped him up, and ran screaming to the neighbors' house. The neighbor lady tried to calm her down, and agreed to take them both to the hospital."

The emergency room staff treated him for a broken jawbone, but wasn't buying the "I accidentally ran over my son's head with the car" story. The doctors' doubts turned to chagrin when a bruise unmistakably shaped like a tire track appeared across his left cheek.

The doctors reasoned that Webb's head wasn't crushed because the driveway was made of sand. The weight of the car simply pushed his head deeper into it, cushioning the head-popping pressure.

"When Andrew Webb gets under pressure as an adult," ventured Marty, "he breaks into people's homes, puts a firearm in a person's face, threatening to shoot their head off, and slices people's throats because he fears they are going to rip him off. If anyone wanted to see Andrew turn into a violent madman, all you had to do was mix him with alcohol."

Andrew Webb's alcoholism and chemical dependency came as no surprise to his wife, nor did it elude evaluation by the Tacoma Treatment Alternatives to Street Crimes (TASC) staff who evaluated him after his arrest. "We would be willing to work with this individual, based upon his substance use history," reported TASC, affirming their commitment to helping Webb achieve ongoing sobriety, "though we are concerned about the alleged incident that brought him here." Because of this evaluation, an additional legal requirement insisted upon by the judge was that Andrew Webb remain drug and alcohol free, not possess a firearm or dangerous weapon, and that he "stay out of trouble" until his sentencing.

"Andrew Webb was sentenced on those assault charges on June seventh," recalled Detective Yerbury, "exactly two days before Paul St. Pierre shot him." Judge Thompson, who sentenced him on the assault charges, didn't know Webb was involved in the Damon Wells homicide, and Andrew Webb wasn't about to tell him or Probation Officer Woolf. Had Judge Thompson known that Webb was involved in two murders, both of which happened while Webb was on probation, the sentence imposed would most assuredly not have been deferred, nor would Webb's debt to society have been paid by 700 hours of community service.

"Simply put," commented Detective Yerbury, "I was of the opinion then, and I hold that opinion today, that Andrew Webb killed Damon Wells in a desperate act to avoid going to prison."

Six

Charged with murder, and locked up in the Pierce County Jail, Andrew Webb and the St. Pierre brothers weren't speaking to the authorities, but they talked profusely to friends and family. "They were continually calling me on the phone collect from the Pierce County Jail," remembered Marty Webb. "Each of them had a different story, and none of them were the same. I wasn't the only one they called. They were calling Mark Ericson, Jim Fuller, and all sorts of family members."

In one version of the Salmon Beach events, Paul and Chris St. Pierre tackled Damon Wells, then held him down. "Chris said he had kicked the guy in the head a few times. They then held him while Andrew came up from behind, grabbed his hair, pulled back his head and, with the knife Paul had given him, drew it across his throat from ear to ear. Then Andrew turned and walked away. When Andrew called, he told me that he threw the knife down after that," explained Ben Webb, "but Chris said that Andrew didn't throw it down. He said that Andrew turned back, threw the knife, and it stuck in the guy's back. Paul was the heavy that night, and I'm sure at this point he took a stab at Wells and he would have made Chris do the same.

I think the idea was that doing that would link them all together—if one falls, they all fall."

"Chris called me from jail, too," recalled Mark Ericson. "He said that Paul killed that kid out there in Salmon Beach. 'Paul killed that kid.' And then Paul would call me up and say, 'Gee, those guys are nuts, man. Andrew killed that kid.' Chris said they'd beat him up, took him out there, but he didn't want to go. In one version, maybe Andrew's, Paul pulls his gun out and tells Chris to 'take care of him.' Chris says, 'No, you can't shoot him because it will make too much noise.' Paul goes, 'Yeah, right,' puts the gun back, and Andrew and he chased the guy down. Paul pulls his knife out and says, 'Andrew, you gotta take care of him.' I guess he handed the knife to Andrew, and Andrew slit his throat. But first Chris kept telling me that Paul slit Damon Wells's throat. All I know is what they said to me on the phone, and they all said something different. I hated even hearing about it. It was horrible and heartbreaking for everyone involved."

Paul and Chris St. Pierre also shared their consistently conflicting versions with auto mechanic Jim Fuller. "Paul told me that he shot one guy in the head, but it was Chris who said that it was over a bad drug deal," Fuller later told police. "Then Paul told me that Andrew is the guy who cut the guy's throat, and Chris backed that up with one of his phone calls. He told me they dropped him at Salmon Beach and that Andrew ran after him and pushed him down and cut his throat while Chris and Paul were looking on."

"Jim Fuller was not involved in any wrongdoing," confirmed Detective Yerbury. "He contacted us because he was aware that we were told that Damon Wells and he left the party together, and he feared accusations of being an accomplice." When Jim Fuller saw the front-page headline of June 21, 1984—2 MURDER VICTIMS IDENTIFIED—he picked up the phone.

Reporter Bill Ripple's compelling article in the *Tacoma News Tribune* named Damon Wells and John Achord as the homicide victims. Police would not release the murder suspects' identities until formal charges were filed in superior court. The savvy reporter, however, easily discerned and printed the two most probable names: Paul St. Pierre and Andrew Webb.

"That wasn't too difficult to figure out," newsman Chet Rogers later commented. "The police released information that two of the guys were involved in an earlier assault incident where one of them hauled off and pumped hot lead into the other—not the official police wording, of course. Well, the only earlier Tacoma assault case fitting that exact description transpired at, amazingly enough, the same house next to Ericson's that the cops got the search warrant for. Our brilliant, analytical minds—Bill Ripple's included—quickly discerned that two of the arrested men were (a) the guy who pulled the trigger, and (b) the guy who caught the bullet—Paul St. Pierre and Andrew Webb."

The news media also reported that police found the suspected murder weapon. Recovering the double-edged Gerber knife in a brushy area near the SR7 Freeway Interchange with South Thirty-eighth Street was not accomplished by simply foraging through the bushes. The successful search required thorough professional planning, including careful coordination of three distinct search groups under the direction of Officer Donald E. Moore, search and rescue (SAR) coordinator for the city of Tacoma.

Given the assignment, Moore teletyped a message

to the Department of Emergency Management requesting an Evidence Search Training Mission Number, and the following search groups were called into action: Evergreen SAR Tacoma CB Radio Association, and Explorer SAR.

Detective Price took Officer Moore to the freeway interchange, and pointed out where Tony Youso allegedly threw the knife from a moving car. Moore returned Price to Central Station, ordered traffic barricades and ROAD CLOSED UP AHEAD signs, and contacted the Washington State Patrol.

"It was my intention," reported Moore, "to block traffic completely from the ramp area to insure the safety of the volunteer searchers. The Washington State Patrol was further advised of the intention to close the ramp with an estimated start time of seventeen hundred hours." The Tacoma Fire Department Station #11 became the search base, and it was here that the Tacoma Public Works Department delivered twelve traffic barricades.

"With the arrival of Explorer Search and Rescue, all search groups were briefed," said Moore, "and all traffic onto the SR seven ramp was diverted with search base being moved onto the ramp. Using the streetlight standards, string gridlines were set in at the light standards," he explained, "and halfway between each two light standards. Shoulder-to-shoulder grids were used, starting from the pavement and working northbound up the hill.

"Heavy rain and five-knot winds made the brush and grass wet enough to cause them to be laying down with the weight of the moisture," Moore reported. "Searchers were on their hands and knees each time they went uphill."

At approximately 1755 hours, Marvin E. Thompson, a member of the Tacoma CB Radio Association, located the double-edged knife. "It was not touched by any volunteer," stated Moore, "and it was left in the field location until later when the knife was taken into evidence. At twenty-one oh-nine hours, the Washington State Department of Emergency Management was notified that the search was completed with positive results."

Moore also arranged the equally complex same-day search for evidence at Salmon Beach. "The actual field operation started at seventeen hundred hours, and at seventeen twenty-five hours, we located a small white-and-black Nike tennis shoe approximately one hundred feet from the Upper Salmon Beach Road," said Moore. "Per standard operating procedure, the shoe was not disturbed. The shoe was in reasonable condition with the shoelaces intact. The search continued for an additional three hours before the second tennis shoe was located approximately twenty-one feet, nine inches from the first find."

Evidence searches and homicide investigations are invariably challenging and time consuming. They require teamwork, patience, dedication, and persistence. "It seems that when we get called to a homicide," remarked Yerbury, "it's at three in the morning, it's an outdoor crime scene, and it's raining. Whatever the situation, you arrive at the crime scene, you get told the circumstances, and there are always lots of things that need to be done, and lot of doors that need to be knocked on. It's not uncommon to have to go back to the same door four or five times. You have to keep working at it and working at it. You never know when you're suddenly going to find out some important new piece of information."

Captain William Woodard of the Tacoma Police Criminal Investigations Division announced at 1:30

P.M. on June 22, 1984, that four suspects held in connection with the homicides of Damon Wells and John Achord were formally charged by the Pierce County Prosecutor's Office. The names of those charged—Paul and Christopher St. Pierre, Anthony Youso, and Andrew Webb—were officially revealed for the first time.

Stew Johnston of the Department of Assigned Counsel represented Paul St. Pierre, entering his plea of not guilty to all charges. On that same day, notice was sent to the Tacoma Police Department, the Pierce County Sheriff's Office, and the Pierce County prosecuting attorney that Paul St. Pierre was henceforth represented by the Department of Assigned Counsel. In addition, on that same June 22, 1984, Paul St. Pierre, as client, signed a notice that demanded legal representation during any contact with police authorities.

Stew Johnston filed the complete text of the notice with the court, saying, "My client is asserting in this notice his demand that legal counsel be present during any and all contacts by police authorities and their agents. All future contact can be made only through defense counsel, excluding contacts limited to administrative jail purposes. He does not wish to discuss waiver of his legal rights except in writing and in the presence of his or her legal counsel." Paul St. Pierre's assigned legal counsel would be Ellsworth Connelly and Jeffrey Gross.

"The document may be filed," said Judge Healy, presiding, "and the prosecutor's office is charged with the responsibility of notifying law enforcement agencies."

Representing the prosecutor's office was Assistant Deputy Prosecutor Carl Hultman. He immediately accepted this court-ordered responsibility. "We'll do that. We'll do so, Your Honor."

Less than a week later, Tacoma Police detectives took a sworn statement from Paul St. Pierre without presence of his legal counsel. Connelly and Gross were not present because the prosecutor's office did not bother to inform them.

"It was Paul St. Pierre who contacted us, not the other way around," explained Detective Yerbury. "He sent a message to Detective Price saying that he wanted to talk to him. Before we talked to Mr. St. Pierre, we asked the prosecutor's office if it was permissible. We even talked to Carl Hultman's boss. Everything, they said, was OK."

The Tacoma detectives' ethical action—seeking advice from the prosecutor—is admirable behavior. Many police departments simply go ahead with such interviews, and tell no one about it.

"Prosecutors are bound by ethics," explained Mike Grimes, former head of the Anchorage, Alaska, elite Homicide Response Team, "but police have none. We're not obligated to adhere to American Bar Association standards—we're not lawyers. If we tell the prosecutor's office that a suspect wants to make a statement to us, the prosecutor is ethically obligated to inform the defendant's lawyer. We have no such obligation. In many police departments, the policy is to get the statement first, inform someone about it later."

At 4:50 P.M. on June 28, Paul St. Pierre supposedly said, "I hereby make the following free and voluntary statement to Detectives Price and Yerbury, who have identified themselves to me as police officers of the Tacoma Police Department." The wording is a pre-written template fulfilling legal obligations, and not the spontaneous statement of Paul St. Pierre. The next paragraph contains other required identifiers.

"My name is Paul Joseph St. Pierre, I am twenty-five years of age, and was born in Bellingham, Washington. I am single and reside at [house number] South Pacific, Tacoma, Washington. I have lived in Tacoma for twenty-one years. For the last two months, I was employed at Royal Donuts in Tacoma."

Paul St. Pierre's description of Damon Wells's Salmon Beach demise closely matched his brother's version. "Andrew Webb told me he was going to go grab my knife. The knife is a double-edged Gerber Fighting Knife. He went and got the knife." Missing, however, was any reference to Wells's threats of retaliation or attempts to run away. Despite bragging to Roy Kissler about cutting Wells's throat, Paul St. Pierre gave all the credit to Andrew Webb.

"My brother, Andrew, and I were beating up Damon Wells. He was almost unconscious when Andrew took out the knife, grabbed Damon by the hair, and slashed his throat about four times and then stabbed him in the back."

As for the death of John Achord, Paul St. Pierre said that Achord and he were watching the *Rambo* video *First Blood*. Everything was fine until, "John got up and started walking around my house. I told him to sit down and watch the movie. He just looked at me and pulled out his pocketknife. I told him he should sit down. At that point, I thought he was going to stab me. I had my forty-five in my hand and he could see it. He started coming at me with the knife. I told him to stop, but he wouldn't, so I shot him in the head in self-defense. The reason I'm telling you this is because I don't want to take a murder rap that I didn't commit, and I shot John Achord in self-defense. Sometime last year, I picked up this girl hitchhiking. . . ." Paul St. Pierre inexplicably segued directly into a brief narrative seemingly unrelated to the deaths of Damon Wells or John Achord.

"When we got to her apartment," St. Pierre continued, "I dropped her off and she told me to come back later that night. When I returned, there were two Banditos that are in an outlaw motorcycle club. These two Banditos told me they were going to kill me and take my motorcycle. They started coming at me, and I pulled out my forty-five, which I have a permit for, but I did not shoot them because I felt my bike was not worth killing them over. So I let them steal my motorcycle. This is all I want to talk about, thank you."

The significance of this motorcycle incident eluded both police and prosecutors. The answer, if there were one, would require an extensive investigation with no apparent bearing upon either homicide. Hence, the matter was never pursued. In truth, this peculiar narrative was Paul St. Pierre's convoluted way of revealing his motive, admittedly oblique, for "teaching Wells a lesson." Andrew Webb's motive was one that police and prosecutors could easily identify, back up with evidence, and present to a jury. It was a motive, however criminal, that "made sense." Paul St. Pierre's motive made less criminal sense, but it was sensible to Paul St. Pierre. For him, everything was about "getting even," explained Ben Webb. If he couldn't retaliate against individuals, he would "get even" with the event or experience. Paul St. Pierre would re-create scenes of personal humiliation, acting them out with himself as victor rather than victim. That night of terror for Damon Wells was one of those reenactments. The Bandito incident to which St. Pierre referred was more violent and degrading than portrayed in his statement. They beat him up severely, took his shoes, and made him walk home in the dark to "teach him a lesson." In the Salmon Beach reenactment, Damon Wells played the part of Paul St. Pierre; Andrew Webb, Christopher St. Pierre, and brother Paul played the Banditos. Paul St. Pierre's intention was to give this small, weak stand-in for himself the beating and long shoeless walk home that would make things somehow "even." The treatment by the Banditos was another instance of Paul St. Pierre suffering the humiliation reserved only for the weak and the outnumbered.

All hell broke loose when Paul St. Pierre's lawyers found out police took a statement from him without requesting their presence or asking their permission. Ellsworth Connelly, assigned counsel for St. Pierre, was furious. "Do you think for one second that would have happened if they had simply picked up the phone and said, 'Your man wants to make a statement. We have him down at the police station, will you come down?' Of course it wouldn't!"

"A person in custody can only waive the assistance of counsel in the presence of his or her lawyer," explained Jeffrey Gross. "The presence of the assigned counsel restrains the suspect who is motivated by fear, intimidation, ignorance, or unreasoned impulse. Our client had been given his Miranda rights. He'd been arraigned in court. On top of that, he already told them that he wasn't waiving his constitutional rights. A judge would have to rule on whether or not the statement of Paul St. Pierre could be admitted in court."

Those who knew him theorized that what motivated Paul St. Pierre to contact Detective Price was simply that he couldn't let Chris be the only St. Pierre to have his version of events professionally noted and transcribed. Paul St. Pierre wanted equal time and equal attention.

"It's difficult to describe," offered Marty Webb, "but if you heard the way these guys talked on the phone, and the way they acted, it would be real clear that Paul St. Pierre thought the whole thing was really cool. Just take a look at his mug shot—the booking photograph—the picture they took of him when he was arrested. He's smiling, for God's sake! He liked being in the newspaper, and he probably just loved being a well-known murder suspect. I think the whole thing made him feel powerful, tough, and control-ling—and that's what he liked best."

Paul St. Pierre's official statement to the police was different from his informal statement to Roy Kissler. The possibility that he exaggerated his participation in Wells's death when confessing to Kissler gained credibility when he also bragged to fellow inmates at the Pierce County Jail.

Inmate Gordon Gibson voluntarily shared details of St. Pierre's jailhouse confession with Detective Yer-bury. According to Gibson, on June 22, the day St. Pierre was formally charged, St. Pierre was eager to see if there was anything about him in the newspa-per. "The guard came and got the newspaper from us and gave it to him," Gibson explained. "I and Mike Compton [another inmate] asked him why he murdered those two guys. He said the guys were pricks." Concerning the decapitation of John Achord, St. Pierre said that he had to cut the head off because of evidence. He also told his fellow pris-oners about putting the head in cement and throw-ing it in the river.

Paul St. Pierre, a well-practiced braggart, added to his list of informed confidants by sharing details of the Achord incident with Terry Kauslarich, a pal of

Jim Fuller's. "The first part of June, I was at Paul St. Pierre's house working with Jim Fuller on Paul's brother's car," said Kauslarich. "Every time I see Paul, he's always bringing up the subject of doing somebody in. So when the subject came up, Paul said that what he would do would be to shoot somebody in the head and cut off his head so there would be no ballistics nor dental identification. He said he would throw the head somewhere separate from the body. He admitted shooting three or four people. I was also talking to him about some people who had ripped me and Fuller off—Cindy Brewer and Gary somebody—and Paul wanted to go out that night and take care of them. He said, 'Let's just waste them.' I didn't realize that he was serious."

"More and more people came forward with their own stories about Paul St. Pierre," acknowledged Yerbury. "And once those guys were in the Pierce County Jail, we heard from other prisoners and we got more anonymous phone calls. Some of them were valuable, some of them not. Someone called Crime Stoppers and told us that John Achord's head was buried under a doghouse in the St. Pierre's backyard, and someone else called to say the head was thrown into the Nisqually River." Jim Green, who'd known Paul St. Pierre since grade school, told Officer Hargrove that Paul St. Pierre bragged to them that he "shot someone in the face and ditched him."

"It seems everyone had something to say to the police except Andrew Webb," recalled his former sister-in-law. "While Chris, Paul, and Tony Youso were telling plenty, Andrew just got his court-appointed lawyer and kept his mouth shut tight."

Assistant Deputy Prosecutor Carl Hultman filed for amended charges against the St. Pierres and Andrew Webb on July 2, 1984. Originally, the three were charged with murder in the first degree, kidnapping in the second degree, and third-degree assault. The requested revised charges, if approved, would specify first-degree aggravated murder—a death penalty offense. Hultman was not done upgrading criminal charges, and on July 12, he requested increasing the kidnapping charges against the St. Pierres to first degree.

Thursday, July 19, 1984, in the courtroom of Judge James Healy, all of Hultman's amended charges were approved. Andrew Webb, however, was not subject to any increased charges. Carl Hultman asked the court for a continuance in the case against Webb, declined to provide the reasons for his request, and, as a result, was attacked by an outraged Paul St. Pierre.

"He jumped from his seat and lunged for the prosecutor. It was wild—St. Pierre was chasing Hultman around the table," recalled Detective Yerbury, "while jail guards were chasing St. Pierre. The guards caught Paul and wrestled him to the floor. It was potentially a very dangerous situation, and it's one of those very tense emotional moments that only takes on a hue of humor several years later."

St. Pierre was forcibly removed from the courtroom, and Judge Healy ordered a special room prepared with closed-circuit television monitors. "This was so Paul St. Pierre could see and hear what was going on in the courtroom without being able to go after poor Carl," Yerbury said. "He just won't be able to behave himself," Ellsworth Connelly confirmed to the court, "if he sees Carl Hultman."

"Paul was throwing one of his famous fits," commented Wesley Webb's ex-wife, "and as for Tony Youso—he got his case separated from the murder trials altogether. The big deal was what was going on with Andrew. The court proceedings that were supposed to happen against him were all . . . postponed. There was something going on."

What was "going on" was Prosecutor William "Bill" Griffies of Pierce County was authorizing Carl Hultman to cut a deal with Webb. On the afternoon of Thursday, July 19, Hultman and Webb's attorney, Larry Nichols, severed Webb from the others and assigned him a separate trial date.

Shackled in leg irons, hands cuffed to chains around their waists, the three defendants appeared in Judge Healy's courtroom on Friday, July 20. Tony Youso's lawyer requested that his client be released to his parents until the trial. Carl Hultman objected, insisting that there was a high risk that Youso might make a run for it. Judge Healy agreed, and Youso remained behind bars. Paul St. Pierre's bail of $1 million precluded any similar request.

While Youso and the St. Pierre brothers were in Judge Healy's courtroom, the Pierce County Prosecutor's Office announced that accused murderer Andrew K. Webb was now the prosecution's "star witness" against his former codefendants. Webb's newfound status as witness for the prosecution was universally surprising; Paul St. Pierre's July 20th plea of not guilty by reason of insanity surprised no one.

Six days later, forensic psychiatrist Dr. Donald F. Allison examined Paul St. Pierre in the Pierce County Jail. Forensic psychiatry entails interpreting and combining concepts involving mental health, psychiatry, and the law. Associated with the Criminally Insane Unit at Western State Hospital since its formation in 1973, Dr. Allison evaluated offenders and alleged offenders concerning their sanity at the time the offense was committed, and/or their competency to stand trial. His findings were then provided, as requested, to judges and lawyers. "We did from fifteen to sixty evaluations a month in that unit," Allison confirmed.

"July 26, 1984, was a very hot day in the jail," recalled Dr. Allison. "Paul St. Pierre was in his shorts, and he showed some disturbing signs of the heat. I sat right next to the door, and the door was left open. He would occasionally stick his head out the door to see if anyone else was listening."

Allison's diagnosis, based on his interaction with Paul St. Pierre, was that he suffered from a paranoid personality. "He wasn't psychotic. He wasn't neurotic," explained Dr. Allison. "He had the feeling that people were out to get him. The prosecuting attorney was out to get him. The victim of the case was out to get him. He stuck his head out the door to see if anybody else was out to get him. It only took a little over an hour to make this diagnosis."

In their time together, Paul St. Pierre willingly shared his feelings and beliefs regarding his role in the family, his discharge from the Marine Corps, and concern for his younger brother, Christopher.

"He was pretty mad at the Marine Corps because they kicked him out," said Dr. Allison. "And he was somewhat unhappy concerning his relationship with his father—he felt that his father expected more out of him than he delivered. As for Christopher, Paul St. Pierre was especially concerned about his well-being."

Christopher St. Pierre, the one defendant who delivered evidence and information to the police, anticipated favorable treatment from the Pierce County prosecutor. When Andrew Webb cut a deal virtually to deliver the conviction of the St. Pierres, the brothers were infuriated.

"Christopher was very upset when the police said they would help him, and then didn't," confirmed Father Matthew Demaria, a Catholic priest and frequent jail visitor. "He was very angry about that, and most of the time on our visits, I had to hear that over and over again, how the authorities said that they would help him by giving this evidence, and then they didn't. He was very angry about that, and vented that frustration out on me." This venting, however, didn't prevent Father Demaria and Christopher St. Pierre from sharing an amicable relationship.

"He was always pleased that I came to visit him in the Pierce County Jail," the priest recalled. "He prayed and received Holy Communion, and he was very grateful for my visit." On the topic of Christopher St. Pierre's involvement in the two homicides, Father Demaria said, "I get the impression that he was in the wrong place at the wrong time." Paul St. Pierre emphatically restated the identical sentiment during his meetings with Dr. Allison.

"He insisted that his brother Christopher shouldn't be in jail," Allison reported, "and that his brother was in the wrong place at the wrong time, and should have no involvement in this case."

Christopher St. Pierre was irrevocably involved, as was Tony Youso. On July 31, during a pretrial hearing for Youso and St. Pierre, Judge W. L. Brown Jr. refused a defense motion to suppress Christopher St. Pierre's sworn statement. A similar motion regarding Youso's typewritten remarks was also denied. Brown ruled that both men's statements were voluntary, given without coercion, and within legal guidelines. As of July 31, Youso and St. Pierre were scheduled to stand trial on August 13 on one count each of rendering criminal assistance.

Chris St. Pierre wasn't upset about the criminal assistance charge; it was the first-degree aggravated murder charge that concerned him.

The Honorable Thomas Sauriol's involvement with

the St. Pierre case began with his assignment as presiding judge of the Damon Wells trial. "Judge Sauriol is professionalism personified, and his ethical standards are above reproach," said Detective Robert Yerbury. On September 4, in Tacoma's County-City Building, the trial began with a bang.

Seven

One solid gavel bang by Judge Sauriol signaled the onset of the most significant and closely followed Pierce County legal proceeding in decades. "The *State of Washington* versus *St. Pierre, Paul St. Pierre, Christopher St. Pierre,*" began Sauriol. "I take it those are the only defendants that the court is concerned with at this time."

After a brief discussion of potential scheduling problems and probable resolutions, Assistant Deputy Prosecutor Carl Hultman presented his first pretrial motion. The state requested that the signed statement made to Detectives Price and Yerbury by Paul St. Pierre while in the Pierce County Jail be admitted as evidence.

Hultman recounted how on June 20, 1984, Detectives Price and Yerbury visited Paul St. Pierre in the Pierce County Jail. They advised him of his rights and arrested him for the murders of John Achord and Damon Wells. St. Pierre signed a form acknowledging that his rights had been explained to him, and when asked if he wanted to waive his rights, he declined to do so. Twenty-eight days later, Paul St. Pierre sent a written request from the jail, commonly referred to as a kite, directly to Detective Price. The kite read: "I would like to talk to you please. Thank you."

Aware that they were not to initiate contact with the suspect outside presence of counsel, Detectives Price and Yerbury consulted the prosecutor's office for advice. They spoke both to Carl Hultman and his superior, Ms. Chris Quinn-Brintnall, and were advised to go ahead and take St. Pierre's statement without notifying Paul St. Pierre's attorney. "The detectives acted responsibly, the statement was voluntary, and the court should admit it as evidence," said Carl Hultman.

Ellsworth Connelly, Paul St. Pierre's attorney, vehemently disagreed. "My client can only waive the assistance of counsel in the presence of his lawyer, and he had already served official notice that he wasn't waiving his constitutional rights."

It was clear and inarguable that on the day of his arraignment, June 22, 1984, Paul St. Pierre signed a notice advising that he wanted counsel present anytime he was questioned. The notice further stated that the Department of Assigned Counsel, representing Paul St. Pierre, demanded to be present "during any and all further contacts made by police authorities and/or their agents except during administrative jail contacts."

"It is phrased as a demand," countered Hultman in his argument to the court, "but the Department of Assigned Counsel has no rights in this situation with respect to whether or not Mr. St. Pierre talks to detectives or not. It's Mr. St. Pierre who has those rights. These are not Mr. Connelly's rights. He doesn't have the privilege and the power, and with all due respect to Judge Healy, nor does the court have the power to prohibit Mr. St. Pierre's communications with the rest of the world."

The circumstances surrounding St. Pierre's communication with Detectives Price and Yerbury were, in Connelly's view, highly irregular and suspect. "Was there one court reporter present who wrote down one single word as it happened at the time in shorthand, on machine, or otherwise? No. Was there one single inch of tape recording to take down the two hours that are represented in this page and a half that takes five minutes to read? No. Why? I don't know why," said Connelly to Judge Sauriol, "and you don't know why, and neither of us know what was said and done in there simply because they chose not to do this. Do you think for one second that would have happened if they had simply picked up the phone and said, 'Your man wants to make a statement. We have him down at the police station. Will you come down?' Of course it wouldn't."

The fact that neither Price nor Yerbury saw the court order insisting that St. Pierre not be contacted or questioned without his lawyer present was an endless source of dismay to Connelly, and an embarrassment to Carl Hultman. "Judge Healy directed the prosecutor to make copies available to everybody," Connelly informed the court. "Well, did he? No. The prosecutor never told the detectives about this, and they never received copies as directed by Judge Healy.

"Was there any effort made to contact Paul St. Pierre's attorney, or the Department of Assigned Counsel, or myself?" asked Connelly rhetorically. "No, none at all, she—Chief Deputy Prosecutor Brintnall— just said, 'Well, go ahead and talk to him.' They could have phoned, but they didn't. Why? Because they were simply eager to get a statement from Paul St. Pierre, and to do that, to hell with any kind of court order, or direction from the court, or notice or anything like that.

"Had they called me," he further explained, "the

first thing that would have happened would have been a conversation with the defendant discussing the advisability or inadvisability of giving the statement. If he decided to do it, I would demand that it be taped in full so that we don't have two or three pages of boilerplate, which the officer says is what he dictated to them, and we know that simply is not so. Do you think that if I had been there I would have gone along with this? I say it should never come in," he told Judge Sauriol. "It's contrary to law. It's contrary to common sense and good morals and it shouldn't come in. That's all I have to say, Your Honor."

"Do you want to try to top that?" Sauriol asked the other attorneys, indicating his admiration of Connelly's presentation.

"I'm almost devastated, Your Honor," responded Hultman. The prosecutor's sardonic delivery didn't impress the court. "Don't make light of it," said Sauriol. Hultman then assaulted Connelly's argument, entreating the court to accept St. Pierre's statement.

"It was Paul St. Pierre who initiated contact, motivated by a desire to explain and express his part in some grisly incidents, and to describe and explain other people's conduct in those same incidents. There is no indication that he was motivated by fear. There's no indication that he was motivated by intimidation. He sent out the kite saying he wanted to talk to the detectives."

The court could not find that St. Pierre was motivated by ignorance because he was advised of his rights, said Hultman. "Paul St. Pierre did something that he would not have done if Mr. Connelly had been there. I don't think that rises to the level of unreasoned impulse. Detectives Price and Yerbury specifically asked Paul St. Pierre if he were initiating the contact of his own free will." As verification, Hultman called attention to this phrase in St. Pierre's statement: "They were not to talk to me without my attorney being present, but I chose to talk to them."

"This is a very unusual case," Hultman said. "I've never seen one like this before. I'm impressed with the detectives, the way they honored what they believed was his assertion of rights, the way they checked with counsel before they made a decision, and that they took his statement in a way free from interrogation. They simply let him tell them what he wanted to say, and I think the statement should come in."

The entire scenario did not sit well with Judge Sauriol. "The court has been in the profession of law since 1953," he stated emphatically, "and I can honestly say that during that entire time when I practiced law, I never had a communication with my opposing litigant under any circumstances while the litigation was going on."

Sauriol was blatantly upset that Hultman's superior, Chris Quinn-Brintnall, approved of Yerbury and Price taking St. Pierre's statement without first contacting Mr. Connelly. "I don't want anything I say to be taken in any way to condone the chief deputy prosecutor for doing what she did in this case. The reason I'm putting the blame at that doorstep is because I know, Mr. Hultman, that she's your boss, and whatever you may have said would have her stamp of approval if she didn't do anything to countermand it. This is a very serious case. It is as serious a case as this court has ever encountered as either an attorney or as a trial judge.

"The rule of law involved is whether or not the defendant's statement to the police officers was voluntarily made with no evidence of duress, force, threat, intimidation, or the like," said the judge. "In this particular instance, the situation has been complicated by the actions, and I'm not blaming the police officers, complicated by the actions of the chief deputy prosecutor. It annoys me. This case is going to be difficult enough without flirting with disaster, and that's what's happening. This better be a message to somebody," insisted the judge. "I don't want to see anything like this occurring again in this case. First of all, it's probably going to give me an ulcer and, secondly, it may very well create reversible error. This case is going to be tried according to the rules from day one, and this is day one.

"I think the only thing that saves the state's neck is the fact that Paul St. Pierre initiated this contact," Sauriol said. "I don't think we would be dealing with the violation of the canons of ethics in this case but for the fact the police were concerned with what they should do. They went to the prosecuting attorney's office, and Chris Quinn-Brintnall said, 'Go ahead, do your thing.' She then made these two police officers an arm of the prosecuting attorney's office. In my judgment, there is a violation of the canons and that's flirting with disaster.

"Secondly," continued the judge, "Judge Healy indicated that this order shall be complied with. Mr. Hultman took it upon himself to say, 'I'll advise the police officers,' and he didn't do it." Sauriol then leveled his gaze directly at Carl Hultman. "I don't know, Mr. Hultman, whether it's because you have such a horrible workload, and the pressure of having to deal with that, that you didn't do it, but you should have.

"I don't think that the violation of the canon of ethics should have anything to do with the voluntary nature of the statement," he said, speaking to the heart of the issue, "nor does the ethical violation make a difference as to the admissibility of the confession."

The judge remained irritated and dismayed with the

prosecution's behavior, and offered additional critical comments. He noted that when Paul St. Pierre sent a second kite, Chris Quinn-Brintnall immediately notified Connelly's office. "She should have done it with the first one, but I don't think that should suppress the confession, but it does not speak very well of the chief criminal deputy's adherence to the canon of ethics. The reason I'm saying all this is because the chief criminal deputy in Pierce County is one of the chief law enforcement officers, if not the chief law enforcement officer, in this community. The court will deny the motion to suppress the statement."

Police officers acting as adjuncts of the prosecutor's office, or any similar unethical behavior, is a sensitive topic for Tacoma residents. The slightest hint of corruption triggers unpleasant memories of the police department's well-earned and decidedly unsavory postwar reputation.

Homecoming World War II veterans found their city in decay and notorious for vice. Racketeers, vice lords, thugs, and gangsters were the primary architects of Tacoma's law enforcement policies. Honest cops treaded softly on the underworld-controlled streets while an undercurrent of civic dissatisfaction was rising day by day. Detective Yerbury's father, Robert L. Yerbury, joined the Tacoma Police Department in 1947 when the troubled port city had devolved almost to the final depths of its downward spiral. At age twenty-three, Yerbury was either exceptionally brave or remarkably naive. The late-1940s Tacoma Police Department was riddled with corruption.

In 1946 through 1947, the times, if not rapidly changing, were shifting. The new consumer-centered climate of cold war America was inhospitable to what had been formerly acceptable. Corruption and the elimination of vice were the hot topics for political platforms, crusading district attorneys, grand juries, and citizens committees.

Tacoma's change came from the Tacoma Police Department. On Thursday, March 28, 1946, forty rogue, or vigilante, Tacoma police officers raided seven gambling and "bootleg" operations downtown, arresting fifty-four persons and seizing over $1,000 in cash. Neither the chief of police nor the commissioner of public safety, tangentially connected to these enterprises, was informed of the raids, and both were furious.

The Thanksgiving weekend saw seven more raids and forty-two arrests. The twelve arresting officers were immediately suspended. Vigilante raids on illegal gambling dens continued through 1947, sparking a firestorm of controversy. Four officers were dismissed, and denounced by Chief William Farrar as "tools of the underworld."

By summer, however, two constables from neighboring towns joined forces with the fired Tacoma cops and pulled a joint raid on the infamous Star Social Club. They arrested sixty-seven people and shipped them by bus to the town of Roy, where they each posted $25 bail for being in a place where gambling was being conducted.

By July 27, 1947, the four dismissed patrolmen were reinstated with back pay, and the raids ceased. But the reverberations continued to be felt throughout city hall. A succession of chiefs, some lasting as little as three months, began. Between March 1946, when the first raids were made, to July 1953, when the department was reorganized, eight men served as police chief.

Political interference in police operations was a daily fact of Tacoma life due to the commissioner form of local government. The commissioner, a de facto police chief, often knew nothing about law enforcement.

The proliferation of prostitution fueled accusations that police and vice lords were in bed together, and that the cops were accepting payoffs for protection. The American Social Hygiene Association declared Tacoma diseased, and the United States Army threatened to put the entire city of Tacoma "off-limits" to soldiers. Tacoma captured the title "America's #1 City for Sexually Transmitted Disease." This dubious distinction was not easily overcome.

Tacoma was America's first major city to implement the city council–city manager form of local governance. This bold step directly attacked the roots of political and police corruption. On July 9, 1953, Chief Roy D. Kerr, an experienced officer with impeccable credentials, assumed office.

"That day marked the beginning of a new era for the Tacoma Police Department," said Yerbury. "Chief Kerr was a true 'professional' police chief, having previously served as chief of Topeka, Kansas, as well as a deputy sheriff and deputy U.S. marshal. He was also a graduate of the FBI National Academy."

He put an end to graft and corruption, appointed the straitlaced John Hickey to head up the Morals Squad, and together they attacked vice throughout the city. Kerr also introduced the first classroom training for new recruits, revamped department forms, procedures, and policies. Gradually, Chief Kerr rebuilt the police department into a professional, modern agency.

"What made the Tacoma situation so unique is that it was the members of the police department, and not an outside investigation, who demanded the change that ushered in a new era for the police department and the city," commented the second-generation Yerbury. "Today my son carries the same badge number that my dad carried. When he graduated from the state academy, Dad and I jointly pinned the badge on him. Of course, my dad is incredibly proud of him."

The senior Mr. Yerbury, an eyewitness to his city's turbulent history, served twenty-seven years with the Tacoma Police Department. "Through thick and thin, even in the toughest times, we had a great police department, and we still do," he said. "I was always proud to be on the Tacoma Police Department, and I loved the job. As for corruption, I never took a dishonest dime in my life, and I can name lots of other good cops who didn't get into that corruption at all. There were a few—that's a fact. They were into small deals—none of them were getting rich at it, I don't imagine. A few bad ones make even the good ones look bad—and that's a shame. There were plenty of good, honest cops—and those are the ones I remember and admire. Of course, folks around here are sensitive to Tacoma's old reputation, and that helps keep things on the up and up."

The community's sensitivity amplified the importance and relevance of Judge Sauriol's strongly worded admonitions to the prosecutor's office against even the appearance of impropriety.

Sadly, His Honor's stern warnings against "flirting with disaster" were repeatedly violated. The next crises generated by an alleged act of questionable ethics involved a conversation between Chief Deputy Prosecutor Quinn-Brintnall and Paul St. Pierre's co-counsel, Jeffrey Gross. The St. Pierres and Andrew Webb all faced the death penalty if convicted of first-degree aggravated murder. There was, however, a way to avoid this. Quinn-Brintnall told Gross, "The first one through the door gets the deal." The clear message inferred by Gross: "If your client doesn't want to die, your client should make a deal." The first one "through the door," in all truth, was Christopher St. Pierre. However, it was Andrew Webb who got the deal. Gross and Connelly, backed up by Christopher St. Pierre's lawyer, John Ladenburg, complained bitterly to the court and in the press.

"I recommended that no bargain be given to Andrew Webb," insisted Quinn-Brintnall, countering this allegation. "I felt that Andrew Webb was a very dangerous individual and, for that reason, I would not bargain with him." If there was going to be a deal cut with anyone, Quinn-Brintnall knew who shouldn't get it. "Neither Andrew Webb nor Paul St. Pierre would have been my choice," she admitted. As for a race down the hall, Quinn-Brintnall confirmed there was a race—but not between defendants.

The reason for the race was a stipulation in Washington State law that would prevent the prosecutor from upgrading the charges against the defendants from first-degree murder to first-degree aggravated murder—a death penalty offense—if the accused filed notice to plead guilty to the original lesser charge.

"There was basically a race to the clerk's office door," said Quinn-Brintnall, "between Larry Nichols and myself, and I think Tom Larkin representing Christopher St. Pierre at that time, and Ellsworth Connelly and Jeff Gross who were representing Paul St. Pierre at that time."

Quinn-Brintnall filed her amended charges at 12:17 P.M. on June 29. Larry Nichols, according to the clerk's office, filed the notice of intent to plead guilty as charged to murder one on behalf of Andrew Webb sometime between noon and 12:17 P.M.

After Webb won the race to the clerk's office, the result was the same as if he had indeed run to the prosecutor's office. The Pierce County prosecutor, Bill Griffies, and Assistant Deputy Prosecutor Carl Hultman negotiated an "agreement" with Larry Nichols on behalf of his client. Quinn-Brintnall was out of town during these negotiations.

The deal was supposedly clean and simple: the kidnapping and assault charges against Andrew Webb would vanish, as would any possibility of the death sentence. In exchange for his life and the possibility of parole, Webb would testify against Paul and Christopher St. Pierre.

"He was allowed to escape a possible death sentence by pleading guilty to the lesser charge of first-degree murder and turning state's evidence," complained Ellsworth Connelly. "I don't think it is appropriate and I don't think it's right."

"There is no 'deal,'" countered Prosecutor Bill Griffies. "He has the right to plead guilty. Andrew Webb feels that the time has come for him to tell the truth, and to testify and attempt to cleanse what he's done and that's what he's doing. He's doing it out of a sense of what he feels is right."

"Webb's willingness to talk to police," added Carl Hultman, "shows mitigating circumstances. Reports of a history of violence in the St. Pierre household do not." The St. Pierres had no previous criminal records, Connelly pointed out, while Webb was convicted of assault in a case where he held a gun to a victim's mouth.

"The 'mitigating circumstances' for Webb is that he won the footrace to the prosecuting attorney's office and literally saved his neck," said Connelly, "when he was the one who used the knife."

Griffies acknowledged that he considered Webb's "willingness to testify" against the St. Pierre brothers "a mitigating factor in itself. We have got to be practical." He further explained that if there is no evidence to support a murder charge, and one member of the group of offenders is willing to testify against the others, then the prosecution would have its evidence. "It is not unusual at all," said Griffies. "It is something that becomes necessary, and it is something that is done routinely in murder cases."

The St. Pierres immediately moved to strike the death penalty, charging misconduct by the prosecutor in selecting which defendants would face a possible death sentence. They also requested that the trial be moved out of Pierce County. The court reserved ruling on the death penalty issue, but granted the change of venue. Under intense press scrutiny and local interest, the case against the St. Pierre brothers began.

Tony Youso was the second one through the door, but there was no one racing against him. Attorney Karl Haught told the court that Youso participated out of fear for his life, and his client readily admitted tossing the cement-encased head of John Achord into the Puyallup River. Charged as an accomplice in both homicides, he pleaded guilty to tampering with physical evidence. Youso received a one-year deferred, and forty-seven days in the county jail. Having served almost forty days, Youso was released within a week. As part of his plea-bargain agreement, he would testify against his former housemates.

Beginning September 20, prospective jurors in Pacific County were individually questioned in the privacy of Judge Sauriol's chambers. "I know you're a little bit nervous about that type of procedure," said the judge, "but these questions are not designed to pry into your private or personal affairs or to embarrass you. All three of these lawyers are professionals, and very good ones. The purpose of this is to secure and to determine that the case is tried before an impartial jury.

"The prosecuting attorney has filed a notice of intention to seek the death penalty in this case," Sauriol reminded the potential jurors, and detailed the degree of their sequestration. "You will not be able to have any communication with anyone other than yourselves, and you will not be able to discuss this case or any of the evidence until the case is finally submitted to you." There would be no calls back home; they would be bused to Tacoma and kept in a hotel until everything was over. "You will be virtually out of touch with members of your family. That is virtually what sequestration means." With that, the individual questioning began.

Chief Prosecutor Bill Griffies personally took charge of this high-profile case, with Assistant Deputy Prosecutor Carl Hultman acting as his aide. During the jury selection process, Griffies asked several potential jurors if they would give the death penalty to the St. Pierres even though Andrew Webb avoided it by cooperating with the prosecution. Any juror acknowledging reluctance in the matter was immediately excused. The defense strongly objected, insisting that the prosecution's line of questioning was inappropriate and illegal. "They are making the challenge," said Ladenburg, "that the jurors are unwilling to follow the court's instructions."

"Essentially," John Ladenburg later elaborated, "Griffies was asking them, 'If you find these guys guilty, will you hang them?' You just can't do that. It is not legal at all." So intense was the objection, and the argument given in its support, the prosecution took the objection seriously, looked closer into the applicable policies, and recognized their error.

"The defense counsel were correct in their objection," Hultman finally acknowledged. "We were prejudging some of the issues of the case." When the situation's perilous nature was realized, Chief Prosecutor Bill Griffies quietly withdrew from direct participation.

"I walked into the courtroom one morning," recalled John Ladenburg, "and saw Carl Hultman sitting by himself, and he seemed upset. I asked him where Griffies was. He told me that Bill wasn't going to be there. I knew right then something was up. Sure enough, poor Carl was left alone to face both the embarrassment and the uphill task of arguing against a mistrial. I felt sorry for Carl that day, I really did."

Hultman valiantly argued for devising a remedial strategy that would satisfy legal requirements while still excluding the same proposed jurors. "It is the state's belief that this error can be sufficiently cured," he suggested. "Simply bring back those jurors and excuse them all over again. This time they would be properly excused," Hultman told the court, "and the trial can proceed."

The prosecutor's office also offered up some of their remaining jury challenges in appeasement. Ellsworth Connelly remained quiescent; John Ladenburg never quavered.

"Paul St. Pierre would object to that procedure," said Connelly. "I just want to be on the record as having objected to that procedure," added Ladenburg. The defenses' objection fell upon sympathetic ears. Judge Sauriol, already aggravated by the prosecution's previous borderline behavior, gave Chief Prosecutor Bill Griffies another stern lacing. "Should a similar incident occur again," he snapped, "the attorney who caused it would be held personally responsible for the cost to taxpayers of the aborted proceedings."

The trial was over and everything was back to square one. "At that point," recalled John Ladenburg, "there was really only one thing we defense attorneys could do that made sense to all of us—we went out to lunch."

Paul and Christopher St. Pierre's attorneys commiserated over sandwiches and coffee.

"Ellsworth Connelly ran against William Griffies in the previous election," recalled Ladenburg. "Connelly was considered the front-runner, and was favored by the local Bar Association." As the election approached, Connelly, because of his prestigious endorsements, extensive experience in the prosecutor's office, and strong name familiarity, was far ahead in the polls. When Election Day drew near, he was targeted for what some considered a "smear campaign" in the press. Griffies won the Pierce County election, but not Pierce County's hearts.

"He was not the predetermined choice," acknowledged attorney Ben Bettridge, Pierce County's 1985 Republican party chairman at that time. "I think a lot of people wanted him to fail and I think a lot are angry because he hasn't. It's hard to argue with results."

The results lauded by Bettridge were, for many residents, insufficient. Corrections officers openly complained of too many plea agreements, and several police officers, while complimenting the efforts of Hultman and Quinn-Brintnall, said that the prosecutor's office was "giving our cases away."

In Connelly's estimation, a good man to replace Griffies would be John Ladenburg, Christopher St. Pierre's defense attorney. The concept was not initially appealing to Mr. Ladenburg. "I had a successful practice, had won quite a few high-profile defense cases, and was quite happy doing what I was doing. I'm a real Tacoma 'hometown' type of guy. I like doing a good job in my profession, and being of service to the community. I just never really seriously considered running for chief prosecutor."

At age six, John Ladenburg was the third of sixteen children when his family settled in Tacoma. He graduated with honors from Stadium High School, then took off for Spokane, Washington, to attend Gonzaga University. In 1969, he married Connie Chapman, his high school sweetheart. To support his family and his education, Ladenburg worked in gas stations and grocery stores. "I also bused tables and cooked at a Denny's restaurant," said Ladenburg. "I would attend classes during the day and then often work until two in the morning. This paid off in 1974 when I graduated from Gonzaga Law School and passed the bar exam. That's when Connie, the kids, and I returned to Tacoma, and I joined Binns, Petrich, Hester and Robson, a well-known law firm. In 1976, a good friend from childhood and I formed our own firm, Ladenburg and Haselman."

It wasn't simply Ladenburg's legal background and expertise that prompted Connelly to suggest that he run against Griffies. A significant aura of civic service surrounded Ladenburg's career—he served as the president of the South Tacoma Business Club, several advisory committees to the Tacoma City Council, including the Urban Policy Committee. In 1982, he was appointed to the Tacoma City Council over twenty-seven other applicants, and was elected for another term in 1983, immediately prior to the St. Pierre case. During his tenure on the council, he chaired both the budget committee and the utilities committee. A strong and practical environmentalist, he was instrumental in saving local taxpayers tens of millions of dollars by pioneering energy conservation standards.

"Despite being an attorney who represented 'the bad guys,' law enforcement personnel respected me because I strongly endorsed increased police and fire services for Tacoma," Ladenburg said. "The police union and the sheriff's guild earlier suggested that I run for chief prosecutor, but I didn't seriously consider it. Everything was going great for me both personally and professionally. I appreciated Connelly's complimentary suggestion, and I tucked the idea away in the back of my mind. The defense of Christopher St. Pierre and the Sixth Amendment of the United States Constitution were my top professional priorities at that precise point in my career, and at that general point in our pleasant mealtime consultation."

Eight

The bold-type headline of the *Tacoma News Tribune* on October 9 was a surefire attention grabber: KILLER GIVEN LIFE SENTENCE; MURDERER IMPLICATES ST. PIERRES. The opening paragraph referred directly to a new elaborate confessional statement by Andrew Webb in which he claimed that he "slashed Wells's throat because he feared he would be killed himself if he didn't."

Webb's narrative of Damon Wells's tragic fate differed dramatically from those of Perez, Marshall, and the brothers St. Pierre. In Webb's version, he bravely opposed each and every instance of violence, came to the aid of Damon Wells, and did everything possible to mitigate the severity of the situation.

He and Wells were having a friendly postfight chat, he asserted, when Paul and Chris suddenly burst into the bathroom. "They started hitting and knocking him into the corner," said Webb. "I stopped them and told them that Damon was OK, but Paul would kick him and tell him to shut up. I gave up arguing with him because he was getting mad at me, so I helped him walk Damon out to the car."

Wells possibly died, according to Webb, from being kicked in the head by Christopher St. Pierre. "We all chased him and tackled him," Webb said of Wells's attempted escape at Salmon Beach. "He was on his hands and knees and he raised his head up to yell for help. That's when Chris kicked him in the head, which either knocked him out or killed him. I thought he was dead because he wasn't breathing."

It was then, said Webb, that Paul St. Pierre compelled him under implied threat of death to slit the throat of the already lifeless Damon Wells. "Paul then grabbed the knife from me and said, 'This is how you kill somebody,' and stabbed him in the back. He then handed the knife to Chris and told him to stab him, so Chris did that once that I know of."

"How did the newspaper get hold of Andrew Webb's blatantly self-serving plea-bargaining statement?" asked Ellsworth Connelly. He also provided the answer. *The Tacoma News Tribune* got it courtesy of the Pierce County Prosecutor's Office.

"Here's how they did it," offered Connelly, explaining that an ordinary guilty plea has a simple defendant's statement that merely acknowledges the essential elements of the offense. "They put in as part of his plea the entire statement that he gave when he wanted to make his deal. Yes, the whole statement covering every alleged murder, the decapitation, everything you can think of. The prosecution knew full well the press was dying to get their hands on that, and as soon as they got their hands on it, they'd print it. Which they did!"

The newspaper story, accompanied by a large picture of Andrew Webb, gave prominence to his recent version of events. "Andrew admitted slicing Wells's throat—although under pressure from Paul—and he absolutely threw the knife into that kid's back just like he used to throw knives and hatchets into his folks' garage door," said Marty Webb. "In this version, almost all the blame or guilt is put directly on Paul and Chris, and he makes himself out to be the most innocent of the three. By pleading guilty and cutting this deal, he got a twenty-year minimum sentence, but he could serve as little as thirteen or fourteen years."

Connelly, outraged by the apparent manipulation of Tacoma's print media by Prosecutor Griffies, was equally angered when Griffies and Chief Deputy Prosecutor Chris Quinn-Brintnall granted a special in-depth interview to television station KSTW. Broadcast two weeks before the trial, the "St. Pierre Case" was discussed in remarkable detail.

"We see the prosecutor and his chief deputy go on television, channel eleven, and talk about *this specific case,*" Connelly said with ill-concealed anger. "The purpose of this apparently is some sort of means by which the general public can be reached, every potential juror. This station goes out all over the state on cable. Presumably hundreds of thousands of people could have watched this program. Is that proper? No. Is it legal? No. Is it a violation of our ethical rules? Yes. Why is it done? Why would a man do this? The obvious reason is so he can have some sort of advantage outside the courtroom before anything really gets under way."

Connelly sought dismissal of all charges, claiming that the prosecutor's reprehensible conduct made a fair trial impossible. "I submit to Your Honor that there has been a concerted effort of misconduct by the prosecutor in an effort to give themselves an edge with reference to Webb, and to hurt and prejudice St. Pierre in every way possible that they can. Not by coming and putting on a strong case in court, but before we even get there with this publicity business, this TV, this leaking to the newspaper, and finally this thing on the plea.

"I say it's an abuse of process," Connelly insisted. "I say that it is misconduct, and I think that what you should do is to strike the death penalty. I don't know how they can act like this with someone's life hanging in the balance and expect to salvage a death penalty case."

John Ladenburg joined Connelly in the motion to strike the death penalty, and filed a few of his own. Among those were a motion to drop the entire case against the St. Pierres because of prosecutorial misconduct, and a motion for a restraining order to gag the prosecutor from any further public comment on the case.

Judge Sauriol immediately granted the gag order silencing Bill Griffies and his staff, bringing the prosecution's recent media career to a dead halt.

"It is nothing short of amazing," said Ladenburg, "the continual abuse of the rules and procedures in this case by the prosecuting attorney's office." The court viewed the TV interview of October 6 on videotape, and studied a verbatim transcript. After watching the video, John Ladenburg quoted directly from Bill Griffies's comments about Webb's plea-bargain deal, drawing attention to several incongruent statements, including "there is no deal."

"He's saying on TV that there is no deal with Andrew Webb," stated Ladenburg firmly. "Well, that's hogwash! That is a blatant violation of disciplinary rules for attorneys in this state."

"Griffies also said that Andrew Webb was pleading guilty because 'it was the right thing to do,' and that was complete bullshit," commented Anne Webb several years later. "Oh, yeah, sure. Andrew Webb: altruistic snitch and ace manipulator. He manipulated me for years, burying me under layer upon layer of fear, lies, and intimidation. He enjoyed burying those poor guys they killed, too," she recalled. "Honest to God, he told me that when he was burying the bodies, the earth spoke to him—the ground opened up and spoke to him. Then he quoted something from the Bible about the ground speaking. There's probably nothing in the Bible like that, and if there is, I'm sure whoever wrote the Holy Bible wasn't talking about Andrew K. Webb."

"I have practiced law for eleven years here," Ladenburg told the court. "I have never had to accuse a fellow attorney in court of violating the rules, but I can see no way around it. Frankly, I am appalled at the conduct of the prosecuting attorney of this county."

John Ladenburg presented a detailed legal argument, buttressed by extensive precedents and rulings. The prosecution's reprehensible behavior, he insisted, equally violated ethics and law, including the right of his client to a fair trial.

Carl Hultman, of course, did not agree with either Connelly or Ladenburg, and presented extensive arguments refuting their accusations. He also opined that Tacoma's television broadcasts and newspaper stories have little or no impact on citizens of nearby King County, the county from which jurors for the new trial would be selected. Results of his own unofficial poll concluded that only one out of fifty-four people in the prosecutor's office on the ninth floor knew about the television broadcast—hardly a major impact. Hultman did, however, agree that the so-called "gag order" was a fine idea.

"We never asked for a gag order before," Connelly later explained, "because it never occurred to anyone on the defense side that the prosecutor was going to go on television with his chief criminal deputy and talk about the case. We never thought that was going to happen because nobody has ever heard of anybody doing that sort of thing in a death penalty case."

Thomas Sauriol's reaction to "the first one through the door gets the deal" was dismay and disgust. "I am very troubled by that undisputed and obviously undenied remark," said the judge. Sauriol recalled previously reprimanding the prosecutor, and his declaration from the bench that there must be no more "flirting with disaster," and absolutely no ulcer-inducing aggravation. By the time Connelly, Ladenburg, and Hultman exhausted their arguments, Judge Sauriol was exhausted as well. "Right now I have Excedrin Headache Number four-sixty," he loudly declared. "It's all generated by this case, and it's fierce!"

"Do you think for one minute that I don't consider a felony, first-degree aggravated circumstances murder case serious?" the angry judge asked rhetorically. "I wasn't on the bench five months when I had to impose the death penalty, and I choked it out. It hurts to say, 'You shall be hanged by the neck until you're dead.' "

His Honor then aimed his piercing gaze at Pierce County's chief prosecutor. "Do we have any more surprises now, Mr. Griffies?"

"Not that I know of, Your Honor," replied Griffies politely. During a moment of stressful silence, Judge Sauriol collected his thoughts and found them disturbing. From his years of experience, he knew that disgruntled lawyers, having lost a case, often blame "the guy in the black robes. He's the reason we lost the case. I'm not going to take the blame for what's happened in this case," Sauriol strongly asserted. "Just in case anybody has any funny ideas to lay it on my shoulders, I've got news for you, I'm going to fight back this time. It won't happen!"

The judge made it clear that he placed no blame on Carl Hultman. "There is no way in which Carl Hultman, the deputy prosecutor who was assigned to try this case, is at fault for anything that occurred here." Sauriol put the blame one hundred percent on Prosecutor Bill Griffies.

Only steam shooting from his ears could have made Sauriol's anger more apparent. "Does it seem like I'm angry? You better believe I'm angry!" He then addressed Hultman's argument that the TV program had few viewers and little influence. "It's known by practically everybody in this building what happened on channel eleven that night," said the judge. "You can't have Sauriol walk down these halls without somebody saying, 'That's the judge that got to hear about the prosecutor going on channel eleven.' I'm not totally deaf. I hear these things.

"I'll tell you something about the code of professional responsibility," Sauriol said to the prosecutor. "The disciplinary rules, unlike the ethical considerations, are mandatory in character. You don't have a choice; you don't have an option. The rules state the minimum, not maximum. I suggest you take a look at that. It's not that hard to read. It's stated in very simple language."

For his finale, Judge Sauriol announced that "considering what this is doing to my blood pressure, there's no way in the world I can hear this case." Judge Thomas Sauriol, for reasons of conflicting commitments, extended trial dates, and rapidly rising bile, stepped down from the case on October 15, the same day Dr. Lacsina, Pierce County medical examiner, performed an autopsy on the recently recovered severed head of John Achord.

* * *

The police knew John Achord's head was inside the orange five-gallon metal bucket filled with cement that Tony Youso tossed off the Lincoln Avenue Bridge into the Puyallup River. Tacoma Police Department divers had attempted retrieving the bucket on more than one occasion, but without success.

"There had been two unsuccessful attempts by the Tacoma Police Department to recover the head from the Puyallup River," confirmed Sergeant Parkhurst. "Due to unfavorable river conditions—the current being extremely strong, visibility zero, and the depth of the river quite high—recovery attempts were discontinued until river conditions improved."

On October 8, 1984, Lieutenant Moorhead and Sergeant Parkhurst requested Officer Donald E. Moore, SAR coordinator for Tacoma, to organize a comprehensive evidence search of the Puyallup River below the Lincoln Avenue Bridge. "Going through the chain of command," recalled Parkhurst, "Officer Moore obtained permission from the Tacoma Police Department to obtain an evidence search number. Lieutenant Moorhead and I acted as police department liaison between the search and rescue operation and the Tacoma Police Department."

"The subject of the search," Moore confirmed, "was an approximate five-gallon metal bucket containing the partial remains of a homicide victim. I had previously indicated to Lieutenant Moorhead that the use of volunteer search and rescue personnel should provide the expertise to allow for the recovery of the partial remains."

Granted permission to use voluntary emergency service personnel, Moore marshaled his resources. "I contacted Evergreen Search and Rescue, and the Pierce County unit of Explorer Search and Rescue. I then got hold of the Tacoma Citizens Band Radio Association, the Amateur Radio Emergency Service, and the Puget Sound Sea Rescue Association. In combination, these groups provided the necessary personnel to conduct a safe and detailed search of the Puyallup River below the upriver side of the Lincoln Avenue Bridge."

After several meetings with Denny Guy, the Puget Sound Sea Rescue (PSSR) Association's diving expert, October 13 was selected as the target date for evidence recovery. As an additional safety measure, and at the urging of PSSR, a specific type of divers float was constructed at Moore's home. The float would be attached to a span line, and positioned via hand lines to specific search grid areas.

"The approximate center of the Lincoln Avenue Bridge was located with six-foot grids marked off on the upriver railing," explained Moore. "The depth of the river was twenty-four feet, but the average river depth in the center span area was only eight feet."

The search effort, from conception to execution, was complex, elaborate, and demanding. Extensive preparation, coordination, and interagency cooperation were imperative.

"We involved Puget Power, Tacoma City Light, Army Corps of Engineers, the National Weather Service, and the Tacoma Fire Department," said Moore. "We also contacted Tacoma Public Works and requested forty traffic barricades, four Detour Ahead signs, and ten portable No Parking signs for the early morning of October thirteenth."

Moore also enlisted the command duty officer of the USS *Implicit*, whom he contacted at the Naval Reserve Training Center. The simple request of four 400-foot of "long line" (rope) was easily honored, and an additional offer of navy-trained divers was forthcoming from the USS *Implicit* watch officer.

The coordination and cooperation among diverse state, local, and county agencies and associations was exemplary, as was the international teamwork. "We used eight different volunteer organizations for time handling, diving, and safety. There is a current problem on the river, plus tidal backwash and mud. The depth of the water varied from one side of the river to the other. Additional hazards were fishing nets in the river just prior to undertaking this search. Thankfully, that problem was resolved. The Puyallup Nation's Tribal Council was contacted via Sergeant Evans of the Tribal Police," said Moore, "and a letter of request was forwarded to the Tribal Council regarding the temporary closure of the Puyallup River to net fishing and boat traffic by tribal fisherman. The Tribal Council cooperated fully, closing the river for the duration of the search."

At noon, on October 13, 1984, the Lincoln Avenue Bridge was closed to all traffic, and the rigging of the span and in-hand lines, supplied by the USS *Implicit*, began. Everything was ready by 4:00 P.M. when the Pierce County Sheriff's Office jet boat transported PSSR divers Peter Reese and Ronald Campbell to the divers' float. "Deputy Dillon and Sergeant Schmidt piloted the boat," stated Moore, "and the divers worked a grid search of the river bottom starting to the east of the center span and working westbound."

After fifty minutes underwater, Reese and Campbell's search of the first grid neared completion. The river was extremely muddy with near-zero visibility at the river bottom. Then, in eleven feet of water, the two divers spotted the protruding bottom edge of a five-gallon orange bucket, lid end down, nearly covered by silt and sand.

"The dive team first cited a possible metal five-gallon bucket at approximately fifteen-fifteen hours," reported Parkhurst, "this was brought to the surface at fifteen-thirty hours." Schmidt, Dillon, and Parkhurst lifted the bucket to the jet boat's rear dive platform.

Once ashore, the bucket was photographed several times by Identification Technician J. Dunatov. "Approximately twelve photos were taken," the official report stated. "There were two of the bucket, two of a distant view of the bridge, three of the approximate location of the find, two of the concrete survey marker used to mark the site, and two photographs of Reese and Campbell."

"The bucket had a lid, and this was removed by Officer Keen," said Parkhurst. "The reason for removing the lid was to ascertain if the bucket was, in fact, full of cement. There was about a half-inch layer of silt at the top of the bucket, and once this was rubbed away, the bucket was completely filled with cement. Then, as prearranged through the Pierce County medical examiner, the bucket was transported to the medical examiner's office. The bucket was X-rayed, and the results revealed a skull encased in the cement. The bucket was released to Deputy Medical Examiner Jack Tropriano."

"Lists of all volunteer workers were obtained from each unit," reported Officer Moore, "and there was a sketch drawn by Ronald Campbell of the bucket as it was found on the river bottom. The complete derigging and release of volunteer personnel was accomplished by seven-thirty P.M., and all involved were requested to not talk about the recovery until completion of any court trial."

The Tacoma Police Department quickly called a press conference where Dean R. Phillips, director of Tacoma Police Services, announced that important evidence in the Achord homicide case was recovered at 3:30 P.M. "A preliminary investigation by the Pierce

County medical examiner's office has confirmed that the container contains the evidence the Tacoma Police were searching for," Phillips said. "However, police are awaiting a confirmation on the identity of the body part by the medical examiner."

Two days later, October 15, 1984, Dr. Lacsina and his staff peeled the bucket away from the cement and exposed the skull by chipping away at the cement casing. "The skull was found to be in remarkably good shape," Parkhurst reported. "There was a bullet entrance to the mouth region on the front of the skull. However, there was no exit point noted by Dr. Lacsina. There also was no bullet found inside the skull."

Dr. Lacsina explained the absence of a bullet, despite no exit wound, as "resulting from the bullet having lodged in the area where the head was removed from the main body, and it may still be at the grave site. Lacsina also noted," recalled Parkhurst, "that the skull had a hole on the right side of the head, just above the hairline, which also corresponded to an injury that the listed victim had suffered. Dr. Peter F. Hample, DDS, an expert in forensic odontology, charted the skull's teeth and dental work."

"I arrived at the Pierce County Medical Examiner's Office on October 15, 1984," recalled Dr. Hample, "at which time I was shown the specimen of what appeared to be a human male head and neck in an advanced stage of decomposition. I was told that the head and neck had been in a five-gallon paint bucket filled with concrete and had been recovered from the Puyallup River. After my initial examination, I felt it would expedite matters and allow for a more complete forensic dental examination if I could resect the maxilla and the mandible from the remains."

Dr. Lacsina granted Hample permission to undertake the task, and after doing so, Hample reported that the maxilla and mandible were shattered into many pieces, and many teeth were severely fractured. A thorough examination of the specimen also revealed numerous tooth and bone fragments. After cleaning the fragments, the tedious task of reconstructing the maxilla and the mandible was performed using cyanoacrylate adhesive (superglue). Following this reconstruction, the postmortem dental charting was prepared, and postmortem dental X rays and photographs were obtained.

On October 16, Dr. Hample received a photocopy of the most recent dental chart of John L. Achord from the office of Dr. Alan D. Brooks covering the period of November 8, 1974, through November 17, 1975. Hample also received from Dr. Brooks dental X rays of Achord taken during that same time period. From this material, Dr. Hample prepared the antemortem dental chart of John Achord.

"The comparison of the postmortem dental chart and dental X rays . . . with the antemortem dental chart and X rays stated to be John L. Achord show no inconsistencies. Therefore, I feel that within reasonable dental certainty that the specimen noted as Pierce County Medical Examiner case number . . . and John L. Achord are one and the same."

On November 14, Carl Hultman used these confirmed autopsy results as his primary justification for launching a new charge against Christopher St. Pierre—first-degree aggravated murder.

Nine

Originally, only Paul St. Pierre was charged with the premeditated murder of John Achord; his younger brother had been charged with rendering criminal assistance. Hultman now requested superior court judge Robert H. Peterson to amend the charges. Christopher St. Pierre would now be held equally responsible for John Achord's death.

"When Chris St. Pierre gave the police his statement describing the killing of John Achord, he did not mention the fact that John Achord was stabbed," asserted Hultman. "He indicated that this man was lying there, apparently dead on the floor from gunshot wounds to the head, and then described how the body was disposed of. When he gave his statement to the police, he hid the fact that he was present and watched his brother stab John Achord twelve times or more in the back. He didn't mention it at all."

The complete autopsy of John Achord, involving a thorough examination of the body and the head, revealed that Achord was very much alive after a gunshot wound to the jaw. According to Andrew Webb's "official statement," it was Christopher St. Pierre who objected to summoning aid for the injured Achord.

"When Andrew Webb suggested that they call the

police," explained Carl Hultman, "Paul said it would be self-defense, and that he would be all right because this had happened before when he shot someone. Christopher St. Pierre said, 'No, we can't do that. They will never believe Paul. He's high on acid,' therefore suggesting that they had to hide the crime of shooting John Achord. Perhaps worse, he expressed concern that the police, looking into John Achord's shooting, might discover something about Damon Wells, who had been murdered in February."

"I would urge the court," said Hultman, "that reading the words of Chris St. Pierre suggests nothing more than this man has to be killed; this man has to be dead before we can bury him. Webb's statement said the man 'is laying there making gurgling noises.' There is no indication in this evidence that Chris St. Pierre is deaf, and accordingly, I think the court is entitled to believe he heard those same noises. I think there is probable cause to believe that he aided, abetted, urged, and, in fact, he was the inspiration for Paul St. Pierre stabbing John Achord in the back to hide evidence of him being shot, but more importantly, to hide the evidence of the murder of Damon Wells."

Defense attorney Ladenburg, dismayed at Hultman's attempt to charge Chris St. Pierre with John Achord's murder, strongly opposed the amended charges with a barrage of solid legal arguments. He insisted that the state's "evidence" regarding the nonfatal nature of John Achord's head wound was "cumulative and superfluous to the argument of whether or not they had probable cause—not whether or not they had a great case or the best case, but whether they had a probable case."

Ladenburg further argued that Hultman based his entire justification for the new charge on Andrew Webb's statement: "Chris stopped me and said he didn't think it was a good idea [to call the police] because Paul was high on acid, and the police might not believe him. And if the police came snooping around, they might find out about Damon Wells, so we should bury the body in the mountains like Damon and no one will find out."

"Where is the probable cause that Chris ever encouraged or asked Paul to kill him?" asked Ladenburg. "After the gentleman is pointed out to be alive, it is not Chris that is alleged to take any action, or to say anything at that point. Neither statement from Andrew Webb make any such allegation, that Chris encouraged or asked or did anything to indicate that this gentleman should be killed."

Carl Hultman interpreted the matter differently. "The words of Chris St. Pierre, 'We got to get rid of this person so they won't find out about Damon Wells; we're going to take him and bury him,' suggests nothing more than this man has to be killed, that man has to be dead before we can bury him. It is clear," insisted Hultman, "that the idea for finishing off John Achord came from Chris St. Pierre."

The two attorneys argued back and forth until their words and reasoning became repetitive. At that point, the judge interrupted them. "I'm ready to rule," he announced. "I'm going to permit the amended complaint. I'm going to find that there was probable cause."

The official charges against Christopher St. Pierre were then read aloud in the courtroom. "I'll ask you, Mr. St. Pierre," intoned Judge Peterson, "how do you plead, guilty or not guilty?"

"Not guilty," replied Christopher St. Pierre.

"All right," responded Peterson.

Christopher St. Pierre was now under the same oppressive legal cloud as his brother. On that same day,

Paul St. Pierre, in a self-described show of power, fired his lawyer.

"Paul charges that he has no confidence in counsel," Connelly said to Judge Waldo F. Stone, "he believes that counsel lied to him, and he says that because of my background in the prosecutor's office, I was 'a sellout artist.' "

"I fired him because he was lyin' to me about things," said Paul St. Pierre, "tellin' me I didn't have a right to this or that." St. Pierre could not actually fire his lawyers; he could only officially request that they be replaced.

"This is a transparent effort to disrupt the start of the trial," Carl Hultman insisted, objecting to St. Pierre's demand for new legal counsel. Fred Weedon, director of Assigned Counsel, bemoaned the fact that a new attorney "would have to start from scratch to prepare a defense for Paul St. Pierre. The defense of the St. Pierre brothers has already cost taxpayers ten thousand dollars, and it will cost much more if a new attorney is appointed."

Judge Stone asked Ellsworth Connelly and Jeffery Gross how they felt about being replaced. The two defense lawyers told Stone that they were "perfectly comfortable" with the situation. In light of the seriousness of the case, said Connelly and Gross, dismissing them now would eventually be "less trouble."

The court had to rule on the matter, and Carl Hultman insisted that Paul St. Pierre was simply angry at Connelly for suggesting he accept a plea-bargain deal with the prosecution. "There is no fuckin' way," insisted Paul St. Pierre. Andrew Webb had made a deal like that, and Paul St. Pierre despised Webb.

With reluctance, the court granted Paul St. Pierre's request for new counsel. "There will be only one shift of attorneys," Stone told St. Pierre. "Whoever the new attorney is, that will be it. Period." Weedon's task was to find a new attorney for St. Pierre as quickly as possible.

"I also wish to change my plea," blurted out the defendant. Judge Stone was unimpressed. "I heard that loud and clear. But as I indicated to you, and I indicate again, the court will be dealing with a new attorney, and you will bring that information to his attention if and when appropriate. He will make the proper motion. I don't wish in any way to be rude, but I want to be crystal clear. I am dealing with your attorney and not with you, sir."

The only available qualified attorney with previous homicide trial experience was David Murdach. He introduced himself during a fifteen-minute meeting at the Pierce County Jail. Paul St. Pierre asked one question of David Murdach: "Did you ever work for the Pierce County Prosecutor's Office?"

The honest response was received with marked irritation. Murdach had previously worked in the Pierce County Prosecutor's Office at the same time as the recently dismissed Ellsworth Connelly. Paul St. Pierre was not pleased.

"I would choose not to represent Mr. St. Pierre," Murdach told Judge Stone on the afternoon of November 16. "Obviously, he does not want me because of my background. I think an attorney should be appointed that either did not work at the prosecutor's office," he suggested, "or an attorney who has his offices outside of this county."

David Murdach then turned to his potential client, saying, "I will simply turn it over to Mr. St. Pierre and he can tell the court what he wants." Judge Stone told the defendant to go ahead and speak up.

"I object to be represented by Mr. Murdach on the grounds that he being an ex-prosecuting attorney of the County of Pierce, and that is all I have to say, Your Honor," St. Pierre stated.

"If Mr. St. Pierre is going to be hostile toward me," commented Murdach, "and does not want me to represent him, I don't know if I can provide effective representation. I will need his cooperation in working with him."

Carl Hultman sympathized with David Murdach, called him "an excellent attorney," and insisted that St. Pierre had no right to refuse Murdach's services. "Mr. St. Pierre seems confused about who runs these cases and who runs the courtroom. There has not been any history of performance or basis upon which to discharge Mr. Murdach, and I ask the court to approve the appointment."

David Murdach did his best to get out of it, citing St. Pierre's negative attitude, potential lack of cooperation, possibility of appeal due to the unique nature of the situation, and "from a personal standpoint," he didn't really feel up to it. Judge Stone appointed him anyway. Murdach, despite his best efforts and those of his reluctant client, was now defense counsel for Paul St. Pierre.

To allow Murdach time to prepare his client's case, Chris St. Pierre agreed to a continuance. His brother, whom Murdach now represented, strongly objected. He wanted the trial to begin immediately. His objection was overruled and a new trial date was selected.

On November 16, a week prior to Thanksgiving, Judge Stone set February 13 as the new trial date. The attorneys, judges, and their respective families could set aside thoughts of the upcoming murder trial until the first of the new year. For the heartbroken families of Damon Wells and John Achord, there would be no happy holiday season.

"We're having a holiday coming up—Christmas,

without Damon," said brother Brandon Wells. "We try to make it all nice and neat for Mom and Dad, and try not to mention his name so we don't have to see the hurt in their faces. The night before Damon was murdered, he and I got in a fight, and I tried to call him the next night to apologize. I just never had the chance to tell him I'm sorry, and I loved him."

"We got life with no parole, no nothing," said younger brother Sean Wells. "Never, ever again will we ever have another Christmas, Thanksgiving, or anything with Damon. We're all messed up in my family. I can only speak for my family. Nothing has ever been the same—not Christmas, nothing. Nothing's the same."

Christmas at the Webb household in 1984 was also not the same as previous years. The Webb family, although distraught at Andrew Webb's homicidal behavior, saw him in a more positive light. He was being reinvented in the family's eyes as a transformed and inspired agent of the Lord.

"No sooner was he in the Pierce County Jail," recalled Anne Webb, "than he found God. Since God had forgiven him, everything was fine—maybe inconvenient, but basically OK. Besides, it couldn't be Andrew's fault because Andrew never did anything wrong."

"Christmastime tended to be highly charged in the Webb household. Dolores really went all out to make it warm and wonderful," said Marty Webb. According to her, any big Webb family get-together was when one of the Webbs would most likely reveal some shocking secret or inappropriate behavior. "With the Webbs," she insisted, "no pleasant occasion transpired untouched, and the holiday season brought up more ghosts of Christmas past than Charles Dickens."

Marty Webb, countered her ex-brother-in-law Ben, makes up negative exaggerations because she is bitter about the way his family treated her.

"They treated me like shit," elaborated Marty, "and that was simply because I had some slight bit of backbone. Not enough, but just enough to piss 'em off."

In Ben Webb's memories, Christmas with his family was a Norman Rockwell painting come to life. Ben moved out in 1981, and only returned home for two Christmas celebrations. In his entire experience, he only recalled one unexpected confession, involving drugs.

Anne explained family members' positive memories, "No matter what you or somebody else did, everyone could be forgiven if they were a good Christian, and simply prayed for forgiveness—forgiveness for themselves, or for someone else. Even Andrew Webb facing life in prison for murder was nothing that the power of prayer couldn't overcome."

Opal Bitney, mother of John Achord, was a good Christian woman who, no matter how hard she tried, could not overcome her inability to pray for her son's murderers. She could not forgive; she could not plead with God on their behalf. She tried, but it was difficult. "In fact, I find it impossible," she said. "I hate now. I've never hated before in my entire life. They've taken the compassion, the ability for me to have compassion for them. They have taken that away."

Compassion for all concerned was a virtue best exemplified by Mark Ericson. "It was really a sad thing for everybody involved," he commented several years later, "especially for the families of Damon Wells and John Achord. And imagine what it was like for Lowell and Dolores Webb, and George and Carmella St. Pierre. My God, how tragic it would be for them living with the sadness and shame of their little baby boy turning into a murderer. Another sad aspect of this whole tragic story was that Paul St. Pierre's sister Mary was engaged to a Tacoma Police officer at the time. They already had their wedding plans and everything. He's a policeman—he can't just marry the sister of a killer and have Paul St. Pierre as his brother-in-law, that would be too much. Mary did end up marrying a really nice guy years later, but how devastating what these boys did—it was really horrible, sick, and crazy."

PART TWO

Ten

Sick from solitary confinement in the Pierce County Jail, Paul St. Pierre began New Years, 1985, by almost going crazy. The lack of interaction with the jail's general population was driving him mad.

David Murdach, realizing his client's disturbed state of mind, seriously doubted St. Pierre's competency to stand trial. Paul St. Pierre's attorney wasn't the only one cognizant of his client's bizarre behavior. His family observed extreme suspiciousness and paranoia beginning the day Paul St. Pierre was taken into custody. "When he calls to talk to us on the phone," explained his brother Charles St. Pierre, "he thinks people are listening to his conversations. When we go to visit him in jail, he believes that people are watching him. He's always looking over his shoulder, and wondering who this is, or who that is."

"He's very distrustful of people," added Mary St. Pierre, "and he's really paranoid and thinks everybody is out to get him." His mother, Carmella, noticed the same disturbing behavior. "We try to discuss things, and he says, 'Mom, we don't talk about that because somebody might be listening.' Paul has been a little different," said Mrs. St. Pierre, "he's been sick."

On January 4, David Murdach submitted a motion

for complete psychiatric and psychological evaluations of his client by psychiatrist Dr. Charles P. Tappin and psychologist Kenneth Muscatel. Tappin had previously interviewed St. Pierre as a prudent matter of course in August 1984. Judge Stone granted the motion without delay. In the same court session, defense and prosecution wrestled over a seemingly mundane topic: the unpaid storage fee of over $600 for Paul St. Pierre's car, which had been confiscated by authorities and towed away. St. Pierre was now expected to pay the overdue fee.

"If the car is still there," said Murdach to the court, "Pierce County is holding it and there's a storage fee owed by my client, who can't pay it because he is in custody. Nor can he go out and claim it because he is in custody. There is no reason my client should be stuck with the storage fees when it was Pierce County that stored it." Murdach wanted the county to pay the bill, but that was the least important issue. Due to Paul St. Pierre's unavoidable failure to reclaim his vehicle from storage, the car—seized for possible evidentiary reasons—was designated "abandoned" and put up for sale. John Ladenburg joined in, asking that the record make it clear that, on behalf of his client, he objected "to the disappearance of any evidence in this case. They have not had our consent to release any evidence in this case."

"I don't know if the evidence has been destroyed," said Murdach. "I got a notice that the vehicle is going to be sold. It may have already been sold. This notice did not come from the prosecutor's office; it came from the towing yard. They arrested my client; he is charged with numerous claims and then incarcerated, shackled. And then to file a lawsuit to get this thing paid is not proper at all. He is in custody. He can't march down to the towing yard and get the car, or pay the bill. He can't even use the phone without calling collect. Either the county pay the storage fee and give us the car, or keep the evidence until after the trial is over so we know what we are dealing with."

By 2:00 P.M., Carl Hultman determined that the car had been sold. What he could not determine, however, was the new owner's name, address, or phone number. "The vehicle has gone, it is needed, and Mr. Ladenburg has a motion to compel its production," said Murdach to the judge.

The car's importance was in dispute. Was this car used to transport Damon Wells to Salmon Beach? If so, bloodstains would validate claims that Wells was beaten and bleeding during the drive. If Andrew Webb's original statement that Wells went to Salmon Beach voluntarily was true, the car's interior would be free of bloodstains. With this in mind, the kidnapping charges against the St. Pierres hinged upon a thorough examination of the automobile's interior.

The vehicle was originally impounded on June 19, 1984, and searched on the following day. "At the time, we thought there were bloodstains below the trunk lid," said Sergeant Parkhurst, "but that turned out to be negative. We searched the trunk, which was oil soiled and very dirty. We completely emptied it, and then vacuumed. There were no signs of blood in the 1967 Mercury, the Ford station wagon, or the 1971 Dodge Challenger."

Carl Hultman rightly insisted that the car was examined, that there was no evidence of any kind found, and the defense had copies of the examination report. "I think there was a lack of diligence on Mr. Murdach's part," said Hultman, "when he knew the car was going to be unavailable, and he didn't even ask me to do anything about it." Hultman also insisted that he "was not aware that the car would be sold."

"We are entitled," said Murdach, "to have our own experts examine the car. . . ."

"Hoping to find blood," interjected Hultman sarcastically.

"It's not your turn, Mr. Hultman," said Judge Stone sternly. Hultman apologized.

On January 25, John Ladenburg argued his motion for complete dismissal of all charges against the St. Pierres due to destruction of evidence by the prosecution. The arguments in support of dismissal were heated, elaborate, and extensive. Despite disturbing charges of evidence destruction, and numerous legal references, the result was Judge Stone intoning, "Motion denied."

More disturbing than the defense's allegations were the results of Paul St. Pierre's medical and mental evaluations. Dr. Charles P. Tappin, diplomat of the American Board of Psychiatry, submitted his findings to David Murdach on February 8, 1985. Clinical psychologist Kenneth Muscatel examined St. Pierre three times in the month of January, administering the MMPI, Rorschach, Michigan Alcoholism Screening Test, Rotter Incomplete Sentences Test, and a structured psychiatric interview. He filed his evaluation the same day as Dr. Tappin. Both reports characterized Paul St. Pierre as a "deeply disturbed paranoid individual."

"He is quite pathetic in terms of his social skills," noted Muscatel, "and he relates to others with deep suspicion." He was further described as "extremely paranoid most of the time, and he has threatened to kill other inmates. His understanding of his role in the legal proceedings is superficially intact, but his judgment is quite poor. The quality of his decisions, particularly with respect to helping his attorney in the development of his own defense, is suspect."

St. Pierre's unpredictable and possibly violent court-room behavior—both previously and potentially—supported Muscatel's opinion that St. Pierre could become more overtly psychotic during the trial. As for competency to stand trial, Muscatel found it "shaky" at best.

Dr. Tappin saw St. Pierre three times in January, and again on February 4. "Mr. St. Pierre did not exhibit any symptoms of a profound thinking disturbance," reported Tappin. "He is insightful, and perceives his present difficulty as being directly related to an overly suspicious aspect of his personality. He admits to very poor control over his aggressive impulses. He has difficulty controlling his murderous feelings toward other inmates, and wanted to kill the inmates he believed were talking about him."

The evaluations noted that despite the preponderance of evidence against him, Paul St. Pierre maintained an unrealistic view of his situation, expressed feelings of grandiosity, and insisted that he could be the best adviser in his own case. "He depicts his behavior in the courtroom, with his first lawyer," said Tappin, "as an indication of his 'power.'"

Dr. Tappin believed Paul St. Pierre understood the charges against him, but was incapable of cooperating effectively with his defense attorney. "Because of his highly suspicious attitude, the likelihood of dangerous and explosive behavior in the courtroom, the grandiose concept of himself, and a suicidal tendency," Tappin concluded, "Mr. Paul St. Pierre is not competent to stand trial. He should be committed to Western Washington State Hospital for treatment of his paranoid personality disorder." Tappin added that Paul St. Pierre was "fully aware of the rightness and wrongness of his actions, and therefore should not be considered as legally insane with respect to the crime."

On February 11, 1985, Judge Stone delayed the trial, setting a new date of March 27. He also ordered another complete psychiatric evaluation of Paul St. Pierre by Dr. Joseph Lloyd, MD, staff psychiatrist of the Mentally Ill Offender Program at Western State Hospital.

Lloyd described Paul St. Pierre as "a powerfully built, somewhat disheveled young white man" who denied physical distress, but was obviously anxious during the entire interview situation. "He was cooperative within the limits of his ability to cooperate," said Dr. Lloyd, who also reported that St. Pierre was "globally paranoid," not sure that he could trust anyone except himself, and doubted his ability to cooperate with his attorney. "He was maintaining his self-control only by the narrowest of margins," observed Dr. Lloyd. "Perhaps small amounts of medication might help him think more clearly and organize his thoughts in a better fashion."

Dr. Lloyd's diagnostic impression was identical to those of Muscatel and Tappin: "Paranoid Personality [and] Adjustment Disorder with disturbances of emotions and conduct as a result of incarceration in the isolation cell at the jail. Psychosis is highly possible at any time," said Lloyd, "I concur with Dr. Tappin and Dr. Muscatel that he is barely competent at the present time. Continued segregation is likely to worsen his mental state."

On March 7, 1985, the first competency hearing of Paul St. Pierre began at 9:45 A.M. Prosecutor Hultman delineated the hearing's fundamental purpose. "Today is the date set for the court to determine and review the competence of Paul St. Pierre. His competency was put into question as a result of examinations and reports received from doctors Kenneth M. Muscatel and Charles Tappin, retained by the defense for that purpose, as well as ours, Dr. Joseph Lloyd. The court also directed that the defendant be examined at the Pierce County Jail by a member of the staff for Western State Hospital."

"The obvious issue," interjected David Murdach, "is whether or not Mr. Paul St. Pierre is competent to go to trial. My client, by virtue of these reports, is incompetent to stand trial."

Under Washington State law, the defense attorney's opinion as to his client's competency is accorded great weight. He, as well as the experts, plays a part in the court's decision regarding the defendant's competency to stand trial and assist in his own defense.

The first witness called on behalf of Paul St. Pierre was Dr. Joseph Lloyd. Lloyd, at the request of the prosecutor's office, had interviewed St. Pierre on February 22, 1985.

"He was right on the edge between being able to perceive reality and being psychotic," Lloyd testified. "My impression was that Mr. St. Pierre was in and out of competency." Dr. Lloyd further testified that Paul St. Pierre could get worse if not taken out of solitary confinement, but did not agree that St. Pierre should be sent to Western State Hospital. "I don't know what the purpose of him going to Western State would be. Mr. St. Pierre is not in so bad a shape that it would require in-patient care."

During cross-examination by Carl Hultman, Dr. Lloyd reiterated his opinion regarding the negative effect of solitary confinement, and offered that appropriate medications, and a return to general population, could render Paul St. Pierre competent to stand trial.

Dr. Tappin was the next expert called to the witness stand. "What was significant," Tappin testified, "was a profound disturbance in his ability to trust individuals, or trust the circumstances in which he was living. I felt he was very paranoid. Basically, I came out with the impression that he was suspicious and seemed to bear thoughts of grandiosity to be able to control everything around him, by being a powerful individual. To that extent, I felt his judgment was quite impaired."

Dr. Tappin also stated that St. Pierre's feelings of anger, hostility, and fear would negatively affect his ability to aid in his own defense. "I felt, therefore, that he was not competent. I would state that he did not present a classical picture of an incompetent individual. There is a marginal competency."

Dr. Tappin asserted his firm conviction that two weeks at Western State Hospital could make all the difference, and in his professional opinion, Paul St. Pierre was currently not competent to stand trial.

Dr. Muscatel, the final witness in the hearing, also testified to Paul St. Pierre's "paranoid personality," terming him "deeply disturbed." Muscatel agreed with Dr. Tappin's suggestion that St. Pierre be admitted to Western State Hospital for further evaluation.

Following a ten-minute recess, David Murdach addressed the court, and described his client as delusional, dangerous, unpredictable, and completely incompetent either to stand trial or assist in his own defense. Murdach based these statements upon his own personal experiences with his troubled client, who spoke of spiders crawling all over him during the night. St. Pierre also told Murdach that he was experiencing the same feelings as when he attempted attacking Carl Hultman in the courtroom. Judge Stone, unfamiliar with the incident, looked at Murdach with increased interest.

"The court was not involved in that proceeding," Murdach explained, "but Mr. St. Pierre physically went after Mr. Hultman in the prior proceeding some time ago. He's feeling that kind of emotion coming back on him," Murdach told Judge Stone. "He has begun breathing heavy, and is afraid he will flip out. He says he cannot take the witness stand because of the possibility of his future actions. My client also related to me experiences in the Marine Corps. He saw a demon or a witch through the window. . . . The other soldiers told him that the witch was a sign that he was being shown the road to hell."

Murdach further recounted that Paul St. Pierre saw the ceiling moving when he was in bed, was afraid of talking on the telephone, and assumed there were hidden microphones in the walls. "He also described experiences in the Marine Corps with guerrillas in the jungle, and the marines helping the government hunt them down. He described the combat in that situation." Paul St. Pierre's tour of duty in the marines, his lawyer discovered, was during peacetime. His client never experienced combat, and there was no jungle action against guerrillas.

"My problem with Mr. St. Pierre," stated Murdach, "is the fact that I do not feel he is able to understand the nature of the proceedings. Based on my statements, and all the statements of the witnesses thus far, I think the preponderance of evidence has clearly been shown that Mr. Paul St. Pierre, at the present time, is incompetent to stand trial."

Murdach recommended that St. Pierre be sent to Western State Hospital for up to ninety days of review and evaluation prior to the court setting a firm trial date. "The only reasonable approach," he said, "is to set a firm trial date as soon as a report is received back from Western State concerning his competency to go forward." He also requested that St. Pierre be removed from solitary and returned to the general population.

Prosecutor Carl Hultman expressed his earlier suspicions that Paul St. Pierre was "trying to manipulate things," but acknowledged that expert testimony said otherwise. "He is just not manipulating the system— this is not some transparent or artificial effort to affect our ability to start this trial. There is another trial date right now, which has not been changed, which involves both the St. Pierre brothers charged with aggravated murder in the first degree relating to the death of John Achord. It is still set for March twenty-fifth, two days before this court's case—before Your Honor is to begin. I don't know what more I can say, how frustrating the state finds itself in the position it is in. . . . The state concedes that it has not presented evidence to refute."

Murdach was blatantly stunned when Judge Stone firmly declared, "I am unable to find by a preponderance of evidence whether Paul St. Pierre is unwilling to cooperate with counsel, or whether he is unable to cooperate with counsel. That is the only issue as I see it to competency. The decision the court makes is that I am unable to find that Paul St. Pierre is incompetent. I am unwilling or decline to order him transferred to Western State Hospital for any period."

Disappointed, Murdach asked Stone why he found Paul St. Pierre competent despite expert medical testimony to the contrary.

"The court was presented with two factors as I understand the law," replied Stone. "Number one: a person must be able to understand the charges against him, and I presume the consequences. The experts were in full agreement that he did fully understand.

"We then go to the question of cooperation with defense counsel, and it came down to the question of unwilling versus unable. In the mind of the court," Judge Stone explained, "there has been no preponderance of evidence on that subject. I find him competent today, and I make no apologies for it."

Stone then informed Murdach and Hultman that he'd requested an appearance by the sheriff's authorities. The judge wanted a better understanding of the county jail's policies, especially in regard to Paul St. Pierre receiving the medications suggested by Dr. Tappin and Dr. Lloyd.

Murdach's irritation with both the decision and the planned proceeding was ill concealed. If the court would not rely on the expert testimony of Tappin and Lloyd regarding St. Pierre's incompetence, why would the court heed their recommendations concerning medications?

"Because of the predictions," Stone explained, "the predictions are that as long as he is in isolation, these problems are not going to get better. They will probably get worse. I heard some gloomy predictions . . . and I would like every safeguard."

The following day, March 8, 1985, Judge Stone presided over a hearing he initiated. "Absolutely," concurred Stone, "there is no question this hearing was initiated by the court. It was not initiated by either the defendant or the prosecutor." The defense thought the proceeding useless; prosecutor Hultman said, "none of us would have called it." It was Judge Stone's hearing, and he had his reasons.

"Yesterday the court heard testimony regarding the competency of Paul St. Pierre," began Stone. "The testimony was in dispute, but the court made a ruling on competency. As the court interpreted the evidence, regardless of which doctor you listened to, or which attorney you listened to, it seemed almost total agreement that whatever Paul St. Pierre's condition was, it would not be getting any better in isolation and might very well get worse. I think it is obvious that the court expects to explore the issue on the question of isolation for Paul St. Pierre pending trial."

Stone then called John Shields, chief of the Bureau of Corrections, to the witness stand. Employed by the sheriff's department, Shields was responsible for the corrections bureau's overall operation, including the classification and segregation of prisoners in the Pierce County Jail.

Shields had moved St. Pierre, originally placed in general population, to maximum security. "This is because of his past history of violence, and a future possibility of violence as indicated by his psychologist. The way I see our responsibility," explained Shields, "we have the welfare in mind of the other inmates, the corrections officers, and the individual himself. We have put everyone on notice that he is dangerous to other people. We have no facility for holding mentally ill people."

Judge Stone asked Shields how the Bureau of Corrections would feel about the court, if possible and legal, ordering St. Pierre returned to the general population. The answer was swift, uncompromising, and emphatic: "Resistance on our part."

Stone pondered the situation and found it uncomfortable from whatever angle it was viewed. If St. Pierre stayed in isolation, he would get worse. If returned to the general population, he might improve. He also might kill a fellow prisoner—a possibility honestly acknowledged by St. Pierre himself. The third option, and it was only a possibility, was medication administered in jail whether Paul St. Pierre wanted it or not. The fundamental question Stone needed answered: "Does the court have authority to order the sheriff to do certain things in the jail which is basically the sheriff's jurisdiction?"

"It is probably in violation of the law," offered Carl Hultman. "The Washington Administrative Code makes it clear that the chief of corrections, the person responsible for running the jail, has the responsibility to identify and classify and segregate. There is an awful lot of attention given to safety of all inmates." Hultman referred to specific provisions of the state code stating: "Problem prisoners who endanger the health and safety of other prisoners or themselves shall be segregated."

The defendant unquestionably fulfilled the state's criteria for segregation, and the court had no legal authority to tell John Shields which prisoners should be segregated, and which ones belong in general population.

Judge Stone questioned the safety of other patients and hospital personnel were he to order St. Pierre sent to Western State Hospital. "I didn't advocate Western State," interjected Hultman. "I am very concerned about Mr. St. Pierre being at Western State Hospital except under the most extraordinary tightly supervised security."

David Murdach, advocating his client's transfer to Western State Hospital, advised Judge Stone that St. Pierre would be in a locked ward, not wandering the hallways, strolling the grounds, or stalking its residents.

"What is needed here," insisted Murdach, "is an evaluation of Mr. St. Pierre under the guidance of trained professionals in a hospital setting with twenty-four-hour monitoring. They will have a complete hospital record, and can finally make a recommendation as to competency." The defense felt that allowing two weeks for evaluation at Western State would "fit nicely" with the start of the trial.

Judge Stone, constrained by the law itself, expressed his frustration. "The court has the very distasteful alternative of sending somebody to a hospital when we say he is too dangerous for the jail, or at least a portion of the jail. OK, the court will decline to order the sheriff to do anything. This case won't go away, I know that. The problems of it won't go away. I had hoped they might get better instead of worse, and maybe my hopes are in vain. The court makes a nonruling on my own suggestion."

David Murdach immediately referred Stone's competency ruling to the Washington State Court of Appeals. "I was a little surprised when it was stated that something was before the court of appeals," said Judge Stone. "Not that I'm surprised on the merits, but I didn't know you could take one to the court of appeals before the judge had entered any written order."

The idea of his ruling being reversed by the court of appeals didn't bother him. "Frankly, it's happened plenty of times, and over many years, and it will happen again in what I hope to be many years to go on the bench. There is no question on the competency ruling," said Stone, "this court got led by a capable doctor who made a prediction how he felt the whole problem could be sort of avoided. And frankly, the prediction in my opinion was logical. I don't know whether the court should reconsider or not reconsider the decision."

"In light of the court's comments," Murdach said, "I would move the court for reconsideration of its decision that Mr. Paul St. Pierre was competent to stand trial."

"What is it specifically you are asking the court at this time? What specific remedy?" asked Stone.

"The remedy I'm asking for," answered Murdach,

"is for him to be transferred to Western State Hospital consistent with the recommendation of Dr. Tappin. It's for him to be committed for ninety days. Then, after ninety days, if he is still incompetent, to be committed for another ninety-day period. I urge the court to reconsider its decision, and to have him declared incompetent at the present time. The reason is, he is in and out of competence. Quite frankly, I don't know, from one day to the next, what day he is competent and what day he is incompetent. And if at trial he is fluctuating—going in and out of competency—I don't think we can receive a fair trial. Paul St. Pierre is incompetent as far as Dr. Tappin and I are concerned, and we need to have more assessments done of him to really determine if he is truly competent to stand trial. There is no sense having an incompetent person languishing in some cell if he never is going to regain competency. On the other hand, the state is allowed to proceed in the case if in fact competency is restored."

Stone, faced with endless ambiguity as to Paul St. Pierre's competency, and the rising specter of increased psychosis were the defendant to remain in isolated segregation, reconsidered his previous ruling. "My previous ruling seemed logical at the time," remarked Stone, "but not necessarily consistent with the testimony of the experts or the opinions of the attorneys. The court will, in effect, reconsider, and the court now makes a finding of incompetency."

"I made that finding of incompetence with extreme reluctance," Stone later commented. "I refused to make that finding at the first hearing. I am not a doctor, I am a judge, and the court should not attempt to usurp the prerogatives of the doctors."

Murdach was pleased. His client would be removed from solitary confinement, relocated to Western State Hospital, and receive at least ninety days of professional observation and evaluation. Dr. Lloyd, who previously characterized Paul St. Pierre as incompetent to stand trial because of a mental state bordering on psychotic, would undoubtedly be Western State Hospital's prime evaluator. Although Lloyd didn't originally endorse sending St. Pierre to Western State Hospital, he was familiar with the patient's history, current diagnosis, and most appropriate medicinal needs.

Pursuant to a court order issued March 25, 1985, Paul St. Pierre was admitted to Western State Hospital for ninety days of observation, evaluation, and treatment. The Damon Wells murder trial would begin the following week. Paul St. Pierre's hospitalization for psychiatric evaluation meant the brothers would be tried separately.

Lyhle Quasim, director of the Mental Health Department of Social and Health Services, confirmed St. Pierre's transfer. "He will be treated like any other patient," said Quasim. "The guy was sent to us under provisions of the revised code of Washington, and we are treating him."

On March 25, shortly after 2:00 P.M., Dr. Joseph Lloyd admitted Paul St. Pierre to Western State Hospital's high-security Mentally Ill Offenders Unit. On March 26, Dr. Lloyd's supervisor pulled him from any contact with Paul St. Pierre and replaced Lloyd with retired psychiatrist Dr. Donald Allison. On Thursday, March 28, Dr. Allison and clinical psychologist Dr. William C. Proctor interviewed Paul St. Pierre for approximately one hour and forty minutes. On Friday, March 29, Paul St. Pierre was back in solitary confinement at the Pierce County Jail.

David Murdach didn't know about his client's round-trip visit to Western State Hospital until he read

about it in the Saturday *Tacoma News Tribune*. Judge
Stone was equally caught off guard. "I was a little surprised when I got a call from the newspaper reporter
asking me questions," recalled Stone, "and this was
before I had even read the newspaper. For all I knew,
Paul St. Pierre was still at the hospital. I learned from
the newspaper reporter that St. Pierre was at the jail."

Stone, Hultman, Murdach, and Ladenburg all received copies of Proctor's and Allison's evaluation on
Monday, April 1. The doctors found him competent
to stand trial, a medical determination pleasing to Carl
Hultman. If Stone upheld the report, the Pierre brothers would be tried together after all. The prosecution,
however, had more on its mind than the mental state
of Paul St. Pierre. Hultman's main interest was the
long-awaited, much anticipated, and often dreaded arrival of his star witness, Andrew Webb.

"What Mr. Webb will testify to," Hultman previously
explained, "is that he was kneeling beside Damon Wells
when Paul handed him the knife, and when he was hesi-
tant to do anything, Paul displayed a forty-five that he
regularly carries on his belt." Once reunited, Hultman
and Webb would prepare for his all-important courtroom appearance. A few short hours thereafter, everyone would know, in detail, what exact testimony to
expect from Andrew Webb.

On Tuesday, April 2, Andrew Webb arrived from
the Washington State Penitentiary in Walla Walla.
Marty Webb recalled the day, the date, and the essence
of her brother-in-law's interaction with the deputy
prosecutor. "If my memory serves me well, that's when
Andrew told Carl Hultman to shove it up his ass."

Eleven

"I interviewed Mr. Webb on Tuesday, April 2, after he was flown back by the Department of Corrections," confirmed an exasperated Carl Hultman. "He indicated in my interview with him that he unequivocally is determined to not testify in this case about any of these matters. He had a variety of explanations which range from what he professes to be religious beliefs, to some reference to the fact that he has been threatened three times since he became incarcerated."

"Paul St. Pierre would like to know whether or not Mr. Webb will be a witness in this trial," Murdach told Hultman, "and I think we have a right to know. We heard that he will not testify, or will not give a statement or something, but I need to know. I think it is only appropriate that the prosecutor tell us."

"I think we will undoubtedly call him to the witness stand outside the presence of the jury in order to establish his unavailability," Hultman answered, "but that is a separate question right now. I don't have any anticipation that he will testify. He sounds unwilling, and he says that he's decided to not testify against those two defendants."

This answer wasn't good enough for Murdach. It also wasn't good enough for Judge Stone. "Isn't Mr.

Murdach entitled to know, yes or no, whether you expect to have him come before the judge or jury, or both? You are not guaranteeing what he is going to say, or what happens."

"I do not intend to give any suggestion to the jury that he is available to testify," answered Hultman, "nor suggest any testimony he intends to give, because he has said right now that he will not testify."

"He will be brought before the judge at some point," Stone assured Murdach, "and he will be available in custody in Tacoma, I gather, for any consultation."

The next item on Stone's agenda of April 3 was the controversial competency evaluation from Western State Hospital.

"Paul St. Pierre's ninety-day evaluation at Western State Hospital lasted less than two hours," complained Murdach. "He was immediately pronounced competent to stand trial, and the *Tacoma News Tribune* said that hospital sent him back to the county jail because he was too dangerous."

"Mr. Murdach, the court, and the state received a lengthy report from Western State Hospital concerning the condition of Paul St. Pierre," said Carl Hultman. "The report was completed by [the] doctors Proctor and Allison. Their conclusion in that report is that Paul St. Pierre is competent, and he had already been returned to the Pierce County Jail by the time that report was received."

Dr. William Proctor, PhD, chief psychologist, and Dr. Donald Allison, staff psychiatrist, interviewed St. Pierre on March 28. According to the report, St. Pierre bragged about dismissing his first lawyer, Mr. Connelly. "I fired him because he was lyin' to me about things," said St. Pierre, "tellin' me I didn't have a right to this or that." He complained that Connelly insisted that he plea-bargain with the prosecutor, and that his new attorney had approached him with the same deal. St. Pierre said that there was no way that he would accept a plea-bargaining deal, and complained that his attorney didn't say what he wanted him to say in court. "I might as well go ahead and speak for myself," he said.

St. Pierre explained that the prosecutors had bungled the case, and there was a good chance he wouldn't be convicted. Asked to define a prosecutor's role, he answered, "Mainly, they try to get you to cop a plea. Otherwise, they try to keep railroadin' ya." He complained of being pressured to plead guilty, and insisted that the judge was working with the prosecutors.

"A real judge would have dismissed the case as far as what's gone down," St. Pierre told the doctors, "because I can't get a fair trial in Washington or the Northwest for that matter because of being on the TV. If I were on the jury myself, I would probably give myself the death penalty."

"Mr. St. Pierre clearly would prefer to be in the general population in the jail, rather than to be in an isolation cell," stated the report. "The defendant was alert and oriented throughout the examination. He was generally cooperative in the sense that he answered questions put to him except when they came close to discussions about the alleged events. He was cynically suspicious of the criminal justice system and all those connected with it. The examiners gained the impression that some of the questions were not answered fully because of the context in which the examination was taking place. His speech was normal in terms of quantity and quality, and rate of production. He had a good flow of goal-directed speech and showed good logical progression of thought. As is frequently seen among incarcerated persons, there were a considerable number of expletives used to give emphasis to his cynical thoughts about the criminal justice system. About the criminal justice system, there was an underlying tone of defiance and disdain. His mood was appropriate to the topic under discussion, varying from anger at the thought of being confined in solitary, to cheerfulness at the thought of the informer's peril in Walla Walla. No delusions, hallucinations, or other symptoms of major mental illness were noticed during the examination. He was interrogated about earlier vague reports he had made of seeing things appear and disappear. His response was that while he was in solitary he had the sense that things were moving or changing around him, but he definitely discounted the idea that he might have seen anything moving, appearing, or disappearing. He explicitly denied that he had experienced hallucinations.

"Throughout the interview," reported Dr. Proctor, "he evidenced the desire to defy the prosecutors and jailers, rather than to lose prestige by making a deal. He expressed distrust for all people, but particularly those related to the criminal justice system. He demonstrated a great deal of cynical suspiciousness of the idea that the criminal justice system existed to benefit him in any way."

"At the time of our recent evaluation, there was no question in our minds that the defendant was aware of the nature of the charges against him and the possible penalty if convicted," wrote Proctor and Allison. "The question then hinges on whether or not the defendant is able to assist counsel in his own defense. Intellectually, there appears to be no problem with Mr. St. Pierre's doing so. He is aware of his constitutional rights and errors that the prosecution has allegedly made which rebound to his advantage. He seems, in fact, to have a reasonable layman's working knowledge of the legal justice system.

"It is the examiners' opinion, that the defendant is able to assist counsel in his own behalf. Consequently, it is our opinion that the defendant is competent to stand trial at this time. As the defendant is competent to stand trial, and the evaluation is complete, we respectfully request that he be returned to the court for further proceedings."

"It was my request that this morning the court conduct a competency hearing with respect to Paul St. Pierre," Carl Hultman stated, "and if the court determines that Paul St. Pierre is now competent to stand trial, it would be the state's motion that he be rejoined as a defendant so both defendants could be tried at a joint trial as originally intended."

David Murdach strongly objected. Holding a competency hearing on such short notice allowed him no time for adequate preparation. "Christopher St. Pierre's case is set for trial today," Murdach said, "and we should proceed with the trial. Paul St. Pierre's case should be set in due course and allow a fair hearing to take place in view of the amount of testimony concerning the issue of competency. I think we are rushing to judgment over the issue of competency in an effort to hitch Paul St. Pierre's case along with Chris St. Pierre's case. I think the two are entirely different matters. Christopher St. Pierre's case should go along as scheduled, and Paul St. Pierre's case should be a fair trial, and set after a fair competency hearing where I have a chance to sit down with my witness in an educated setting and go over all the testing that has been done. In fact, I feel I should have the chance to have Dr. Muscatel, or some other clinical psychologist, do some testing of Mr. St. Pierre to see what hap-

pened in one day to change him from incompetent
to competent."

"I will state flatly," Judge Stone replied, "it is the
intention of the court to proceed with the competency
hearing. As I say, it's the order of the court that we
will proceed to the competency hearing at this time."
The judge turned to Carl Hultman. "You may call your
first witness."

The state's first witness was Dr. William Proctor. "I
am a licensed psychologist in the state of Washington," said Dr. Proctor, "and I have testified in superior
court on competency and diminished capacity issues
on many, many cases, and I have reported on these
matters over the years. I am familiar with the tests for
competency, and to my understanding, the defendant
has to understand the nature of the charges against
him, and the possible penalty involved upon conviction, and has to be able to assist in his own defense."

After spending one hour and forty minutes with
Paul St. Pierre on March 28, Dr. Proctor reached the
following conclusion to which he testified. "There is
no question that the defendant at the time of the interview understood the nature of the charges and the
serious possible penalty of death if he were convicted.
There is no question about that. He was knowledge-
able about the legal process. He had at least average
intelligence. I didn't see any reason to feel he was incompetent."

Dr. Proctor acknowledged Paul St. Pierre's suspiciousness of the legal justice system, but interpreted it
as an aid rather than a detriment. "Perhaps it sharpens
his sense of the need to defend himself," said Proctor.

Murdach demanded Dr. Proctor explain how Allison and he determined St. Pierre's competency in
less than two hours, and with no testing.

"I didn't think testing was necessary because one

doesn't assume a person is psychotic without any evidence to that effect," explained Dr. Proctor. "You assume people are aware of reality around them unless something has been presented to make you question that. And, frankly, nothing in my interview with Mr. St. Pierre led me to wonder about that. If I don't see signs of incompetency, then I think the person is competent."

"Do you recall," asked Murdach rhetorically, "that there was a court order finding him incompetent, and he was sent to Western State for an evaluation? He has been found incompetent, and was sent to you with a finding of incompetent?"

Obviously aggravated, David Murdach verbally pushed Proctor into a testimonial corner. "Did you start out presuming he was incompetent? Or did you start out presuming competency?"

Proctor admitted the preconceived idea that St. Pierre was competent before he ever met him, that Judge Stone most likely was in error, and the other psychologists and psychiatrists consulted were equally mistaken.

"What makes you think your view is more clear than someone else's?" Murdach, as irritated as he was curious, honestly wanted an answer. Proctor provided one without hesitation. "Very rarely have I testified in court on this issue when the court did not agree with me. Probably ninety-five or ninety-eight percent of the time, the court agrees with me."

Murdach, taken aback, requested clarification. "Because you have been sustained by the court makes you feel that you have a more clear understanding than other people? It's not because of your training?"

"Training? Well," responded Proctor, "it's part of my experience."

Murdach lost it. "It's because you have been rubber-stamped by the court!"

Hultman objected, and Judge Stone said, "I think the court would object to that, too. I will sustain the objection."

"Dr. Proctor was a professional individual who handled a lot of difficult questions on cross-examination quite well," Hultman later commented. "He is an intelligent man who has been on the witness stand before, and he knows how to deal with these issues."

David Murdach's professionalism prevented him from throwing a fit or punching a psychiatrist when he discovered, in the course of further testimony, that the examination of Paul St. Pierre was inconsistent with Western State Hospital's standard procedures, and the actual hospital record of St. Pierre's whirlwind tour was not provided to the court.

Dr. Allison then took the stand on behalf of the prosecution and described his examination of Paul St. Pierre. "I only did a portion of the interview on this occasion because Dr. Proctor was just now meeting Mr. St. Pierre. I had met him twice before, but we spent a pleasant hour and twenty minutes, and Mr. St. Pierre was quite pleasant." Allison also considered St. Pierre "a good actor."

"It's our job to tell the good actors from the bad actors. He puts on a good show," testified Dr. Allison. "He likes to play games, he believes in hysterics, or his strong personality, and he likes to put on a show to get attention. That's what the hallucinations are. In other words, he wants to be important. He likes to talk about some witch character that whispers to him once in a while to kill himself, but he never quite gets around to it, but that's about it. I'm sure he is competent to stand trial."

Asked further about his professional experience and

career, Allison mentioned resigning his position at Western State Hospital the previous November. Semi-retired, Allison continued working part-time for Western State in sex offender admittance. The most recent Thursday, however, he was summoned from fifty miles away to evaluate Paul St. Pierre.

"Apparently," said Dr. Allison, "it was somebody's opinion that I see him instead of another doctor." Under oath, Allison confirmed that the "other doctor" was Joseph Lloyd. "I heard Lloyd was being moved because he was not doing an adequate job, I guess," Allison testified. "I don't know. I refuse to speculate. I never talked to Dr. Lloyd about Paul St. Pierre."

"Are you aware that Dr. Lloyd wrote a report in this case?" asked Murdach during cross-examination. "Did you read that report?"

"No, why should I? I haven't read Dr. Muscatel's or Dr. Tappin's reports, either. I don't need to read reports; I need to see patients. Patients are what we are treating, not paper."

"Don't you think it would be a good idea," prompted Murdach, "to read what has been done by other doctors in the St. Pierre case before you come to your conclusion?"

"It would be like reading the newspaper before I went to jail to see a client, like reading the newspaper before I came to court to see what I'm doing. I never read the newspaper," stated Allison firmly. "I never read such junk. I don't like my brain occupied by a bunch of garbage."

Murdach requested clarification. "You think Dr. Tappin's report and Dr. Muscatel's report are garbage?"

"I have not seen them," replied Allison, "and I am not going to read them to prove my point. We do tests to tell if the patient is crazy or not, but there are not too many tests to see if they are competent or not. That is what you do by the seat of your britches—being human, paying attention to the patient and not packing my head full of paperwork garbage."

When asked if he actually participated in writing the report on St. Pierre's competency, Dr. Allison replied with uncompromising candor. "I told Dr. Proctor to write it, and then I went home. The secretary called me the next day after she typed it and read it to me over the telephone. She signed it instead of me. I told her to sign it after I heard it. I live fifty miles away, and I wasn't going to ride in just for one report."

"Dr. Allison's testimony was interesting and different," Judge Stone later commented. "We saw the attitude of a doctor who is absolutely totally independent; he doesn't have to answer to anyone but himself. He could care less about the administration of Western State Hospital or the opinion of other doctors. I think he was the ultimate as far as independence is concerned because he wasn't concerned about public relations or administration or internal relations within the hospital. He simply had his opinions."

Following Allison's testimony, Murdach pleaded with Judge Stone to halt the competency hearing. "It's apparent that there are witnesses which need to be present before this proceeding continues. I don't have any witness here to rebut the testimony of Proctor and Allison. I was unaware until I cross-examined them that the examination of Paul St. Pierre was done inconsistent with normal procedure, and the fact that the hospital record is still back at the hospital, and the fact that Dr. Lloyd, who had previously maintained that Mr. St. Pierre was incompetent, especially when in solitary confinement, was lifted off the case for mysterious reasons these experts were not able to explain.

"Quite frankly," said Murdach, "Dr. Lloyd was taken off the case because he found him [St. Pierre] incompetent on the prior occasion and prescribed medications to him, and for some reason"—Murdach pointed toward Carl Hultman—"*they* had to bring in *their* witnesses to find him competent! I think the whole way this was handled, the quick nature of the evaluation, and the way it was done, coinciding with anticipating the start of Christopher St. Pierre's trial, makes it all transparent."

Murdach's implication was obvious: the hospital administration conspired and/or cooperated with the prosecution. The swift competency evaluation assured that Paul and Christopher St. Pierre would not have separate trials. When Murdach accused the prosecution of manipulating Paul St. Pierre's hospital examination, he was pointing his finger above and beyond Assistant Deputy Prosecutor Carl Hultman. His target was Pierce County's chief prosecutor Bill Griffies.

Murdach's belief that Bill Griffies masterminded his client's revolving door evaluation in consort with Western State Hospital may have sounded as if the defense counsel was taking on the paranoid characteristics of his client. There were, however, understandable reasons for his accusations. First, the case's history was already stained by several allegations of prosecutorial misconduct. Judge Sauriol had scolded Griffies on several occasions. Western State Hospital was fighting a protracted and costly lawsuit involving a settlement or judgment of staggering financial proportions. The attorney handling the suit against Western State Hospital was David Murdach. Based on these facts, coupled with the "dual defendants on trial" outcome, Murdach surmised that Paul St. Pierre's medical evaluation and declaration of competency had been manipulated and/or controlled by the prosecution.

"He's a controlling manipulator," Carl Hultman said of Paul St. Pierre. "He caused substantial delays and an awful lot of resources have been expended on his behalf to explore this competency issue thoroughly. I think the court can conclude without any question that Mr. St. Pierre is competent to go to trial."

Murdach took the opposite view. Only a few days earlier, the court had ruled that his client was incompetent. The court also ruled that his client should spend ninety days in Western State Hospital for observation and evaluation. "Now we have the benefit of an hour and forty minute examination by [the] doctors Proctor and Allison—one doctor who wrote the report, and the other doctor who had the report read to him over the phone, didn't examine him, and had his secretary sign it. Also the reason Proctor and Allison performed the evaluation is of some question. Dr. Lloyd was familiar with the case, and Dr. Lloyd had previously examined Paul St. Pierre. Suddenly, Dr. Lloyd is replaced on the evaluation by Proctor and Allison. Instead of examining my client, Dr. Lloyd was getting chewed out in the superintendent's office for something he supposedly did wrong in this case. We also have the newspaper coming out with that quote about St. Pierre being too dangerous to keep out there."

Murdach offered a quick, if sardonic, recap of current events: "We have a finding of incompetency, he goes out to Western State, he is there for three and a half days, and he's seen for an hour and twenty minutes and found competent by one of the examining psychiatrists who does not read the reports of the other doctors because he thinks it's a bunch of garbage. I don't think that is a thorough examination.We are not dealing with just a question of evidence," argued Murdach, "we also have to deal with the appearance of fairness to the defendants. That appearance has been shattered by the quick transfer of Dr. Lloyd off the case and bringing in Dr. Allison, a retired man, to examine Mr. St. Pierre. I don't think there has been an appearance of fairness to Mr. St. Pierre in these proceedings as far as what has been done at Western State."

Judge Stone asked John Ladenburg if he had any comments or observations, and he most certainly did. "It's the court's responsibility to decide competency, and not that of the doctors, because competency is a legal question and not a medical one. I think Dr. Proctor misunderstood the legal definition, and the problem is that he thinks that if the defendant is somewhat cooperative with his counsel, he is therefore competent. That is not the law. Paul St. Pierre's mental defect, the elements of his paranoia, is affecting his relationship with his counsel. I don't see how the court, based on the evidence before it, can find this gentleman competent, since the evidence is clear that he is suffering from a paranoia affecting his ability to deal with his counsel, and that, in and of itself, makes him incompetent."

Judge Stone faced a surging sea of conflicting opinions, definitions, arguments, and diagnoses. "The court will proceed on the basis of the evidence and the testimony that I had before me this morning," said Stone after serious reflection. "The court was impressed in all the hearings that those who had absolutely no responsibilities at Western State Hospital felt that would be an excellent place for Paul St. Pierre, while those who had responsibilities at Western State Hospital expressed different opinions in varying degrees."

As for Murdach's suspicion that Western State rushed St. Pierre's evaluation simply so the brothers could be tried together, Stone gave the concept no credence. "I'm not willing to conclude all that speed with which Western State acted had anything to do with the court dockets, or whether two defendants should be tried together or separately. I think that Western State Hospital, and particularly administration, perhaps not the doctors, were very much concerned with public relations, with news media, and less concerned with a particular result.

"I'm not thrilled with some of the things Mr. Murdach has pointed out—the quickness of the review, and sending back, and people drawing their own conclusions—Murdach has his conclusions and the judge has his, and other people will have their own. I don't think there is any question that the court is looking for some reassurance that it would be doing the right thing if it were to proceed to trial. The court has now found that reassurance that it was looking for, and I find it in two doctors. The court makes the finding of competency."

Hultman immediately moved for "a court order that Paul St. Pierre be rejoined with Christopher St. Pierre and that their trial commence as soon as practicable. He told the judge, "The state would be prepared to begin jury selection tomorrow in King County."

"I need a few days before this case starts," said Murdach, "and there are a couple of reasons for that. We learned this morning that Mr. Webb is not even going to be a witness in this case. It seems I should be elated about that. I am concerned because it was my understanding that Mr. Hultman was going to call witnesses concerning statements that my client had made about whether or not he participated in the homicide. For example, statements he made to Mr. Kissler about stabbing this individual and so forth. Mr. Webb has stated that my client did not stab Damon Wells. So I've got a real challenge to the prosecutor if he starts presenting evidence which he knows is not true, although my client maybe said the statement as boasting or whatever."

Judge Stone granted Murdach a five-day extension, and ruled that Paul and Christopher St. Pierre were once again joined. "The cases will be tried together," he said, "and we will start jury selection on Monday, April eighth."

Jury selection is an arduous process, and the previous mistrial added additional pressure to all involved. All three attorneys exercised discretion and caution, avoiding another potential upheaval or delay. Jury selection was completed without incident. Opening testimony was scheduled for April 18, 1985.

On April 17, Andrew Webb and the St. Pierre brothers were reunited in a Pierce County courtroom. Also present were defense attorneys Murdach and Ladenburg, prosecuting attorney Hultman, and Webb's legal representative, Larry Nichols. In this pretrial hearing, Judge Stone would rule on whether or not Andrew Webb's statement, given as part of his plea-bargain agreement, could be admitted as evidence against the St. Pierre brothers.

Using out-of-court statements is seldom allowed, exceptionally controversial, and most often unconstitutional. It was Carl Hultman who made the motion, and he knew full well the legal dangers inherent in his request.

"I basically pointed out in my memorandum," said Hultman, "that there is a provision under state law that would support that the out-of-court statements made by Andrew Webb may be admissible if they can be shown to be accurate, whether or not there is sufficient basis to show their reliability."

If Andrew Webb was unable to testify, and the court knew that the state intended to use him as one of its main witnesses, then (according to Hultman) Webb's out-of-court statements should be admissible.

To buttress its argument, the state set forth what it considered an essential and imperative point of fact: Webb made a deal, and that deal involved his promise to testify against the St. Pierres. Webb, however, recently informed Hultman that he'd changed his mind. The state's star witness now refused to testify.

"He supplied, through his attorney, a handwritten first-person statement describing what he would be willing to testify to as part of a plea agreement," recounted Hultman. "The state agreed that if Andrew Webb testified truthfully, the state would not seek to have the death penalty as punishment for him, but permit him to enter a plea of guilty to a crime of first-degree murder."

In addition to Webb's plea-bargain statement of July 17, there was the earlier statement given to Detectives Yerbury and Price. Hultman encouraged Judge Stone to determine reliability by comparing Webb's statements to those of Chris and Paul St. Pierre.

"We are asking the court to rule today on the issue," said Hultman, "and we intend to call Andrew Webb to the stand and determine if he's going to testify." Stone agreed, advising the prosecutor that the court would hear Webb's testimony or nontestimony.

Stone then asked Nichols if he wished to make any brief statements.

"Mr. Webb is on the witness list," stated Nichols, "and he related to me, as his attorney and as an officer of the court, that he does not wish to testify in these proceedings against the two individuals."

"The court respects Mr. Nichols's statement," responded Judge Stone, "but Mr. Nichols is an attorney and not the client. The court needs all the information it can get to make the ruling, and regardless of what the testimony or nontestimony is, there may be some questions the judge wants to ask Mr. Webb. Whether he answers them or not remains to be seen. I will direct Mr. Webb to come forward and be sworn and take the stand, and I note the exception to Mr. Nichols on the court's ruling."

Andrew Webb, duly sworn, testified that he would not testify. Hultman, visibly irked, reminded his recalcitrant witness that they made a deal after Webb's arrest for the aggravated first-degree murder of Damon Wells. "At a certain point, you asked your attorney to let me know that you were interested in pleading guilty if we would not pursue the death penalty, and that you were willing to testify."

"That was the agreement made," confirmed Webb. "And yes, I was intending to plead guilty." He further acknowledged the formal written statement to Yerbury and Price, but did not recall it being a sworn statement. Hultman asked if the statement was "the truth," Nichols objected, and Webb refused to answer.

"What is your response if you are called as a witness to testify truthfully about what happened concerning the death of Damon Wells?" inquired Hultman.

"I will not testify," replied Webb.

"I think the court will direct Mr. Webb to testify," said Judge Stone. "If he continues his refusal, then he is subject to contempt. We can all speculate how effective contempt would be." The court then specifically directed Andrew Webb to testify.

"I refuse to testify," he said once more, making the phrase his witness-stand mantra. He chanted the noncommittal phrase in repetitive, predictable monotone, occasionally adding qualifiers, such as "at this time" or "about that also." When Carl Hultman exhausted all relevant and unanswered questions, Andrew Webb explained why he wouldn't testify against Paul and Christopher St. Pierre.

"I intended to testify against these individuals out of vengeance," said Webb, "and I also wanted to testify for selfish reasons—making myself look good in the public eye. And there was another reason. It has to do with the agreement. I was going to testify because I was threatened with death if I did not. In the agreement there were certain elements which were to be provided for me in exchange for my testimony."

According to Webb, one of those "certain elements" was protection while incarcerated. "As soon as I was turned over to the Department of Corrections, no provisions for protection were made whatsoever." Webb further asserted that verbal death threats were made against him in prison on at least three occasions. Because he was entered into the prison population without any provisions for protection—inmates have a low regard for informants and snitches—he believed that the state "negated the agreement they made, and therefore released me from any responsibility of honoring that agreement."

Alan Achord, John Achord's older brother, regarded Webb's excuse as total nonsense. "From my own experience from being in prison," he said several years later, "any time that you feel you need protective custody you can check in. You do not need to be assigned that. All you have to do is go to the sergeant, one of the guards, tell them that you're in fear for your life, and they will put you in protective custody. So the deal where he says the state did not live up to their part is wrong. All you have to do is ask and you are put in protective custody."

When attempting to question his uncooperative star witness, Carl Hultman tried once more, and he was willing to ask it whether or not an answer was forthcoming. "You do understand one of the possible options that the lawyers will be arguing about is whether the statements you made will be presented to the jury. Are you aware that is part of what this hearing is all about? You are aware of that possibility, that your statement will go to the jury?"

Webb simply said, "Yes."

The prosecution insisted Webb's statements were sufficiently reliable to qualify as evidence. "The indicia of reliability are substantial in this case, and that is why we supplied the court with all the statements made, so the court would have the ability to read the statements made by all the participants in this crime, and determine for itself how accurate they are."

John Ladenburg, defense attorney for Christopher St. Pierre, spoke strongly against the motion. He pointed out that the prosecution was attempting to use an exception in the state's conspiracy law that says that out-of-court statements of conspirators are admissible as evidence if they were made "in the furtherance of a conspiracy, and during a conspiracy.

"The state has not alleged a conspiracy," insisted Ladenburg, "and the statements made by Mr. Webb were not made in the course of a conspiracy, they were made *after the arrest,* and in the furtherance of a plea bargain." He then quoted directly from the state of Washington's legal advisory commission's admonitions: "A statement admitting guilt and implicating another person made while in custody may be motivated by a desire to curry favor with the authorities."

In Ladenburg's view, the prosecution attempting to admit a plea-bargaining statement as evidence was exactly what the advisory commission feared and condemned. "Going beyond that argument," he continued, "there is a question of reliability of the statements."

Ladenburg assaulted Webb's plea-bargain statement from all angles, including Webb's recent admission that it was inaccurate and self-serving. "What I call one big inaccuracy," declared Ladenburg, "is that now he remembers that Paul did not participate in the homicide, and that he himself threw the knife into the gentleman's back. What happened here is that Mr. Webb is, in effect, admitting it is he who did the homicide, and these gentlemen had nothing to do with it. If that is not an indication of unreliability, I cannot imagine what would be. What we have here is contradictory evidence to the heart of the matter. I cannot imagine how the court could be any more convinced that his statements are inherently unreliable because they are repudiated by the gentleman who made them."

If all that wasn't enough, the exception the prosecution was attempting to invoke required the state to provide proof that the witness was unavailable, and that the unavailability was not the state's fault. "The state is responsible for the failure of Andrew Webb to testify," said Ladenburg, "and therefore cannot claim his unavailability."

David Murdach, Paul St. Pierre's attorney, opposed the admission of Webb's out-of-court statement for similar reasons. "Mr. Webb has confessed to slashing the throat of Mr. Wells. Mr. Webb has pled guilty to that crime. Mr. Webb is being punished for that crime.

The prosecutor now wants to attempt to show that Mr. Paul St. Pierre slashed Mr. Wells's throat. That is unethical and should not be allowed."

"The jury should only be exposed to evidence that, on its face, is credible," asserted Murdach. "I am not suggesting the court second-guess what the truth is. But we know that he has recanted his testimony, and changed his testimony. If we allow the statement to come in, I can't cross-examine, and the jurors can't judge the witness's credibility because he is not going to take the stand. It's not right; it's not fair. Obviously, what happened in this case was that there was a mistake made by the prosecution a long time ago as how they approached the case. The prosecutor elected to choose one man's position over another. They chose not only the wrong person, but their deal is burning up in their face. If the court allows Mr. Webb's statement, it will not be seeking fairness and it will not be seeking the truth."

"Mr. Webb told two people that his statement was inaccurate," continued Murdach, "and I will call those two people as witnesses for the defense." The two people were Webb's attorney, Larry Nichols, and prosecutor Carl Hultman.

"I don't know how to handle it," admitted Murdach. "I don't know if it disqualifies Mr. Hultman, as a witness, from prosecuting this case." The defense then launched into a recitation and interpretation of various previous legal decisions that contradicted those provided by the prosecution. In turn, Hultman did much the same, advising the court why he believed the rulings cited by Murdach did not apply.

When all the attorneys completed their impassioned and often sophisticated arguments, the judge offered personal commentary prior to announcing his decision. "The cases of Paul St. Pierre, Christopher St.

Pierre, and perhaps Andrew Webb are unique. There may never be another case like it. There has never been another case like it. The court today makes an evidentiary ruling only. The ultimate justice of the case for Paul and Chris will be determined by the jurors and not this judge and not by the attorneys out front. And in this proceeding," continued Judge Stone, "we are not trying the prosecutor. He may or may not have handled this thing the way he should, but the prosecutor did not create the crime, and the prosecutor has a responsibility to prosecute crime.

"The particular statement which the court is asked to rule admissible is hardly a statement designed to curry the favor of law enforcement, or the police, the only purpose of it to implicate somebody else, so I will get off the hook. Mr. Webb says, 'I cut his throat with a knife.' That certainly is no currying of favor when he alleged he is the person who slit a throat.

"The question here: is there sufficient indication of reliability to admit this statement, or is there not? No one denies that Damon Wells is dead. Nobody denies that a homicide occurred. No one denies that there was a party at [house number] Pacific Avenue and Wells was beaten up in the bathroom." Judge Stone enumerated other areas in which the statements of all three participants agreed. "The total picture has indicia of reliability. The court will rule that the statement is admissible. I am ruling that it does not run afoul of the evidentiary ruling, and I am ruling that it, in effect, fits with the hearsay exception."

"Is the court ruling that the unsigned *and* the signed sworn statements are admissible?" asked Ladenburg.

"I have my own marks and indications," answered Stone, "of where the statement should start and where it should end, and one place where a deletion should occur."

The out-of-court statement Andrew Webb made as part of his plea-bargain agreement, despite his new assertion that it was inaccurate, would be admitted as evidence for the prosecution against Paul and Christopher St. Pierre.

"The court would also observe that Andrew Webb has changed his mind at least twice, perhaps more than twice. It is entirely possible that he may change his mind on the third or fourth time. The court will specifically direct the prosecutor to take all necessary steps to see that Mr. Webb is retained here in the Pierce County Jail so that he can be available for testimony if he changes his mind one more time."

The court then inquired about other motions on behalf of the defendants. As a matter of law, defendants are required to renew their motions at the beginning of trial. Judge Stone denied each of the renewed motions made by Ladenburg on behalf of Christopher St. Pierre, and reminded all three attorneys that there must be no mention of the Achord case to the jury. "Any lack of care could very well cause a mistrial," said Stone, "which certainly the judge does not want."

Murdach's motions, for the most part, were also denied. The court did rule that the prosecution could make no reference to Paul St. Pierre's shoot-out with Kevin Robinson at the IGA. Stone also ruled that the full file on Andrew Webb's criminal history and psychological evaluations be available to the St. Pierres' attorneys.

The first day of testimony in the trial of Paul and Christopher St. Pierre for the assault, kidnapping, and murder of Damon Wells would begin the following morning, April 18, 1985.

Twelve

April 18, 1985

"Good morning, ladies and gentlemen from King County," said Judge Stone as the jury entered the courtroom, "perhaps the first thing you noticed when you came through the door was that there is a television camera here. Yes, there is media coverage today. The television cameraman is ordered to take no pictures whatsoever of any of the jurors. There will be television coverage during opening statements, and that is all. We will now proceed with opening statements. Mr. Hultman?"

"Thank you, Your Honor." The assistant deputy prosecutor for Pierce County stood and addressed the jury. "Now is when you really begin the work that you were sworn to undertake—the part where you sit and listen to the evidence. I think to go through the evidence in this case, you will need to know what we are talking about."

Hultman was talking about Paul and Christopher St. Pierre being guilty of premeditated murder, a murder committed for one or both of two reasons. Reason #1: to conceal assault and kidnapping. Reason #2: to conceal the identity of the persons committing assault and kidnapping.

"In other words," said Hultman, "this murder was committed to hide two crimes that occurred before. The evidence we are going to produce on those charges, and that we are satisfied will convince you beyond a reasonable doubt of the defendants' guilt, is going to consist of a succession of witnesses. Initially, we will call several young men who lived at the same house where the St. Pierre brothers lived, and where they resided with a third man, Andrew Webb."

First the prosecution set the scene at the house on Pacific Avenue the night Steve Wood and Damon Wells dropped by the St. Pierres' "beer bust." He covered the violence between Webb and Wood, and told the jury that after Steve Wood fled the house, Damon Wells accompanied Andrew Webb into the bathroom to help tend his injuries.

"The evidence will show that while Damon Wells was in the bathroom, Paul St. Pierre, the gentleman in the blue suit," Hultman explained, gesturing toward the defense table, "came into the bathroom. And then Christopher St. Pierre, the other defendant, came into the bathroom. I will not go through the details. I will let the evidence do that. But you will assume a brutal beating of Damon Wells occurred in that bathroom. It occurred because he happened to be a friend of the man who beat up Andrew Webb, and he was still there."

Hultman advised the jury that Donald Marshall, one of the St. Pierres' roommates, would testify that he had to wait a half hour before Paul St. Pierre allowed him in the bathroom. Marshall had access to the toilet, asserted Hultman, only after the badly beaten Damon Wells was spirited out of the house.

"Donald Marshall and Mark Perez were told that

Andrew Webb was being taken to the doctor for treatment of his nose injury," said Hultman. "Paul St. Pierre asked Marshall and Perez to clean up the blood in the bathroom while Chris and he took Andrew Webb to the doctor. The evidence will show, from the statements of the defendants themselves, that they didn't go to a doctor. The took semiconscious, five-foot, one-hundred-ten-pound Damon Wells out to Salmon Beach to 'teach him a lesson.' I'm tempted to argue for what that would mean, but that is for you to decide."

The jury heard how Wells was transported to the isolated darkness of Salmon Beach and how the defendants took his shoes, threw them in the bushes, and told him to walk home. Damon Wells, angry and upset, vowed to "get even." Worst of all, Wells threatened to call the cops. The defendants' response was to give chase. Damon Wells ran for his life.

"He was tackled, his throat was slashed, and he was stabbed twice in the back," said Hultman. "And then the defendants, by their own statements, indicate that they stood there for five to ten minutes and watched him bleed to death. Then they threw his body in the bushes. You will hear that from their own statements—Chris's statement and Paul's statement—they apparently tried to remove any blood they could from their clothes. They couldn't remove all the blood, so they built a big fire in the fireplace and burned up their clothes."

The jury sat spellbound, morbidly fascinated by the prosecution's description of the defendants' alleged behavior. "The next night, they took a sleeping bag and drove back to where the body had been thrown in the bushes, and they stuffed Damon Wells into that sleeping bag, took him up to an area near Elbe, and buried him in a shallow grave."

The jury would hear testimony from Damon Wells's mother about her efforts to file a Missing Persons report on her son, followed by Detective Price of the Missing Persons Bureau detailing his investigation into Wells's disappearance. "The testimony of Detective Price will take us into about the thirteenth or fourteenth of June," said Hultman, "when people began contacting the Tacoma Police Department. Based on information from Donald Marshall, Mark Perez, James Fuller, and Roy Kissler, the police got a search warrant and went to the house at [house number] Pacific Avenue."

Brief mentions of the thorough search for evidence at the Pacific Avenue house, and the subsequent arrest of Christopher St. Pierre, were preludes to the detailed description of Christopher St. Pierre's voluntary statement to Detectives Yerbury and Price. The prosecution acknowledged Christopher St. Pierre's assistance in recovering Damon Wells's body, and explained the complexity of legal jurisdiction—the burial site was in Lewis County; the homicide occurred in Pierce County.

"As soon as the grave had been identified, and the body determined to be there, Detectives Yerbury and Price took Christopher St. Pierre back to Tacoma. On the way, he pointed out the location where he believed they could find—because he and Anthony Youso had thrown it—the Gerber knife used to kill Damon Wells, the Gerber knife belonging to Paul St. Pierre. The knife was found one day later, June twenty-sixth, exactly where Christopher St. Pierre said it would be. That knife will be introduced as evidence by Officer Lindamann, an identification officer with the Tacoma Police Department."

The prosecution list of forthcoming evidence and significant testimony included the autopsy report by

Dr. Lacsina of the medical examiner's office. "The autopsy revealed that Mr. Wells died of three wounds, and Dr. Lacsina will testify that any one of those injuries could have caused his death, particularly given the fact that he was allowed to lay there and bleed to death."

The jurors were allowed a moment to absorb this before Hultman enhanced the disturbing imagery with further gruesome details. "He was slashed once, and maybe as many as two or three or four times in the throat. He was stabbed twice in the back, both wounds extremely deep—four inches or more in depth, with actual injury to the internal organs. He bled from all of the wounds, meaning he was alive when inflicted, and any one of those wounds could have been an independent cause of death, as Dr. Lacsina will tell you."

This would all lead up to the testimony of Andrew Webb. Carl Hultman tackled Webb's new, uncooperative attitude head-on. "And finally, the state will call Andrew Webb, the third participant in this crime. Andrew Webb, who was allegedly slicing Damon Wells's throat. I don't suppose there is anything wrong in telling you up front that there is an indication that he is going to refuse to testify. If he does so when he is called to the witness stand, the court will permit the state to introduce a statement he gave concerning his involvement. We will introduce it like the other statements from Detective Yerbury. He heard this evidence, and you won't have any questions in your mind that these defendants are guilty of the crime charged. Thank you."

Carl Hultman sat down, several jurors audibly exhaled, and Judge Stone prompted John Ladenburg, defense attorney for Christopher St. Pierre, to make his opening statement. "I would first like to speak about the order and presentation of the trial," he began. "I think one of the key things for you to remember is that there are certain elements you should look for in order to see any kind of a crime, or whether it has taken place at all, or implicates any particular individual at all."

Ladenburg, much as a teacher in a classroom, drew illustrations on a dry-erase board. "There are three different things that are essential. First, a person has to have the means to commit the crime. Second is the motive to commit the crime, and third is the opportunity to commit the crime. The most important thing about criminal trials," said Ladenburg, "is for the jury to keep an open mind, and wait for all of the evidence. Don't jump to conclusions. Let's gather all the evidence first, and then make a decision."

The jury, for neither the first nor the last time, heard about the Wood-Webb slugfest. "During the course of the fight, Christopher St. Pierre got upset because they were destroying the house and the furniture," said Ladenburg. "He told them to move outside, which gave Mr. Wood the opportunity to escape. He ran up the block and disappeared. We expect the evidence to show that Chris then went back into the house, and was drinking with Donald Marshall and Mr. Perez. At some point, he went into the bathroom and found a fight taking place with his brother Paul, Andrew Webb, and Damon Wells."

In Ladenburg's version, the fight erupted because Webb and the St. Pierre brothers suspected Damon Wells of being a rip-off artist. They imagined he was in the house to "case the joint" for a later burglary. Wells, according to Ladenburg, was continually saying, "I am not a rip-off artist; I am not with Wood. I don't know him that well."

"Paul St. Pierre, or Andrew Webb, suggested that they take Mr. Wells across town and make him walk home to teach him a lesson, and Mr. Wells said, 'that's fine. You can do that. I agree to go along with you and show you that I'm not a rip-off artist, and leave me alone.' The evidence will show that there was no intent to kidnap him, and he was not held for ransom. They were only going to take his shoes and make him walk barefoot as some sort of punishment because they thought he was a criminal attempting to set them up."

According to Ladenburg, this was the turning point in the case. "After the trip to Salmon Beach, as much mentioned by Mr. Hultman, Damon Wells became angry, upset, and threatened the three individuals who had driven him out there saying, 'I will get back at you. I will go to the police and tell them what you did to me, beat me up' et cetera, et cetera. Then Mr. Wells begins to run away from the three, and the evidence will show that it was Andrew Webb who suddenly began chasing down Mr. Wells, knocked him to the ground, facedown, and pulled his head back up by the hair, and slices his throat. It happened as fast as I told you while Chris and Paul stood there."

Months later, when police came to his house with a search warrant, the attorney informed the jury, Christopher St. Pierre was more than cooperative. "You will find from the police officers that Chris spent the entire day of June nineteenth telling them everything that happened. Chris explained that Mr. Webb chased down Damon Wells, slit his throat, then stood there watching him bleed to death, and took the knife and threw it into his back two times. Mr. Webb did that. Christopher St. Pierre spent all day with the police, and took them to where the body was buried. Mr. Webb was then arrested and taken to jail. He didn't make a statement the day he was arrested, he did not give police any evidence, and he did not cooperate with them at any time during his arrest."

Ladenburg then related the undisputed details of Andrew Webb's "deal" with the prosecutor's office. "He gave a statement to the police on July seventeenth that said both St. Pierre brothers helped in the murder, and that the knife wounds in the back were caused by the St. Pierre brothers. By including the St. Pierre brothers, Andrew Webb then became the key witness for the prosecution against the defendants.

"Mr. Webb now admits that he made his original statements out of convenience," Ladenburg said emphatically, "and I believe evidence will show that his statement, given to the police in turn for the bargain, was a lie. Christopher St. Pierre made his statement to the police on June nineteenth, immediately and without reflection, or fabrication. Mr. Webb made his statements on July eighteenth, after being in jail almost a month—after plenty of time for thinking of how he was going to avoid the death penalty."

The defense counsel's next remark had Carl Hultman bolting from his chair. "The evidence will show you only one man that dark night at Salmon Beach had a motive to commit that crime. You will find out during the course of this trial that Mr. Webb—"

"I will object to this, Your Honor," declared Hultman. Judge Stone overruled the objection, and Ladenburg continued. "You will find from the public records of Pierce County that Mr. Webb was awaiting sentencing for a prior assault conviction." The now enraptured jury learned that whether or not Andrew Webb went to prison for that previous conviction depended upon two very important conditions: First, Andrew Webb must have no further run-ins with the law. Second, Andrew Webb must refrain from alcohol and drugs.

"When Mr. Wells threatened to go to the police, only one man had a reason to shut him up to avoid prison," declared Ladenburg forcefully, "and that one man was Andrew Webb. It wouldn't be a coincidence that Mr. Webb was the one that chased him down and slit his throat in a matter of seconds."

Ladenburg's compelling narrative, solid reasoning, and appealing demeanor made a powerful courtroom impression. "Impressive may be an understatement," Detective Yerbury later remarked. "John Ladenburg is an excellent attorney who distinguished himself as both a dedicated defender and also a top-notch prosecutor. In his opening remarks, he really got across his point that Andrew Webb was really the only guy, in my opinion, who had any kind of motive to kill Damon Wells."

Softening his tone and altering his theme, Ladenburg brought his opening remarks to conclusion. "This trial is the last chapter in this story, and in the death of Damon Wells. Yours will be the final decision of who shall bear the guilt. One man has already gone to prison, and perhaps we can argue that he did not receive enough punishment for what he did, but I am asking you to consider all of the evidence before making any decision that Chris and Paul should pay for this crime. Thank you."

David Murdach, counsel for Paul St. Pierre, decided against giving his opening remarks at that time. Some jurors seemed baffled by this departure from expected routine, so Judge Stone explained that defense counsel has the option of making an opening statement later if they so choose.

The court then issued instructions concerning jurors' personal notes and notepads. "Under no circumstances are the notes or notepads to leave the court or jury room. After you have reached a verdict," Stone said, "your pad will be collected and the notes torn off and destroyed. You don't discuss the case, and you don't in any way start to deliberate or make up your mind on anything."

Court reconvened without the jury for another battle over intended testimony for the prosecution. Murdach and Ladenburg strongly objected to Hultman's plan to put Roy Kissler on the stand. "He's changed his story from what he originally told the Tacoma Police Department in his sworn statement," complained Murdach, and Ladenburg agreed. "We also object to the admission of Roy Kissler's testimony on the grounds of hearsay. He changed his testimony from the prior statement, and implicates Christopher St. Pierre by inference, saying, 'they' slit his throat."

"They were upset with me because I altered my story," Roy Kissler later recalled. "Between when I gave that first sworn statement to the police, and when I went to court, I had plenty of time to think about all the things that were said to me by Paul when he went with me up to the cabin. In June, when I went to the cops, I was under a lot of pressure. These guys had already assaulted my brother, and I felt pretty threatened at the time. I wasn't sure what was going to happen. I was nervous and shook-up. When Hultman brought me before the judge, and they argued about whether or not I could testify, the big deal was what they called inconsistency. The defense attorneys thought I was changing things to bring them in line with what the prosecution wanted me to say, but that wasn't the case at all. I was doing the best I could at recollecting what really went down."

David Murdach offered the court an overview of the situation, explaining the problematic nature of Roy Kissler's proposed testimony. "Mr. Andrew Webb recently told the prosecutor unequivocally that Mr. Paul St. Pierre did not cut Mr. Damon Wells's throat, nor did he stab Mr. Damon Wells in the back. Those were statements made after the deal was made, after Mr. Webb returned here to testify. Mr. Kissler has now changed his story from the true and accurate statement he subscribed to before. Now he says that Mr. Paul St. Pierre on one occasion stabbed Damon Wells in the back, and we know that is not true."

"The court will rule that the taking of [the] testimony of Roy Kissler is appropriate," said the judge. "I will overrule any objection based on inconsistency. That is a matter for the jury to deliberate. Now, Mr. Hultman, do you have a brief witness we could accommodate at this time?"

"I certainly can put Steve Wood on the stand," he replied. "I expect we'll have to interrupt him just when his testimony is getting interesting." When the jury returned, Carl Hultman called Steven Christopher Wood, age nineteen, as witness for the prosecution.

"Did you attend a party in later February 1984 with Damon Wells at the residence of Paul and Christopher St. Pierre and Andrew Webb?"

"If Andrew did live there, I didn't know that," answered Wood. "I knew the St. Pierre brothers resided there." Hultman inquired how it was that Wells and Wood attended the party on Pacific Avenue.

"That night, Damon had a bloody ear. I think an orange hit him in the ear." The prosecutor didn't request details of the ear and orange incident; Steve Wood continued his narrative uninterrupted. "We went to the emergency room at the hospital. He was wanting to get it checked out. The doctor said he couldn't get it looked at until two or three hours from now because they were pretty busy. We decided to forget it and go on home. We walked up the street a ways, and I remembered that my friend Mark . . . lived there and was a roommate of the St. Pierre brothers.

We thought we would stop by and say 'hi' on the way back home. We went in there."

"Did at some point," asked Hultman, "a fight break out between you and Andrew Webb?"

"Yes, I guess he mistook me for someone else who had ripped him off, or ripped off a friend of his, because I had a black car and he just jumped on me and lunged at me and it turned into a fight. Damon Wells had nothing to do with the fight at all. He was a bystander and looking at it."

Pressed for details, Wood described the altercation as "a rumble-type thing involving lots of fighting and lots of pushing and banging of the furniture. I know I was getting punches from Andrew," Wood testified, "but I was feeling kicks and stuff like that from behind. I didn't know who was doing it, but it—"

Murdach interjected a forceful objection, asking that the last bit of testimony be stricken. "The court overrules," said Stone. "I don't think I have to rule."

"You were being attacked," asked Hultman, "by more people than you were looking at?" Murdach again objected, and Stone sustained the objection this time. "Disregard both the question and the answer," Stone told the jury.

"Fine," said Hultman; then he asked Wood about Andrew Webb's nose injury.

"He had three fingers in my mouth trying to rip my jaw apart," replied Wood. "He started biting on my fingers and wouldn't let go, and I was on top of him and I told him I would bite his nose if he didn't let go, so I bit his nose."

Wood confirmed that they were told to take the fight outside, and when Webb grabbed his arm at the doorway, Wood bolted and ran. "I ran in a quick hurry because I figured I was going to get ganged up on. I was worrying about my own skin at the time."

John Ladenburg had no questions for Steve Wood, but David Murdach inquired if Andrew Webb seemed in control of himself the night of the fight. "He seemed drunk to me," said Wood. "Everybody was partying, but he was out of control."

Judge Stone called for the lunch break, and again admonished jurors to not discuss the case. Court reconvened at 1:38 P.M. The prosecution's next witness was Donald Marshall, the St. Pierre brothers' childhood chum and former roommate. Hultman had him list who was at the party, what it was like, and how he knew the various participants.

"I came later after I had dinner at my brother's house, and when I arrived, there was Chris, there was Paul, and Jim Fuller and Damon Wells and Steve Wood, Mark Perez, and some friend of Paul St. Pierre's that I'd met once or twice, and Andrew Webb. I met Steve Wood about a week or so before, and when he arrived, Damon Wells was introduced to me as a friend of Steve Wood. Damon Wells had kind of long hair and he was shorter than I. About one hundred ten pounds or so, and he wore a leather coat—kind of a tannish leather coat—and he had a long nose, like mine, I thought. He was a pretty good guy."

Marshall testified that he showed up at [the house] between 6:00 and 7:00 P.M., everyone was drinking, and a beer was thrust into his hand immediately upon arrival. The other participants' intoxication levels ranged from mild to obnoxious. Marshall's recollection of Andrew Webb's condition included neither sobriety nor serenity. According to Marshall's testimony, Andrew Webb was edgy and argumentative.

When Steve Wood mentioned in casual conversation that he had "borrowed some things from some guys who were being really kind of rotten," Andrew Webb first tossed accusations, then threw punches.

"Wood wasn't even talking to Andrew," Marshall told the jury, "but Webb just broke right in and stated that Wood was a thief, and he was the guy who ripped him off, and all that stuff, which was pretty far-fetched. Then Mr. Webb threw a physical punch toward Mr. Wood, who was trying to diplomatically get himself out of the situation. I would say that at this point, Wood had no choice but to fight back."

The inebriation-fueled fisticuffs proved unfavorable to Andrew Webb. "He had a bloodied mouth," said Marshall, "and I believe he was bit across the nose. His eyes were scratched up. Andrew was getting the worst of the deal. When Steve Wood got on top of him in a hold, he couldn't maneuver very well. At that time, Chris kicked Steve Wood in the spinal area, but he still held on. And then Paul St. Pierre gave him a couple blows to the back while Steve Wood still had hold of Mr. Webb.

"I scurried across the room closer to the kitchen," he continued. "Damon Wells and I were there, and a few other people in the house were pushing the guys away from the furniture, stereo and things, so that they weren't damaged. Then the fight broke up in front of Damon Wells and me. As Steve Wood walked toward the front door, he was making remarks like 'I thought you were my friends,' and I told him he should just leave and get out of the house, and I opened the door and he went out.

"Mark Perez had gone into his bedroom, Chris St. Pierre was standing by the bathroom doorway, and Paul St. Pierre was in the bathroom. As for Damon Wells, I was told he had left. I went back to my bedroom to get a fresh pack of cigarettes, dropped them in the hallway near the bathroom door, and I heard voices being raised—Andrew Webb's voice, and Paul St. Pierre's, and then I heard the scuffling and a fight.

I heard some banging against the wall, and the sound of a toilet—like the plastic from the toilet—I heard it hit the floor, and then I heard the sputtering noise like nerves of a person connecting in pain."

"I object," Murdach exclaimed. "He is obviously going far beyond what he heard." Judge Stone overruled Murdach's objection, reminding him that he'd have the opportunity to cross-examine the witness.

"What did you do then?" Hultman inquired.

"I got big-eyed," admitted Marshall. "I said to myself Paul and Andrew might have a disagreement in the bathroom. I believed Paul was roughing up Andrew because he started a fight in his house and lost. Well, I went back from the hallway into the living room. Paul St. Pierre came out of the bathroom. He came upstairs with a bucket of soap and water and some rags and he said he was taking Andrew to the hospital, and asked me and Mark Perez to clean the bathroom up a little bit."

The floor plan at [the house] made it possible to leave the bathroom and exit the house without being seen by anyone in the living room. "All you have to do," explained Marshall, "is close the hallway door and the kitchen door." Perez and Marshall found the bathroom in significant disarray. "The toilet seat was broken; there was a little bit of blood on the floor in front of the bathroom sink. There was blood on the bathroom sink, a little bit to the left side of the toilet. I cleaned the sink in the bathroom. There was blood all over the sink."

Hultman prompted his witness to describe Andrew Webb's appearance following his alleged visit to the doctor. Marshall said Andrew Webb didn't look any different from when he had left the house. "He had no stitches or bandages and he was still bleeding slightly. When I asked Andrew Webb for an explanation of what was really going on, Webb got angry and said, 'You Marshalls used to be someone. You are no one now. You don't need to know anything. You just live here.' "

Ladenburg read aloud from Marshall's sworn statement to the Tacoma Police, primarily eliciting confirmation that it was Christopher St. Pierre who urged Steve Wood to take the fight outside. "He said that they were breaking up the furniture," confirmed Marshall, "and he was addressing mainly Mr. Wood: 'Look at you, start a fight in my house and break up the furniture.' "

David Murdach sought even more details of the Webb-Wood altercation, asking, "How many blows were exchanged?" and "Can you tell me exactly what the words were spoken between Mr. Wood and Mr. Webb just before Andrew smacked him?"

"Well, Mr. Wood goes: 'I don't fuck and rip you off. I never rip you guys off.' And Andrew goes: 'You're nothing but a fucking thief and I hate thieves.' There was a lot worser than that, but I can't recall it. I do remember those sentences."

He also remembered Steve Wood sitting on the floor when Andrew Webb, standing above him, "unloaded a good one on him. I believe he did hit him in the face." Wood, smaller but faster, immediately retaliated. He knocked Webb's feet out from under him, pulled him to the floor, and the half-hour battle began in earnest.

"It was your understanding that Damon Wells had left the house after the fight, right?" asked Murdach.

"Chris said Wells went with Jim Fuller," answered Marshall, "because they live in the same neighborhood, and they're walking home."

Hultman, on redirect examination, handed his witness Plaintiff's Exhibit #1—Marshall's sworn statement

to the Tacoma Police—and asked him to identify it.
"Why don't you look through it," suggested Hultman,
"and check the signature on the back." Aside from
the singular addition of Marshall's new phone number
written in blue ink, it was identical to the original.

"Your Honor," Hultman said to Judge Stone, "the
state moves for admission of this statement. There is
an evidence rule when one party reads from a statement—"

Stone interrupted him, announcing that he would
defer ruling until the recess. With the witness and
the jury excused, Judge Stone addressed Hultman's
motion. "You stated that because portions of the
statement were read or quoted in cross-examination,
it should go to the jury. Tell me why I should accept
your version rather than what I expect the opposition will be."

Hultman admitted that he never anticipated this issue coming up. However, he felt that Ladenburg reading aloud from Marshall's statement would be an
effort to discredit his testimony about how the fight
began. Once a portion of a statement is used in that
manner, argued Hultman, the opposing party may
then move for admission of the entire statement. It
wouldn't be fair to allow one attorney to read aloud
only part of a statement, using that isolated section to
bolster or reinforce his client's position. "The entire
statement should become part of the record," Hultman said. "Otherwise, the jury can't tell if the portion
read aloud was taken out of context or not."

"I don't believe it would be proper," countered
Ladenburg. "The statement contains a number of
items relevant to the case but not testified to by the
witness. If the court admits those things—in effect admitting statements the witness did not testify to in

court—I think all those statements are inadmissible, and should not be allowed in the course of this trial."

Murdach agreed completely. "You can't allow the witness's testimony to come in twice," he told Stone. "It would be the same thing if Mr. Hultman offered a police report from the policeman in addition to the policeman's testimony. I don't believe it should be admitted under any rule."

Judge Stone noted that the trial was becoming more and more about the admissibility of statements. "Yesterday the court made some rulings on the statements that will come in, and there are certain rules and special circumstances. Certainly, the court should consider admitting the statement, but I simply think it would do more harm than good in this case. It would tend to divert the jurors from their main task, and that is to evaluate the witness from the stand."

Stone declined to admit Plaintiff's Exhibit #1, brought back the jury, and directed Hultman to call his next witness. Mark V. Perez, former roommate of Marshall and the St. Pierres. Perez's testimony, virtually identical to Marshall's, contained one significant addition and a potentially disastrous slip of the tongue. Carl Hultman elicited testimony about threatening phone calls to Perez from Chris St. Pierre, asking, "Did you receive numerous calls from Christopher St. Pierre concerning you talking to the police?" Perez answered in the affirmative, and Hultman asked Perez if he remembered what month the phone calls took place.

"It was during sometime," Perez said haltingly, as if searching for a reference point in time, "well, actually, it was after the second case." Everything, and everyone, in the Pierce Country courtroom came to a sudden, silent standstill. Ladenburg, almost incredulous, was the first to speak. "I didn't hear his answer,"

he said, and requested Perez to say it again. Judge
Stone jumped in immediately, saying, "I think it's time
for the afternoon recess. . . . The jury will be excused,
and the court will remain in session momentarily."

"Tell me what I said," offered Perez, and John
Ladenburg addressed the issue. "What happened before the judge excused the jury was that the prosecutor asked about a phone call allegedly made by
Christopher St. Pierre to this witness. At first, I didn't
know what he was talking about. Then the witness answered, I believe his answer was, 'after the second
case'—exactly what we are trying to prevent the jury
from finding out about."

Judge Stone saw where this was heading, and offered sage advice to Carl Hultman. "If the prosecutor
is concerned about a mistrial, I think that during the
recess the prosecutor should have a long talk with the
witness, and make sure that nothing occurs that re-
quires a recess."

Murdach wanted more than Hultman having a long
talk with Perez; he wanted Stone to declare a mistrial.
"He made the statement about the second case," insisted Murdach. "We move for a motion for mistrial
based on that statement." Ladenburg joined Murdach,
but Stone denied the motion, the jury returned, and
Mark Perez continued his testimony.

Hultman asked Perez to repeat Chris St. Pierre's
threats. "I object to any statement Mr. Chris St. Pierre
supposedly made to this witness over the phone," asserted Ladenburg. "I join that objection," added Murdach. "The court will overrule," said the judge, and
Stone told Perez to answer Hultman's question.

"What did Christopher St. Pierre say to you," asked
Hultman, "about Donald Marshall going to the police?"

"He said that he thought Donald Marshall had a

big mouth," replied Perez, "and if he went to the police that him and his family would be dead."

Ladenburg had a few important questions for Perez,
but requested they be asked outside the jury's presence. "Probably time for the jurors to stand and
stretch, anyway," offered Stone. "I will stand up and
stretch with you."

Mark Perez was handed a copy of the last page of
his signed statement to the Tacoma Police. "You said
that Christopher St. Pierre said, and I quote from your
statement, 'Here's the scoop,' " Ladenburg read
aloud, " 'the police were just inquiring about the
shooting and didn't want me for anything.' He said
he thought Donald Marshall had a big mouth and if
Don said anything to the police, Don would be dead
and so would his family." Perez agreed that this was
the gist of his statement. Ladenburg had only one
question: "What shooting was being referred to?"

"The one where Andrew Webb was shot," replied
Perez, and Ladenburg immediately moved for a mistrial. "On the basis of this," he stated firmly, "I move
for a mistrial because the statement has to do with a
different crime and a different case, altogether. The
prosecutor knew it when he introduced it, and now
he's attempting to say Chris St. Pierre was threatening
a witness in *this* case. That is not a fact, and the prosecutor knows it's not a fact."

"The fact of the matter," responded Hultman, "is
that Mr. Ladenburg knows that the statement to the
police covers everything that happened, including the
murder of Damon Wells."

"Just a few basics," interjected Judge Stone. "Number one: When people who are involved in one incident and one incident only, the court and the
attorneys don't have a whole lot of difficulty sorting
things out. Number two: When there are multiple in-

cidents, it gets more difficult. Participants frequently make statements that we lawyers and judges can later say, 'Oops, that was not very wise to say that.' But we don't have the luxury of editing out what people said or didn't say. I don't think the court has to sprain its brain. The court denies the motion for mistrial, and I think it is entirely proper."

Back in session, Carl Hultman wanted to bring Donald Marshall to the witness stand for additional testimony. "I object," said Murdach. "He's had his shot." Judge Stone ignored the objection. "Would you get the jury, please, and bring Mr. Marshall back in?"

"Did Andrew Webb, Christopher St. Pierre, and Paul St. Pierre do anything unusual," asked Hultman, "when they returned to the house on the night in question?"

"Yes, it was very unusual. They came in and Chris started making a fire in the fireplace, and they all started taking their shoes off, and all their clothing, and disbursed it in the fire and let them burn. It was all the clothing they had on. Their coats, their shoes, socks, pants, shirts, and even Andrew spotted some blood on one of my coats that was hanging on the hall tree, and he grabbed my coat—a thin windbreaker—and he looked at me and I turned the other way, and he burned my coat, too. At this time, I questioned them. I said, 'Is anything you guys done? Tell me, is there something you got going or you are not letting me in on?' That was when Webb and Chris and Paul looked at each other and Webb stood up and said, 'You Marshalls used to be something and you are nothing now,' and all this, 'you just live here.' "

Murdach only wanted to know if Marshall was drunk that night, which he wasn't, and Ladenburg had no questions at all. Hultman then called Patricia Wells to the witness stand. She was only there a few emotional

minutes, presenting photographs of Damon with his
puppy, and snapshots of Damon and his girlfriend at
a high school Tolo dance. The state offered the various photographs as plaintiff's exhibits, but Stone deferred ruling until the end of the day.

Officer Meeks, Hultman's next witness, merely
stated basic facts of the Missing Persons report taken
February 27, 1984. Ladenburg had neither questions
nor comments. "I move the testimony be stricken,"
said David Murdach. "It adds nothing to the case."
Stone denied the motion, then addressed the jury.
"The court has some details it needs to take care of.
This is probably the only time in the whole trial we
break early. We will cherish it."

Stone excused the jury, reminding them again not
to discuss the case or listen to media reports on it.

With the jury gone, Stone asked to see the photos
of Damon Wells. "I think the jury should have the
opportunity," said Hultman, "to see him as they do
see the defendants seated here." The court intended
to admit one, and only one, of the submitted photographs.

"The idea of evidence," commented Murdach, "is
to give some assistance to the jury to assist them on
some point in the case. It has been testified to and
repeatedly stated and stipulated that he is five feet tall,
or short, or whatever. I don't see why these pictures
for anyone would add or aid the jury or help on a
particular point in the case."

"I think the victim in this case is entitled to some
consideration," Hultman countered, "and justice demands that the jury have an opportunity to see him."
The court agreed; one photo of Damon Wells was admitted as evidence. "The jury is entitled to realize that
the individual was a human being," said Judge Stone.
"It's admitted for that purpose."

Victim John Achord, 22.

The St. Pierre brothers' home in Tacoma, Washington, where victims Damon Wells and John Achord were last seen alive. (*Photo courtesy Tacoma Police Department, Tacoma, Washington*)

Wells was beaten almost unconscious with the lid from this toilet before he was stabbed to death. (*Photo courtesy Tacoma Police Department, Tacoma, Washington*)

Police found blood on the floor and a bullet hole in the refrigerator after Paul St. Pierre shot Andrew Webb. (*Photo courtesy Tacoma Police Department, Tacoma, Washington*)

St. Pierre hid the gun between two stacks of roofing tiles. (*Photo courtesy Tacoma Police Department, Tacoma, Washington*)

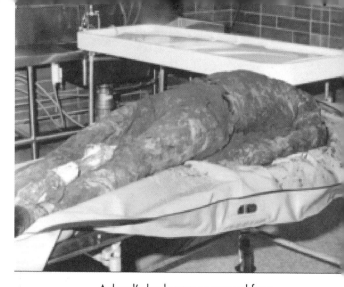

Achord's body was recovered from
a shallow grave on June 19, 1984.
(*Photo courtesy Tacoma Police Department, Tacoma, Washington*)

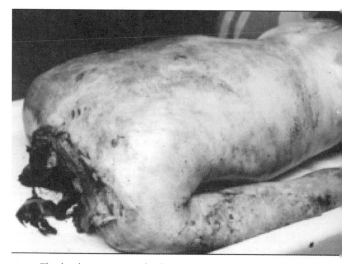

The body was severely decomposed and missing its head.
(*Photo courtesy Tacoma Police Department, Tacoma, Washington*)

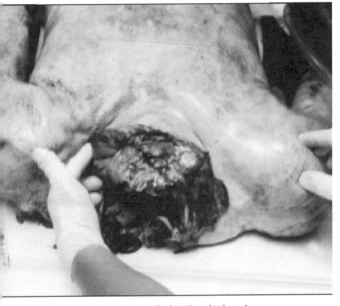

The autopsy revealed Achord's head
had been cut off after he had been killed.
(*Photo courtesy Tacoma Police Department, Tacoma, Washington*)

Police later recovered Achord's missing head in a
cement-filled bucket from the Puyallup River.
(*Photo courtesy Tacoma Police Department, Tacoma, Washington*)

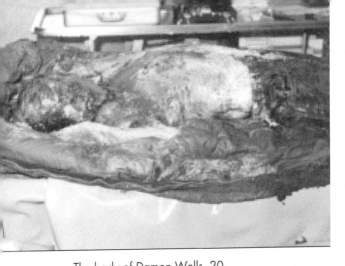

The body of Damon Wells, 20,
was located near Achord's body.
(*Photo courtesy Tacoma Police Department, Tacoma, Washington*)

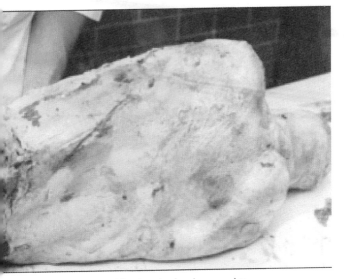

Wells was stabbed in the back several times.
(*Photo courtesy Tacoma Police Department, Tacoma, Washington*)

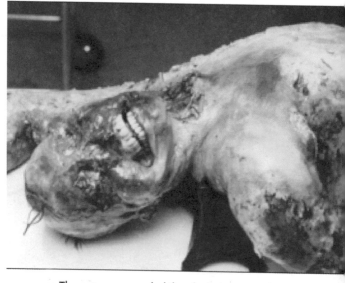

The autopsy revealed that the large open throat
wound in Wells's body was actually three slashes.
(*Photo courtesy Tacoma Police Department, Tacoma, Washington*)

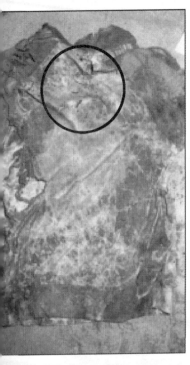

Cuts in Wells's shirt showed where he had been stabbed. (*Photo courtesy Tacoma Police Department, Tacoma, Washington*)

Wells's tennis shoes were thrown into the bushes by his killers. (*Photo courtesy Tacoma Police Department, Tacoma, Washington*)

Paul St. Pierre, 25.
(*Photo courtesy Tacoma Police Department, Tacoma, Washington*)

Christopher St. Pierre, 21.
(Photo courtesy Tacoma Police Department, Tacoma, Washington)

Andrew K. Webb, 24.
(Photo courtesy Tacoma Police Department, Tacoma, Washington)

Paul St. Pierre was given the choice of enlisting in the Marines or spending several years in a juvenile correction center.

istopher St. Pierre as enior at Lincoln High School in 1981.

Paul St. Pierre, Roy Kissler, and Christopher St. Pierre (*right to left*). Kissler provided information to the police linking Paul St. Pierre to the missing Wells and Achord. (*Photo courtesy Roy Kissler*)

Webb's personality changed for the worse when a badly broken collarbone resulted in the loss of his job.

Detective Robert Yerbury.

Defense attorney
John W. Ladenburg.
(*Photo courtesy Pierce County,
Washington Prosecutors Office*)

Prosecuting attorney
Carl Hultman.
(*Photo courtesy Pierce County,
Washington Prosecutors Office*)

Judge Waldo F. Stone.
(*Photo courtesy Waldo F. Stone*)

Andrew Webb in Washington State Prison in December 1994.

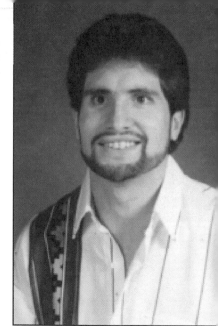

Now diagnosed with multiple sclerosis, Christopher St. Pierre remains in prison.

Patricia Wells, Damon's mother, wanted to attend the entire trial, but didn't know if it was permissible for a witness to remain in the courtroom after giving testimony. "It's a public courtroom," answered Stone. "She is welcome to stay." Ms. Wells returned the following day.

Thirteen

April 19, 1985

Court reconvened at 9:30 A.M.

"With total predictability, there was media coverage in the newspapers, radio, and television," began Judge Stone in his welcome address to the jury. "Anybody here have any trouble following the court instructions? I assume that whatever you know about this case, you got right here in the courtroom. Anybody disagree? Let's proceed. Call your next witness, Mr. Hultman."

Detective Price took the stand, and essentially provided continuation of Officer Meeks's testimony regarding the investigation of Damon Wells's disappearance. Hultman had Price testify that both Chris St. Pierre and Paul St. Pierre provided voluntary statements to the police.

Murdach, on cross-examination, pursued the circumstances surrounding Paul St. Pierre's statement. "Are you aware," he asked Price, "that he requested that interview with you even though there had been a court order—"

"I will object to this!" Hultman was on his feet.

"—for him to not speak to anyone without counsel present?"

"I will sustain the objection," said the judge, "and I admonish the jurors to disregard the last question."

Detective Price was thanked and excused. Roy Kissler took the stand and told of his adventures with Paul St. Pierre at the cabin. David Murdach questioned why—despite Andrew Webbs's recent recantation and acceptance of full responsibility for slashing Damon Wells's throat—Kissler continued attributing confessional statements to Paul St. Pierre?

"What they didn't seem to understand," Kissler later commented, "was that I could only tell them what I remember hearing directly from Paul St. Pierre. It doesn't matter what Andrew Webb may have said, or what he confessed to or didn't confess to. That doesn't matter as far as what I actually heard from Paul St. Pierre. Paul told me that he, Paul St. Pierre, chased down Damon Wells, cut his throat, and all that. Now, maybe Paul was bragging. Maybe he wished he had done something like that. That wouldn't be out of the question at all, but I had to testify as to what I remember Paul saying to me that day, not something that made his lawyer feel better, or the prosecution, either."

"Have you ever," Murdach asked Kissler, "made a statement to anyone that you would like to get back at Paul St. Pierre?"

"I haven't any reason to get back at him," Kissler said. "What I was thinking at that point was for protection for myself and my family." This response, however, did not answer Murdach's question. Paul St. Pierre's attorney asked it again. "The question is: have you ever made a statement that you wanted to get back at Paul St. Pierre?"

"The first few days after this incident happened, because I had nothing but his word to go on, and by the other things he said to me—"

"You are asked," interrupted Murdach forcefully, "have you ever made a statement that you wanted to get back at Paul St. Pierre?"

"Yes," came Kissler's honest reply, "I have."

Carl Hultman returned for further direct examination, requesting clarification from Kissler. "Mr. Murdach asked you if you made the statement about you wanting to get back at Paul St. Pierre. What was that statement you made?"

"OK," said Kissler, "I talked to my minister about it."

Neither Hultman nor Murdach pursued the issue. The prosecutor was happy the jury knew Kissler made this comment to his minister; Murdach was pleased that the jury knew Kissler admitted expressing a desire "to get back at Paul St. Pierre."

"What that was all about," Roy Kissler explained several years later, "is that two months after Paul St. Pierre told me about killing people, I went back up to the church and talked to the pastor. This was a different pastor than was there the first night I went into the church, so we didn't have the same relationship. I told him everything, and I told him that I was thinking of solving this problem—the problem of Paul being a killer who obviously attempted doing to my brother what he did to Damon Wells, and who wanted to do the same thing to me. I had it all figured out how I was going to get rid of Paul St. Pierre."

Kissler knew the neighborhood, and his plan was remarkably simple. Dressed in black, he would go behind Ericson's with a 12-gauge shotgun, throw a rock through the back window of one of their cars, and when Paul came out, a fusillade of double-barrel firepower would spell curtains to the killing spree of Paul St. Pierre. "Then I would just disappear down the alley in the middle of the night. They're up all night, anyway. It wouldn't have been too tough, I don't think, to pull off. The pastor said, 'You can't do that; you're a Christian.' I said, 'Yeah, I can, too.' " The pastor insisted they pray about it, and that's exactly what they did. Prayers concluded, Roy Kissler decided that killing Paul St. Pierre was not appropriate behavior for a man who had given his life to the Lord. "Later, after the arrests," he recalled, "that same pastor went down and talked to Paul St. Pierre at the jail. Honest. It's in the records."

His testimony concluded, Roy Kissler stepped around the rail and signed the witness sheet. Carl Hultman asked the court to instruct the jury on how they should regard the out-of-court statements of Paul and Christopher St. Pierre. Stone agreed.

"Ladies and gentlemen, this instruction that I'm going to give you may apply to several witnesses throughout the case. The jury is instructed that out-of-court statements by one of the St. Pierres are not to be considered by you as evidence against the other one. We will now take the morning recess. You have heard only a portion of the case. You don't start to deliberate or discuss or in any way make up your mind."

From the jury box came an unexpected interruption. "I do not understand your instruction," said the woman.

"The jury is instructed," repeated Stone, "that out-of-court statements by one of the St. Pierres are not to be considered by you as evidence against the other St. Pierre. Now, take the morning recess."

When court reconvened, Detective Yerbury began his testimony. Early in the prosecution questioning, Hultman asked Yerbury to read aloud from the signed statement given by Christopher St. Pierre on the day of his arrest.

"I would ask you then," said Hultman, "beginning

about the third paragraph of that statement, to tell us what Christopher St. Pierre told you about what had occurred with Damon Wells at the house."

"I object," Murdach proposed. "I would like to be outside the presence of the jury." The jurors were again shuffled off to their anteroom while Hultman and Murdach wrestled over law and application. The essence of the disagreement was as follows: The prosecution wanted Yerbury to read selected portions of Christopher St. Pierre's statement. Paul St. Pierre's defense attorney did not want Yerbury to read any portion of the statement because it would contain remarks "out of the mouth of Christopher St. Pierre" concerning alleged illegal conduct by Paul St. Pierre.

"There is no way I can cross-examine Mr. St. Pierre, and no way I can call him to the stand for the purpose of cross-examination," objected Murdach. "The court should not use any portion of Chris St. Pierre's statement that refers to anything of which Paul St. Pierre is accused. We will have the same problem with Paul St. Pierre's statements if he made statements about Christopher St. Pierre."

"I agree," said John Ladenburg, "we will have the same problem with the confession of Paul St. Pierre." The lawyers had previously tossed around the idea of editing the various statements—a troublesome and complex task—and Stone agreed to at least consider the idea. "The court indicated we would have some period of talking about edits and excisions," Ladenburg reminded the court, "and we might as well do it now. We might as well settle it all at once."

Hultman had already marked where he wanted Yerbury to start reading, and where he wanted him to stop. Murdach and Ladenburg did not want Yerbury to read anything at all; the prosecution completely disagreed. "The state's position is that Christopher St.

Pierre doesn't say anything about Paul that Paul
doesn't admit by himself, and Paul says very little
about Chris, and certainly Chris does not admit about
himself. It's the intention of the state that both statements will be testified to by Detective Yerbury, so there
is no unbalance created by only one statement coming
in."

"The fact here," Murdach said in opposition, "is
that Mr. Paul St. Pierre's statement is of questionable
ground. I realize that in a previous hearing, the court
allowed the statement to be introduced as evidence.
However, when I say the statement is of questionable
ground, I'm referring to Paul St. Pierre's statement to
the police being given in defiance of an order by
Judge Healy. If the appellate court holds Mr. Paul St.
Pierre's statement in error, we would then have a statement that is improperly introduced. I think to proceed
cautiously in this matter would be better than to leap
into possible theory issues on appeal."

"The suggestion was made by Mr. Murdach," Stone
later commented, "that this judge should make rulings in anticipation of what the appellate court might
do. I think that is the wrong approach. The appellate
court regularly says that they won't rule until the trial
court rules—'You do your thinking in the trial court,
conduct the trial, and then we will make a ruling and
see if the trial judge did it right'—this judge has to
go first."

"The court," Murdach argued, "instructed the jury
that a statement by one St. Pierre cannot be taken as
evidence against the other St. Pierre. One juror asked
the court to repeat that remark, and I observed her
writing that down. If the jury follows that court instruction, they're not even going to consider Christopher St. Pierre's statement against Paul St. Pierre, so

why admit it, and why not delete it, and why not void any reference to it?''

When Carl Hultman insisted that there was no possibility of prejudice against the defendants if the statements, even judiciously edited, were admitted as evidence, Murdach instantly disagreed. "What greater prejudice could there be," asked the defense counsel, "than not to be able to cross-examine the person who makes a statement against you? For the judge to allow the statement in, and at the same time tell the jury that it has a duty to disregard it, what's the point? Why put it in?"

"For the record," said Judge Stone, "the court has previously ruled and made comments on the taking of the statement by Paul St. Pierre which was, at least on the surface, in direct violation of a judge's order. I see no reason to rehash that. I already made a ruling on it. Certainly counsel has hit a subject close to the judge's heart when he said we should be cautious. We should be cautious in each of our rulings. The judge is reminded that there are not risk-free rulings. In this case, every ruling I make has risk. There is a great likelihood of appeal in this case."

Mutual agreement and cooperative like-mindedness were not characteristics attributed to the trio of trial attorneys gathered in Judge Stone's courtroom. For this reason alone, although other justifications were available, Judge Stone declined any editing process.

"I find that the hazard of editing a statement where anyone can second-guess the judge—'You should take this out and should take that out'—and the hazard of editing is just as great, or perhaps greater today, than the specter of appellate review. The court will decline to edit other than the starting and stopping point. We start and stop, but the ruling the court has to make now," concluded Judge Stone. "I decline to edit the statement of Christopher Leo St. Pierre."

Awaiting the jury's return, Hultman advised the court that Damon Wells's mother and Mrs. St. Pierre were both in the courtroom. None of the attorneys wanted these women excluded from testifying at the penalty phase on the grounds that they had attended the trial phase. As all attorneys were in agreement, Stone simply said, "Mrs. St. Pierre and Mrs. Wells are welcome here."

Detective Robert Yerbury resumed his testimony. First he read aloud from Christopher St. Pierre's statement, then from Paul St. Pierre's. John Ladenburg had no difficulty on cross-examination establishing that Christopher St. Pierre was completely cooperative with Detectives Yerbury and Price, and that the information he provided was accurate and offered of his own free will.

In his opening remarks at the trial's beginning, Ladenburg had told the jury that Damon Wells went to Salmon Beach willingly, without being coerced or forced. Ladenburg returned to this theme when questioning Detective Yerbury. "Did you ever ask Chris specifically if Mr. Damon Wells objected to going along or if he was forced?"

"Well, I didn't see anything in the statement saying Damon Wells was taken at gunpoint," answered Yerbury. "He was unconscious. I assumed he could not make any kind of statement one way or other. There was no reason to ask that question as he told me that Damon Wells was unconscious."

The pace picked up, and the prosecution's next witnesses testified free of incident, objections, or interruptions. Sergeant Parkhurst of the Tacoma Police Department described in full detail the recovery of Damon Wells's body from the grave site in Elbe, the subsequent retrieval of the alleged murder weapon (Paul St. Pierre's Gerber knife), and the search of Salmon Beach, where Damon Wells's tennis shoes were eventually discovered.

Identification Technician John Penton then explained the nature of his employment, and presented several photographs.

"An identification technician is to respond to a crime scene and photograph as necessary the scene and also to recover the evidence at hand. The photographs I shot that day," said Penton, "go from showing the roadway and entryway up to the actual grave and the sleeping bag with the body in it." Penton also showed the court a photograph of Damon Wells's tennis shoes recovered from Salmon Beach.

"We are ahead of schedule," noted Judge Stone, "as far as the timing of the case is concerned. Today is Friday. The court appreciates your following meticulously the instructions of the court, and your ignoring of the media, and we will repeat that. No radio. No television. No newspaper."

Witnesses in the trial were not bound by these instructions. "I remember the day after I testified, I got up and opened the morning newspaper," Roy Kissler recalled, "and right there on the front page, they have my full name in there nine times. 'Roy E. Kissler said this and that.' I was thinking, 'Why didn't they just mail me a T-shirt with a target on it at the same time?' Sure, Paul and Chris were locked up, but I wasn't really sure what else, or who else, they were involved with other than this. I mean, those guys traveled in some different circles. Andrew Webb was sort of a different circle all on his own."

Fourteen

"About Andrew Webb—is it the prosecutor's intent," asked Judge Stone on Monday morning, "to put Andrew Webb on the stand in the presence of the jury?"

"Yes, Your Honor," replied Carl Hultman, "the reason for that is because unavailability is one of the critical requirements and I do not think that Andrew Webb is unavailable until he refuses to testify in front of the jury."

"The obvious thing," said Stone, "is that when we are dealing with Andrew Webb, we are dealing in a sensitive area. Are we ready for the jury? Or would you rather do the pictures before the jury?" The pictures to which Stone referred were graphic and disturbing autopsy photographs. The prosecution wanted them introduced as exhibits, explained Hultman, to show the exact injuries sustained by Damon Wells.

David Murdach thought Hultman's reason was absolute nonsense. "Those photographs show a body in an extensive state of decomposition. It's almost like a homicide case where an attempt is made to dig up the corpse and over a period of time, show the bullet wounds to the jury."

"Your Honor," pleaded Hultman, "I think the defendants have to bear the certain burden of this, of that being the condition of the body. They are directly responsible for it not being exhumed any sooner. They are in no position to complain."

The prosecution described the photos and explained why these particular pictures were selected. "A couple show the throat wounds, back wounds, a photograph of a lung to show the jury what was done to that lung, a leg injury with heavy bruising, and there is one photograph that shows an arm with a tattoo on it."

Judge Stone allowed five milder photos, but he did not want the jury viewing gruesome pictures of Damon Wells's decomposed body. "I think the case can be handled without admitting those."

Following brief appearances by identification technicians from the Tacoma Police Department presenting further exhibits, Medical Examiner Emanuel Lacsina took the stand. "I am a forensic pathologist, which means that I am a physician who specializes in the investigation of sudden, unexpected, unexplained, and violent death to determine the cause, as well as the manner, of death."

"At the time I performed the autopsy," testified Dr. Lacsina, "the cadaver was in quite an advanced degree of decomposition. Most of the soft tissue was pretty decomposed. There were no recognizable features of a face."

Several jurors squirmed uncomfortably in their seats as Dr. Lacsina described the severe stab wounds inflicted on Damon Wells. "One of the stab wounds, the deeper wound, was five and a half inches from the skin surface and penetrated the posterior area wall of the heart." Lacsina acknowledged that both the stab wounds and the throat wounds took place before Wells died. "Any of the three wounds would have caused death."

"There is testimony," said Hultman, "suggesting that at the time the body was . . . attempted to be put in the grave, the individual had to jump up and down on the legs to loosen them and make them bend to fit in the grave. Could this be done?" Lacsina confirmed that it certainly could, and that Damon Wells experienced some sort of "strong blunt force" to his left calf muscles.

Under Ladenburg's cross-examination, Lacsina described the slash wounds to Wells's throat. "The wound was rather deep, quite deep," he said, explaining how the blade sliced through Wells's larynx, the carotid artery, and the left jugular vein. The wounds went all the way to the back of the spinal column. "In addition to that," said Dr. Lacsina, "it also penetrated the underlying third cervical vertebrae of the neck. If the individual was left unattended with that kind of wound, he would have died in a matter of a few minutes."

Judge Stone excused Dr. Lacsina, then asked Carl Hultman if he had any more witnesses. Hultman nodded, sighed, and said, "Andrew Webb. I think we need a recess."

"I assumed that," replied Stone dryly. "Ladies and gentlemen, we will now take the morning recess and there is no guarantee that it will be fifteen minutes. It may be longer than that. You heard only a portion of the case, you don't start to deliberate or discuss or any way make up your mind."

Court reconvened without the jury, and Hultman told the court that Andrew Webb was now available to testify or not testify as he chose. "My intention," said

Hultman, "is to ask Mr. Webb whether or not he participated in the beating and killing of Damon Wells on February 24th, 1984, and I expect his answer will be: I am not going to answer. And then I will ask Your Honor to direct him to answer and he probably will refuse. Then I'll ask him if it is his intention to not answer any questions, and then I'll ask you to direct him to answer."

Ladenburg interjected a simplified approach. "The question I propose is: Is it your intention to answer all questions, not for you, but for all attorneys, concerning the death of Damon Wells? If he refuses, or answers no, I would ask the court to order him to answer. If he persists in not answering, he should be excused as a witness and no one should be permitted to ask him any questions at all."

"I agree with Ladenburg," said Murdach. Andrew Webb's attorney, Larry Nichols, rather liked Ladenburg's suggestion as well. Hultman explained why his proposed scenario was of vital importance—in order for Andrew Webb's statement to be admissible, it must first have been determined that Andrew Webb was unavailable to testify.

"In this instance, he is refusing to testify," said Hultman, "and I think it is a better approach to have him refuse to answer a direct question about the crime than to keep asking him: do you intend to testify? It won't delay the proceedings and embarrass Mr. Webb, or hardly cause any hardships to the defendants."

"We are all speculating," stated Judge Stone, "as [to] what the scenario is going to be. Until he enters and actually takes the witness stand, we do not know what it will be. Let's get Andrew Webb on and off the stand."

Called as a witness by the plaintiff, being duly sworn, Andrew Webb testified as follows: "I refuse to testify to that." The court directed Webb to answer whether or not he was involved in the beating of Damon Wells, and Webb refused to answer.

"Mr. Webb," asked Judge Stone, "is it your intention to refuse to answer all the questions put to you by all attorneys concerning the death of Damon Wells?" Andrew Webb confirmed that he had no intention of answering any questions from any attorney. As his lawyer, Larry Nichols, previously made clear, Andrew Webb wanted nothing to do with the proceedings at all.

If the prosecution couldn't have their star witness, they'd settle for his plea-bargaining statement. Using the argument that Webb's refusal equaled his unavailability, the official statement was the next best thing.

At this juncture, Stone excused the jury and set about the tiresome task of wrangling an agreement from all three lawyers regarding which portions of Webb's statement would be read aloud in court. In the process, Murdach asked Stone to read aloud a certain significant portion.

" 'Now Paul did not care because he wanted me to kill him anyway,' " intoned Stone from Webb's statement. "Then it starts out, 'He handed me a knife and then I realized Paul wanted me to cut his throat and I started shaking my head and said no way, and Paul started at me with the knife and said do it.' "

Judge Stone immediately perceived a glaring error in Webb's statement. Murdach gave voice to Stone's observation. "That's impossible. The statement is inaccurate. There is no way that he could have handed him the knife, and then a moment later come at him with the knife," said Murdach, arguing that the court should not allow the jury to hear statements against his client that were blatantly untrue.

Stone sympathized with Murdach, but refused to disallow the troublesome segment. The judge characterized Paul St. Pierre's defense counsel as having "a double whammy working against him. We are all under a double whammy in this case. That is just a fact of life. As for the court allowing something that is totally inaccurate or totally impossible, the court would simply answer that none of us know exactly what happened out there at Salmon Beach on February 24, 1984. I don't expect to ever know exactly what happened."

With those summary comments, Judge Stone let the evidence go in, leaving it up to the jurors to determine what happened. "I will decline any further editing," declared Stone, "and I decline any further removals. Mr. Hultman, you may call your next witness.

"The state calls Detective Yerbury back to the stand," said Hultman. Previously sworn, Yerbury was still under oath. "In the course of this investigation," asked the prosecutor, "did you have occasion to take a statement from Andrew Webb on July 17, 1984?" After receiving an affirmative reply, Carl Hultman said, "Read to us from his statement concerning the death of Damon Wells."

" 'One night in February,' " began Yerbury, " 'Chris and I had been drinking till late at Ray and Gene's Tavern.' " Andrew Webb's plea-bargain version was read aloud in almost its entirety, ending with, " 'Paul told me not to tell anyone, not even a priest, and he said that if I did, he would kill me. He said I had a family to think about, so I better not tell.' "

"Ladies and gentlemen," said Stone when Yerbury

stepped down, "we are not going to cheat you out of
your lunch. You are instructed to ignore the newspaper, the television, and the radio. I won't see you again
until tomorrow morning."

"I have a number of exhibits," began John Ladenburg when court reconvened, and all the exhibits were
certified copies of documents that began *"The State of
Washington vs. Andrew Webb."*

"There were three things Ladenburg wanted to impress upon the jury," recalled Marty Webb. "First, he
wanted them to know that Andrew was already convicted on three assault charges, made a plea-bargain
deal on those, and was facing sentencing at the time
Wells was murdered. Second, he wanted them to understand that the killing of Damon Wells was essentially identical to the three previous assaults—all of
them were about him getting ripped off, real or imagined, he was rip-roaring drunk, and he couldn't control his anger. Third, and most important, he wanted
them to know that my brother-in-law, Mr. Andrew
Webb, was out of his fucking mind."

"This jury should know that before this crime was
committed," said Ladenburg to Judge Stone, "Andrew
Webb was facing two ten-year sentences with a mandatory minimum five-year term." Ladenburg wanted
jurors to fully comprehend the time line of Webb's
assault charges and sentencing. Damon Wells was murdered one month before Andrew Webb's sentencing
on the assault charges, and charges were reduced because he plea-bargained. "He was in fact given a deferred sentence and was released on probation with
certain conditions."

Ladenburg also submitted the presentence report
filed with the court after Webb's conviction. "This re-

port is important for a number of reasons," he insisted. Not only did the report offer a detailed summary of the assault charges, it clearly showed the consistent similarities between Webb's assaults and the murder of Damon Wells. "Mere suspicion on Webb's part is, according to this report, sufficient justification for outburst of anger, physical beatings, and threats against life and property."

" 'I feel if the apparent anger is not dealt with,' " quoted Ladenburg from the probation officer's report, " 'Webb has the capability of more serious offenses in the future.' "

The next submission was, in John Ladenburg's opinion, exceptionally significant. "I can't think of a more important thing for a jury to know." It was the court-ordered psychological evaluation of Andrew Webb, including the diagnostic impressions by Comte and Associates.

Ladenburg, acknowledging the document's length, turned immediately to page 8—"Conclusions and Diagnostic Impressions." The observations and analyses of Michael Comte, and his associate, Dr. Peterson, were summarized as follows: "Andrew Webb has a very low frustration tolerance, an immediate need for gratification, and a hostile capacity to act out his feelings without regard for the consequences in an impulsive fashion." Dr. Peterson also noted that "Mr. Webb is unlikely to experience true remorse or guilt for his behavior."

"The obvious implication Ladenburg was going for," said Marty Webb later, "was that Andrew got drunk, pissed, angry, and didn't give a shit about anyone but himself. He didn't want to go to prison, so he killed Damon Wells. Then, to make sure he didn't get the death penalty for Wells's murder, he makes this weird deal with Carl Hultman, or Bill Griffies more likely, where he blames Chris and Paul, and promises to testify against them. Then, once he's sure he's not gonna get hanged, he admits it was BS. Probably, in his heart of hearts, if he has one, he really didn't want those two guys to die on account of his statement."

David Murdach supported Ladenburg's efforts to have all the documents accepted. "When Mr. Webb was sentenced in those assault cases, a requirement of Judge Thompson was that Mr. Webb obtain a neurological screening and psychiatric mental status exam."

"When Andrew Webb gets under pressure," declared David Murdach to the court, "he breaks into people's homes, puts a firearm in a person's face threatening to shoot their head off, and slices people's throats because he fears they are going to rip him off."

John Ladenburg mildly interrupted Murdach to inform the court that he had another document for submission—an excerpt from Andrew Webb's previous uncooperative testimony before Judge Stone. "Under oath, he says that he intended to testify against these defendants out of vengeance" and for "selfish reasons." The attorney contended that Andrew Webb implicated Chris St. Pierre in the murder of Damon Wells purely out of anger and vengeance. Webb, Ladenburg theorized, was angry at both St. Pierre brothers, and took revenge against them in his plea-bargain statement.

"First of all, he gets shot in the gut by Paul. He almost dies, but survives only to find out that Chris has spilled the beans to Yerbury and Price," recounted Marty Webb, who agreed completely with Ladenburg's theory, "and the biggest bean spilled was that Andrew Webb, and Andrew Webb alone, according to both Chris and Paul, killed Damon Wells."

"I intend to call as witnesses," announced Ladenburg, "Officer Bahr and Detective Yerbury about the assault incidents in addition to having these documents admitted." Hultman, having reached a point beyond saturation, and near the edge of civility, finally spoke up. "Your Honor, virtually all those documents are inadmissible. The reasons are relevancy and hearsay. The defendants are trying to pull up as much evidence as they can that Andrew Webb is such a violent man, and focus all the attention on his past record, and divert the jury's attention from what the defendants did in this case."

"It is the defendants that attacked Damon Wells," asserted Hultman, "a totally innocent person. He was apologizing to Andrew Webb, and taking side with Andrew Webb, when Paul St. Pierre came through the door and started beating him up, and then the two brothers beat him up.

"I have not heard the defendants argue," continued Hultman, "as to how their allegations about Andrew Webb have anything to do with what they did to Damon Wells. Mr. Murdach and Mr. Ladenburg should be offering some evidence that relates to their clients' conduct, and not Andrew Webb's past."

Stone allowed Ladenburg a response, and he spoke most emphatically. "I think it is a travesty of justice if the jury doesn't know about Andrew Webb. All we are talking about is that Mr. Webb had the motive, and he had the tendency, that none of the other defendants had in this case."

Judge Stone sided with Carl Hultman on almost everything. He refused to admit the documents because, in his words, they were "not properly relevant to this case." He did offer to instruct jurors that Webb was previously charged with three counts of assault with a weapon, and pleaded guilty to the charges. Details of those incidents, and their commonalties, were firmly excluded, as was Andrew Webb's under-oath testimony that he implicated the St. Pierres out of anger and vengeance. The reason Webb's explanation wasn't allowed was simply that neither defense attorney asked Webb that question when he was in front of the jury. "Having had that opportunity and passed on it," said Stone, "the court will not be allowing excerpts of what he said in front of the judge three or four days ago."

Ladenburg, anticipating Stone's ruling, had an immediate alternative course of action. "We propose not to introduce those documents, but call as witnesses those who actually witnessed the conduct of Mr. Webb—Officer Bahr, Mr. Comte, the probation officer, and Detective Yerbury."

Stone declared such testimony equally irrelevant, and these witnesses would not be allowed to testify to the jury. "Next motion," said Judge Stone, and David Murdach gave it his best shot. He intended to call Mr. Carl Hultman, prosecuting attorney, as a defense witness. He would also call Hultman's superiors, Chris Quinn-Brintnall and Bill Griffies, and his client's former attorneys, Ellsworth Connelly and Jeffrey Gross.

"I think the jury is entitled to know how Mr. Webb was treated by the prosecutor's office," said Murdach. "Not only was he given the benefit of the plea bargain, they dismissed the kidnapping charges and assault charges, dropped the aggravating circumstances, and he pled guilty to first-degree murder—life with possible parole—he could be out in thirteen years, and he's the one who actually slit the man's throat!"

Hultman argued against the prosecutor and members of that office testifying for the defense. The court, while not agreeing with Hultman, ruled that the circumstances of Andrew Webb's plea bargain were irrelevant. Stone had no problem with a prosecutor testifying for the defense if circumstances made such testimony appropriate. A perfect example was Judge Stone's immediate ruling that the jury should hear testimony regarding Andrew Webb recanting his sworn statement. That testimony, to be most accurate, should come from the individual to whom Mr. Webb recanted. That one person was Carl Hultman, prosecuting attorney.

"If Mr. Hultman is called to testify for the defense, he will be ordered to testify," declared Judge Stone. "In this particular situation, I will clearly order Mr. Hultman to testify."

"This case has some obvious interesting twists," David Murdach told the jury in his opening remarks on April 23, 1984. "And I am about to present another interesting twist—I will be calling the prosecutor as my first witness."

"The state objects to this proceeding," said Carl Hultman, but he was only going through the motions.

"The court has ordered you to testify, Mr. Hultman," said Stone. Called as a witness by the defense, duly sworn, the deputy prosecuting attorney for Pierce County, Carl Hultman, testified. He wasn't happy about it.

"Did Mr. Webb tell you that there were inaccuracies in the statement," asked Murdach, "which has now been read to the jury by Detective Yerbury?"

Hultman acknowledged that Webb did say there were inaccuracies. Pressed for details, the prosecutor acknowledged that Andrew Webb told him that, in truth, Paul St. Pierre and Chris St. Pierre did not stab Damon Wells in the back "as opposed to his earlier statement that they stabbed him."

Carl Hultman, having testified for the defense,

stepped down and resumed his role as prosecuting attorney. He did not, however, cross-examine himself. His understandably unpleasant attitude toward the situation in general, and David Murdach in specific, was not quickly dissipated. In fact, Hultman's displeasure increased dramatically when he later learned that Murdach possibly misled the court, manipulating the prosecution into testifying for the defense.

"David Murdach did not reveal to the judge; he didn't reveal to me; I don't think he even revealed to Mr. Ladenburg—I know he didn't reveal to the state, and he didn't reveal to the court—that he already possessed the information himself that he sought from me. In fact," explained Hultman, "he asserted to the court that I was the only witness available other than Larry Nichols, and Larry didn't remember the conversation. That was not really accurate because David Murdach possessed the same information from an earlier interview with Andrew Webb."

In other words, the testimony Hultman gave in the Wells trial could just as easily have been given by Murdach himself. It was admittedly clever, however, for the defense to have the prosecution testify on their behalf. The canon of ethics, Hultman was quick to reference, says that as soon as the defense attorney realized that he [Murdach] could possibly be a witness, he should have considered withdrawing from the case.

"He didn't do that," commented Hultman later. "There is some questionable action here." Softening his tone and altering his theme, Carl Hultman pulled back from the brink of personal attack. "I like Mr. Murdach, and I don't think it is anything he intended to come out this way."

Murdach's witness list, even with the addition of Carl Hultman, was noticeably light. Those who did testify on behalf of Paul St. Pierre, however, were of all unquestioned integrity and potentially strong impact.

After Detective Price described the area of Salmon Beach, giving jurors a vivid mental picture of the scene and physical circumstances, David Murdach called his potential trump card—Paul St. Pierre's former co-counsel, Jeffrey Gross. In connection with his representation of Paul St. Pierre, Gross had attended a pretrial meeting in the prosecuting attorney's office for the singular purpose of interviewing Andrew Webb. Also present were Carl Hultman, John Ladenburg, and Craig Adams, the attorney then serving as Webb's legal counsel.

Murdach asked Mr. Gross, specifically and directly, if the description of events given by Andrew Webb during that interview were significantly different from the description of those same events given in his plea-bargain statement to the prosecutor. When Gross answered yes, Murdach requested specific examples.

"Well, Mr. Webb stated that Mr. Wells went along voluntarily," began Gross. "That he walked to the car with the other three individuals, and the reason being that he wanted to show that he was not a thief. Apparently, previously [on] that evening he had been accused, I believe by Mr. Webb, of being a thief and apparently he felt that if he went along with the individuals, that it would prove to them that he was not a thief. On the way out to the vehicle, Mr. Webb stated, Mr. Wells was conscious, he was walking, and at most had a bloody nose."

John Ladenburg, on cross-examination, had a few pointed questions of his own. First of all, was Gross familiar with Andrew Webb's typed statement to the police prior to the interview? If so, Gross knew that Webb's previous statements about Wells's condition completely contradicted the interview. In the old version, Webb said Damon Wells was severely beaten and almost unconscious by the time they dragged him out the door and into the car. The statements did agree on one exceptionally important assertion—Andrew Webb took full credit for slashing Damon Wells's throat.

Carl Hultman was undeniably aggressive in his questioning; so much so that Judge Stone interceded, barking at the harried witness, "Don't answer that question!"

"I haven't even asked the question," complained Hultman.

"Ask the question," said Stone to Hultman, "and you," speaking to Gross, "don't answer until I get a chance to rule."

On that note, the defense of Paul St. Pierre rested. John Ladenburg, representing Christopher St. Pierre, simply said, "Mr. Chris St. Pierre calls no witnesses and will rest." Judge Stone then presented some evidence of his own—the previous assault arrests and convictions of Andrew Webb.

"The fact that information comes from the judge does not make it any more or less important than any other evidence you might receive from the witness stand," said Stone. "You heard the evidence, but the case has not been in any way submitted to you formally."

The jurors, advised that they would be back in court at 8:00 A.M. the following day, were excused. Hultman, Murdach, Ladenburg, and Stone then spent the balance of the afternoon hammering out the extensive jury instructions.

The next morning began with Stone reading each and every jury instruction—a long, tedious, yet imperative process. "Well, we've heard the judge talk

Fifteen

"They [the St. Pierre brothers] are clearly guilty of a vicious, ugly, obscene murder of Damon Wells," said Carl Hultman to the jury. "Some of you have watched wildlife shows, have seen films of a pack of jackals as they attack the weak, and take the unfortunate injured down. Look at these two men; look at what they did to Damon Wells. Think about that. It's awful.

"Think what it was like for Damon Wells," Hultman requested. "Imagine the swearing, shouting, the beatings—they each acknowledge beating Damon Wells. Christopher St. Pierre said Andrew Webb dragged him to the car. Paul St. Pierre said, 'My brother and Andrew and I were beating up Damon Wells.' When was he beating Damon Wells? At the beach! He was almost unconscious at the beach. What kind of savage individuals are these two?"

Speaking directly of Christopher St. Pierre, and Ladenburg's efforts to portray his client as an innocent bystander, Hultman reminded the jury that Chris St. Pierre called Mark Perez and said that if Don Marshall went to the police, he and his family would be dead. "What kind of innocence is that?"

The prosecutor directly addressed Andrew Webb's refusal to testify, saying, "We thought Andrew Webb would tell you the truth, but he refused to testify, so the court admitted his statement. We wish it were otherwise. If we had a live witness, you would hear a little bit more of a sense of the feeling of it. You would hear him say how these two defendants stabbed Damon Wells in the back with a dagger Paul St. Pierre liked to call his fighting knife. What civilized human being needs a fighting knife? What does Paul St. Pierre need one for? You know what for—for killing.

"The defense claims that it is unfair for us to use Andrew Webb's statement because they can't cross-examine Andrew Webb. They are right," said Hultman, "they did not get to cross-examine Andrew Webb. Is that unfair? It is not unfair because both of the defendants' statements are before you in exactly the same way as Andrew Webb's. So the state fulfills any problem with fairness on the use of the statement."

"I object," declared John Ladenburg. "I think it is a direct violation of the United States Constitution, Amendment Five." Stone disagreed; Hultman continued.

"He doesn't want me to suggest that it's fair that you have his client's statement in front of you," said Hultman, referring to Ladenburg. "Probably not, because his client is the one that said Damon Wells was beaten by all three of them."

The prosecution then turned the jury's attention to what he termed "the most direct and specific evidence"—the confessional statement of Andrew K. Webb.

"Andrew Webb forthwith in his statement takes the full blame. He forthrightly pled guilty. He made two statements, one was written in longhand to a detective, and the second one to several attorneys in my office. In both these statements he said that each one of these defendants stabbed Damon Wells in the back.

"Andrew Webb says that after he cut the throat of Damon Wells, 'Paul then grabbed the knife from me and said this is how you kill somebody and stabbed him in the back.' "

The prosecution supported this interpretation of events by the testimony of Dr. Lacsina as to the nature of the back wounds. "They weren't flesh wounds and nicks," Hultman reminded the jury. "They were five-and-a-half-inch-deep wounds, that went almost through this young man's entire body. These wounds required, as Dr. Lacsina testified, a large amount of force."

Hultman asked jurors to judge Paul St. Pierre "by his own words," and most specifically, the prideful boasting to Roy Kissler. "He was proud to tell Roy Kissler that he killed Damon Wells, waited while he bled to death; then they stabbed him and they buried him and he is proud of it."

As for the involvement of Christopher St. Pierre, there was no way Paul's younger brother could escape unscathed from Carl Hultman's well-crafted and insightful argument. "There was a complete concert of action by those three in everything they did together. We beat him. We took him to Salmon Beach. Think about the concert of action at the beach. Think about it with Christopher St. Pierre.

"He keeps telling you that he was not part of what happened to Damon Wells," said Hultman, pointing out that when Damon Wells was bleeding to death for five or even ten minutes, Christopher St. Pierre simply "stood there and watched him die."

The prosecution, building upon each and every piece of testimony, constructed, brick by brick, an inescapable cell of "shared intent"—both Paul and Christopher St. Pierre participated 100 percent in the horrid murder of Damon Wells. "They wanted to shut

Damon Wells up, and they did. They did it by stabbing him in the back. They wanted to shut him up about what they had done—beating him badly in the house, beat him in the car, and they beat him at the beach."

Commenting on the clandestine burial of Damon Wells's body, Hultman conjured up disturbing images. "Recall the old Frankenstein monsters and grave robbers. There is an image to think about: hauling bodies many miles in the car and burying it in the night."

For his conclusion, Carl Hultman identified criminal pride as Paul St. Pierre's motive in murdering Damon Wells. His reference point was Roy Kissler's overnight outing with St. Pierre. "What would cause a man to tell a friend he is proud to have been part of the killing and stabbing and the slashing of the throat and the waiting for him to die? A man proud enough to persist over another man's objections," said Hultman, "and proud enough that he wanted to show him the blood on his car."

Hultman asked for a verdict of guilty, Judge Stone called for a recess, John Ladenburg moved for a mistrial, and David Murdach seconded the motion. The grounds for mistrial, according to Ladenburg and Murdach, were the inappropriate and perhaps illegal statements made by Carl Hultman during his closing argument. The defense counsel felt that Hultman implied that the defendants' failure to testify on their own behalf was somehow indicative of their guilt. In the United States of America, the accused is presumed innocent until proven guilty in a court of law. The presumed innocent defendants are under no obligation to testify on their own behalf. For a prosecutor to portray the defendants' silence as an admission of guilt is a major violation of both legal and ethical standards.

"Frankly, we are dealing with final argument," commented Judge Stone. "There isn't any question that I caught an implication—it certainly got my attention that Mr. Hultman was going right about up to the line." In Stone's opinion, the prosecution got close to the line, but didn't cross it. He also expressed his opinion on final arguments in general. "The jurors may swallow all of it, part of it, or they may swallow none of it. It's argument. Period."

John Ladenburg, representing Christopher St. Pierre, then addressed the jury for the last time. He first appealed to their patriotism by recounting a recent visit to Washington, DC, where, under special lights and heavy guard, was the Constitution of the United States—a copy of the Bill of Rights. "It is important in our system of law," he told the jury, "that the proof be in the courtroom. The proof must come from the witness stand, not that you had a feeling, but that there be proof. The burden of proof is a high one—beyond a reasonable doubt."

Ladenburg reminded jurors that they were instructed to judge each witness's credibility. Christopher St. Pierre could be believed, insisted Ladenburg, but Andrew Webb was unreliable and dishonest. St. Pierre was cooperative and forthcoming; Andrew Webb was opportunistic and manipulative.

"Christopher St. Pierre, when the police arrived at his house, gave detectives a detailed history of everything that had happened. He even led them to the evidence, and to the grave of Damon Wells. Nothing that Chris St. Pierre told the police has been proven on the stand to be incorrect. Period. Nothing. I say believe Christopher St. Pierre."

John Ladenburg's opinion of Andrew Webb was far less favorable. He began by reminding the jury that Andrew Webb was arrested for murder because of Chris St. Pierre's immediate statement to Yerbury and

Price. "After sitting in [the] pokey for a month," said Ladenburg, "with plenty of time to think up stuff, Andrew Webb wanted to talk.

"One thing about Andrew Webb's statement that jumps right out at you," said Ladenburg, "is that while admitting some participation, he tries to make it look like he did not do anything." Citing several examples of Webb's reinvention of events, he focused the jurors' attention on one in specific—the beating in the bathroom. "He says Paul and Chris started beating on him and 'I stopped them. Told them this guy is an OK guy. I stopped them. I tried to protect Damon Wells.' How accurate are these statements that Mr. Hultman wants you to believe beyond a reasonable doubt?"

Dissecting Webb's version of the Salmon Beach homicide, Ladenburg pointed out the most glaring error and impossibility in Andrew Webb's statement. "He says 'Paul handed me a knife, but immediately I realized Paul wanted me to cut his throat.' He must have been a mind reader. 'I started thinking in my head, "No way;" then Paul started at me with a knife.' Wait a minute. If we could have cross-examined Andrew Webb, he would look foolish telling you that Paul starts at him with the knife and then Paul hands him the knife. 'I feared for my life, so I took the knife and drew it across Damon's throat.'

"I submit to you," said Ladenburg to the jury, "that the whole case turns on the believability of Andrew Webb, plain and simple. I would like to ask Andrew Webb, 'Tell me, Mr. Webb, why is it that you slit Damon Wells's throat? Were you afraid for your life, is that true, Mr. Webb? Tell me about your prior assault conviction. Were you afraid you might be going to prison, Mr. Webb?'"

Repeatedly referring to Andrew Webb as a liar, Ladenburg detailed copious inconsistencies between

Webb's statement to the police and his statement to the prosecution. It all added up to one very clear conclusion—Christopher St. Pierre did not commit homicide. "He did not slash Wells's throat or stab him in the back. Chris was not armed with any deadly weapon. There was no premeditation involved in the death of Damon Wells, no 'concert of action' between the three men. Andrew Webb killed him and Andrew Webb meant to kill him. Andrew Webb was the only one with a motive, and the only one with such a hair-trigger violent temper that he chased down Damon Wells and slit his throat."

In conclusion, Ladenburg pleaded with the jurors to not allow the emotions of the day, the horrible facts and horrible situations, to sway them from the requirements of the law—beyond a reasonable doubt.

"I ask you not to convict Christopher St. Pierre, or Paul for that matter, for crimes committed by Andrew Webb. Andrew Webb is being punished for the murder of Damon Wells. Perhaps not enough."

Ladenburg left Chris's fate in the jury's hands, Chris put his fate in God's hands, Judge Stone set the time to reconvene for 1:15 P.M., and everyone had lunch.

When they returned, David Murdach addressed the jury. He, too, had no kind words for Andrew Webb. "We all know that Andrew Webb slashed the throat of Damon Wells, and slashed it so deep that the knife penetrated or came against the third vertebra of the spinal column. That wound killed Damon Wells.

"We all know that is what happened," said Murdach, "because there are no disputes as to those facts. After we know those facts, we then say, 'What was the conduct of the defendants?' When you ask that question, you have violated the instructions—the instructions say that the defendants are presumed innocent. We don't go to the list of crimes and say, 'OK, which one of these are they guilty of?' We don't do that. That is not what you have been told to do. This is not a basket of fruit—you don't select the one that is most tasteful to you, or palatable, to salve the wounds of the people affected by this tragedy. This is not a civil case. This is not a suit for damages.

"In a criminal case," he elaborated, "you enter a plea of guilty or not guilty. In the civil case, you either admit that the complaint is true or you deny it. Both civil and criminal charges require you coming to court and having a trial. Why is it that when criminal charges are brought, we automatically assume that the person did something wrong?"

Murdach answered this question with candor, citing that there are "built-in human emotions we can't put aside. In a criminal case, the repercussions are so great, that our United States Constitution has a built-in safeguard—no other country has this safeguard—we have presumption of innocence, proof beyond a reasonable doubt."

"Yet, in this case, we are asked by the prosecutor—not by Mr. Hultman himself—but by the prosecutor's office to hang the accomplices and let the person who slit the throat go free! Now, what is it my client, Mr. Paul St. Pierre, is supposed to have done that makes him a rascal in the prosecutor's office? He drove the car. He admits driving the car. He admits that he was at the scene. He admits to have beaten up Damon Wells in the bathroom." Driving the car, being at the scene, and beating someone up, Murdach advised jurors, do not equal premeditated murder.

"Mr. Hultman, like it or not," Murdach said with a hint of victory, "is a witness in this case. He is a witness because he heard Andrew Webb give a recantation of his earlier statement. That is novel, unique. It doesn't happen often that a prosecutor's own testimony can create, and did create, reasonable doubt as to whether or not Andrew Webb was telling the truth."

Murdach basically defined and explained the legal rules and regulations regarding the various charges and jury instructions, building his argument that Paul St. Pierre may be guilty of something—some degree of assault and a major degree of irresponsibility—but he was not guilty of premeditated murder.

In the final analysis, Murdach appealed to the jurors' sense of duty—not a duty to find someone, anyone, guilty of murder, nor a duty to punish—a citizen's duty to uphold the high standards of American justice, due process of law, and the Bill of Rights of the United States Constitution. Murdach argued more in defense of the law than in defense of Paul St. Pierre.

Despite his professional and personable presentation, hearts remained untouched. No matter how well intentioned or solidly constructed, arguments invoking the shared civil religion of Americanism are notoriously ineffective. David Murdach's final argument was not the exception that proved the rule.

In his immediate rebuttal, Carl Hultman went for the jugular. "Are they guilty of first-degree aggravated murder, premeditated? Of course they are! Mr. Ladenburg, at the beginning of this trial, told you he was going to talk about three things: means, motive, and opportunity. Well, you didn't hear him talk about those three things in his closing argument!"

The prosecution addressed each of the three elements, starting with the means—"Paul St. Pierre's fighting knife. Paul St. Pierre, the man who bragged about the crime, bragged 'we stabbed him in the back, cut his throat, and waited for him to die.' "

The opportunity, defined by Hultman, was "three against one." The St. Pierres had the courage to attack and kill a five-foot-tall, 109-pound individual, asserted the prosecution, "when they have someone else to help them—Andrew Webb."

The motive, Hultman asserted, was nothing more or less than their cowardice. "What kind of man stands by and watches another man—a smaller, weaker man—slowly bleed to death?" Hultman never allowed jurors to forget that Paul and Christopher St. Pierre watched a helpless Damon Wells die without making any effort to save his life, alleviate his suffering, forestall his death, or ease his pain. Together with Andrew Webb, the St. Pierres experienced Damon Wells's demise with the same detachment as all other cold-blooded killers. The three men were completely severed from the event's emotional resonance, the devastation engendered by the crime, and the unavoidable implication that all three of them were, by their heartless participation in the tragic death of Damon Wells, devoid of morality, ethics, compassion, or humanity.

"Make a decision and give them justice," insisted Carl Hultman, "the kind of thing they didn't give Damon Wells. Come back into the courtroom and tell this community you have done the right thing. You found them guilty for what they did: aggravated murder in the first degree and kidnapping in the first degree and assault in the second degree. Thank you."

Carl Hultman's dynamic, insistent, relentless presentation of the horrific crime made an indelible impression upon the jury. After careful and serious deliberation over three days, the jury found Paul St. Pierre guilty of all charges, including first-degree aggravated murder—a death penalty offense.

Christopher St. Pierre was found guilty of kidnapping, assault, and felony murder—not a death penalty offense. Judge Stone, despite Hultman's arguments to the contrary, ruled that Christopher St. Pierre would serve his sentences concurrently rather than consecutively. Paul St. Pierre, unlike his little brother, now faced the possibility of hearing Judge Stone intone, "You shall be hanged by the neck until you are dead."

Carl Hultman wanted Paul St. Pierre hanged, perhaps willing to provide the required rope if so requested. The law to which Hultman is dedicated, however, insists upon sentencing hearings when life or death hangs in the balance.

"In most cases, the jury has nothing to do with sentencing," David Murdach later explained, "but when the death penalty looms as possible punishment, the jury considers and then decides whether the offender gets life in prison without parole, or death. In this state, the death sentence is carried out by either hanging or lethal injection."

The hearing began April 29, 1985, with David Murdach asking that it be canceled immediately. The court should simply "go ahead and sentence life imprisonment," said Murdach. Stone denied the motion, but assured both defense counsels that they would have extensive opportunities to present any mitigating circumstances—reasons why the jury should show mercy and spare Paul St. Pierre's life.

Before hearing Murdach's plea for mercy, extensive jury instructions were debated, revised, and read aloud when court reconvened. The first mitigating circumstance Murdach wanted considered was Paul St. Pierre's inadequate mental capacity. The second reason for mercy was the easily verified observation that Andrew Webb was incapable of telling the same story the same way twice. Murdach argued that the shifting words of Andrew Webb were a poor foundation for the death penalty.

"What you have decided," Murdach told the jurors, "is that Paul St. Pierre will die. The sentence of life in prison without possibility of parole is a sentence of death in prison. What could be a greater punishment than that? To convict Paul St. Pierre of the crime—which you did—you must have believed Andrew Webb's first version of the offense. What if his recantation is true? Do you want that nagging question over your head for the rest of your lives? Andrew Webb will be on parole someday; Paul St. Pierre will not [be]."

Murdach painted a terminally depressing word picture of St. Pierre's dreary prison future—a monotonous, downbeat existence occasionally punctuated by violent beatings or rape. A few jurors squirmed uncomfortably as Murdach continued his horrific depiction of life in the Washington State Penitentiary. This punishment was preferable to execution, Murdach insisted. "None of us get out of life alive," he sagely stated. "To execute Paul, you would have to decide that he has no right to exist. Death is final. There is no appeal. What will Andrew Webb say five years from now? Or ten years from now?"

Carl Hultman countered Murdach's plea, and spoke against leniency. "I suggest, ladies and gentlemen, it's not whether his mother and father and brothers love him and not whether Patricia Wells would like to see a sentence of death that counts so much here. What counts is your judgment about what he did. You have someone you know is very capable and willing to kill, and who can express pride in doing so. Paul St. Pierre was the leader in this action of cold-blooded murder. He bragged about what he had done. He was proud of it. You have not heard that about anybody else in this case. He was proud of killing Damon Wells. He wanted the credit for cutting his throat."

Hultman, without equivocation, apologies, or regrets, demanded death for Paul St. Pierre. After serious consultation, the jury sentenced him to life in prison without possibility of parole. Judge Stone's gavel signaled the proceeding's conclusion, but there was no sense of finality. Nothing was over except the life of Damon Wells.

Andrew Webb, Mark Perez, Tony Youso, Donald Marshall, Carl Hultman, John Ladenburg, David Murdach, and the St. Pierre brothers would, in less than ninety days, reunite in the Pierce County Courthouse to relive the nightmare of John Achord's death and decapitation.

PART THREE

in favor of David Murdach's motion that the prosecution could not ask witnesses, especially the medical experts, any questions about the "future dangerousness" of Paul St. Pierre. Such a judgment by a witness was considered prejudicial, and didn't relate directly to St. Pierre's guilt or innocence.

Thursday morning, July 18, 1985, was the first day of scheduled testimony, but the topic of testimony itself, and its proposed content, delayed the proceedings. "How much testimony should we bring out with respect to the murder of Damon Wells? I have to weigh that question," commented Judge Steiner to the attorneys, "with respect to how much passion and prejudice will be generated by it. The admission of prior evidence concerning the prior murder may be in the area of passion and prejudice. It's a very difficult ruling."

The defense argued against the jury knowing the defendants were convicted of murdering Damon Wells. It was, they insisted, a separate case, and it shouldn't be tried all over again as part of this new trial. Hearing all the horrid details would make it difficult for jurors to maintain any presumption of innocence, insisted the two defense attorneys.

Carl Hultman saw the two homicides as interwoven acts impossible to unravel one from the other. "Despite what Mr. Murdach and Mr. Ladenburg like to say, there are some very unique consistencies in these two homicides. There is consistency in the fact that the victims were both total strangers," explained the prosecutor. "There is consistency in the fact that the crimes were committed initially as assaults in the home. There is consistency in the fact that the victims died of stab wounds in the back caused by Paul St. Pierre's Gerber knife.

There is consistency in that both victims were transported to an identical site and buried within about ten to fifteen feet of each other."

Judge Steiner ruled that the jury could hear it all, or perhaps some or most. Until there was additional research into some remaining, nagging legal questions, neither defense counsel wanted to give an opening statement. "I'll call on each of you after Mr. Hultman is finished. Are you ready to go with two or three witnesses to consume the morning?"

"I have five witnesses scheduled for this morning," replied Hultman, who listed them off in order of appearance. "And then, if we have time, Detective Yerbury or Parkhurst depending on the court's wishes."

"Yerbury is going to be on the stand for two or three or four or five hours, and I think the witnesses you've named will consume the morning," stated the judge before asking an important question directed neither to the defense nor the prosecution. "Can we bring the jury out in five minutes?" The trial would commence, Judge Steiner was told, when the television cameras were ready.

"The television is here now," said the judge, "it's the ruling of this court that the defendants are not to be photographed, and the jurors are not to be photographed. The ruling now is that only the opening statement will be photographed, and I'm going to remind the witnesses that they have the right to not be photographed. Are you ready for the jury?" Everyone was ready.

"Welcome to Tacoma. I'm glad you all made it this morning. Ladies and gentlemen, we're now going to begin opening statement on behalf of the state of Washington, Mr. Carl Hultman."

Establishing a direct connection between the murder of John Achord and that of Damon Wells, Hultman recounted the entire tragic scenario. Beginning with the February 22, 1984, beer bust, fistfight, bathroom beating, and Salmon Beach murder of Damon Wells, he easily transitioned to Achord's demise and decapitation.

"That's a sordid story," said Hultman, "and it's a terribly ugly crime. Once you have examined this evidence and considered it as a whole, I don't think there's any question but that you will find these defendants guilty as charged."

The purpose of opening statements is to prepare the jury for what they will see and hear as evidence. Hultman, in a clear and orderly fashion, provided jurors a concise preview of the first day's witnesses and anticipated testimony. John Achord's mother, Opal Bitney, would identify her son, tell of his disappearance, and then Officer David McNutt of the Tacoma Police would affirm the official Missing Persons report.

"Mark Perez will testify to you," stated Hultman, "how he was told that John Achord had been killed. He was simply told that Achord had been shot in self-defense, no mention of stab wounds. Gordon Gibson will be called, an ex-convict who, while in jail, had a conversation with Paul St. Pierre. He will tell what Paul told him about what he did to John Achord, and why he did it." As the state's last witness for the trial's first day, Hultman would call Tony Youso to share the disturbing details of Achord's head being tossed into the Puyallup River.

"On Monday, we'll resume this case," Hultman continued, "with Detective Yerbury, and then pathologist Dr. Lacsina." The state succinctly encapsulated Lacsina's testimony. "It is his opinion that John Achord died as a result of stab wounds . . . the head wound was more a wound to the jaw."

"As I say," Hultman concluded, "once you have heard the testimony and evidence, you will have no doubt that the defendants are guilty as charged. Thank you."

Ladenburg and Murdach, as previously agreed, reserved their opening statements for another time; the prosecution called their first witness—Mrs. Opal Bitney, the married mother of five boys, the youngest being John Achord. Soon after taking the witness stand, Mrs. Bitney handed Carl Hultman her son's photograph. "When was that picture taken?" he asked.

"It was made for my Mother's Day present in 1984," she answered softly, "six days before he disappeared." The state offered the photo as Plaintiff's Exhibit #1, and Judge Steiner asked if there were any objections. If there were, neither Murdach nor Ladenburg were going to make them in front of the jury, the victim's mother, and in such close proximity to Mrs. Bitney's heartbreaking mention of Mother's Day.

"No," answered David Murdach, "we'll reserve our objections to be heard outside the presence of jury." The court reserved ruling. "Don't show it to the jury," said Steiner, and Hultman set the photograph aside.

Mrs. Bitney ended her brief testimony by insisting that John Achord didn't use illegal drugs. As she stepped down from the stand, the judge kindly asked her to wait out in the hall for a few minutes. Somewhat mystified, Bitney complied. Steiner sent the jury out as well, and David Murdach approached the bench.

"Family members from both the St. Pierre and Achord families will be sitting here in the courtroom," said Murdach. "And there has been a problem generated in this case which you may not be aware of.

There have been threatening phone calls between the
St. Pierres and the Achords, and vice versa. I don't
think it is appropriate under those circumstances for
any witness who testifies in this case to be seated back
in the courtroom—I think every witness should be excluded if they are not going to be called upon." By
excluding every witness from the courtroom, not allowing Mrs. Bitney to attend the trial would not be
"unfair treatment."

Neither Hultman nor Judge Steiner found merit in
Murdach's entreaty. "Mrs. Bitney has been under
enormous pressure since her son disappeared," remarked Carl Hultman. "I think she should be entitled
to sit through the proceedings."

"This is a public courtroom," Judge Steiner said
sternly, "and anyone who wants to come has a right
to be here. This lady has a right to observe." Changing
the subject, the judge inquired about objections to
Achord's photograph. Did they want to hash that out
now or at noon? "Noon," replied Murdach. The jury
returned, and Carl Hultman elicited exceptionally
short testimony from Tacoma Police officers confirm-
ing Achord's official Missing Persons report.

With the overture and preamble of the prosecution's case behind him, Carl Hultman could now begin
building toward his intended climax of guilt beyond
a reasonable doubt. The first player in the state's or-
chestrated exposition was twenty-three-year-old Mark
Perez.

"I object!" It was Hultman raising his voice, inter-
rupting David Murdach's cross-examination of Mark
Perez. Under Hultman's direct examination, Perez testified about the post-gunshot admonition from Andrew Webb that he should stay in his room, and the

corresponding invitation from Paul St. Pierre to come take a look at what was in the dining room. He also gave testimony about the cut-up carpet, and recounted virtually everything found in his statement to the Tacoma Police.

The question to which Hultman objected concerned Perez's experience with LSD, a powerful psychedelic drug. The judge overruled Hultman, and Perez replied, "In my lifetime, I've tried it."

"You've sold LSD to Paul, haven't you?" Murdach's question brought another, more forceful objection from the prosecution. The jury was temporarily excused while Judge Steiner asked questions of his own.

"This question is part of your defense, right? Your defense is that your client had LSD and he must have gotten it from somewhere. Is that right?" Defense counsel confirmed; the prosecution continued objecting.

"You're asking," said Hultman to Murdach, "Mr. Perez to answer a question that has Fifth Amendment strings attached to it that I can't advise him about, and I don't think the court can, either. He needs independent counsel. Whether he sold LSD to Paul St. Pierre sometime in the past is not relevant to this case."

"You can ask Mr. Perez, 'Do you know whether Paul has used LSD?' " advised the judge, "but don't ask him whether he sold it. Now, let's bring the jury in."

"Wait." Murdach wasn't done. He wanted more from Perez than Steiner would allow. "I think I'm entitled to ask whether he or his girlfriend sold LSD to Paul that night. Mr. Perez can figure out his Fifth Amendment rights for himself. We have a right to ask."

The court always has an obligation of protection—protecting the witness's rights. Steiner advised Perez of his right to remain silent, and the right to have an attorney. Hultman and Murdach continued arguing until they were firmly interrupted, but not by Judge Steiner. The man verbally breaking through was Mark Perez.

"I don't like being here as well as anybody else does," stated Perez emphatically, "and if he has a question he wants to ask pertaining to this particular night, I'll just let him ask it. I don't want to postpone it any longer than it has been."

"All right," said the judge, "let's bring out the jury."

Mark Perez answered Murdach's drug-related question, revealing that Paul St. Pierre often purchased his LSD via Perez's ex-girlfriend's cousin. That individual, in turn, had procured it from someone else. On the night of the Rush concert, Andrew Webb, Paul St. Pierre, and Cory Cunningham planned to share five hits. Although they asked Perez to supply the drug, he was bedridden with an ear infection. "I didn't go to the concert," recalled Perez, "and Rush was my favorite band."

The prosecution's next witness was Gordon Gibson, formerly incarcerated with the St. Pierres, who recounted Paul's explanation for killing John Achord: "He was a jerk." Furthermore, recalled Gibson, "he didn't say they buried him or anything; he just said he cut off the guy's head, put it in a bucket, and threw it into the Puyallup River."

Gibson, after assuring everyone that he received no special benefits in exchange for his testimony, stepped down. The jury went to lunch, and Carl Hultman requested special considerations for his next witness—the man who tossed John Achord's head into the river.

* * *

"Anthony Youso's testimony isn't very long," said Hultman. "I know we're expecting Dr. Tappin to begin at one-thirty and that's out of an extraordinary amount of courtesy to the defense." Tappin, recently recovered from heart surgery, was scheduled for a European excursion. Securing his vital testimony on behalf of Paul St. Pierre required an interruption in the state's case.

"Mr. Youso resides in Colorado. We flew him here Sunday night," explained Hultman. "I request that Dr. Tappin wait five, ten, fifteen minutes so I can put on Mr. Youso and he can catch his plane. We have reservations for Mr. Youso this afternoon."

The defense allowed Youso in, but objected to John Achord's photograph. "It's not relevant," objected Murdach, "and it is not material to any element of this case because I am prepared to stipulate that Mr. Achord was a human being. My client shot this man; this man was stabbed and this man was buried. I'm willing to stipulate that the body that was found in the grave is Mr. Achord and that we are talking about him."

To Hultman's surprise, Judge Steiner excluded John Achord's picture. "I think the jury should have an opportunity to see who the victim was. We did the same thing in Damon Wells's case. They made no objection to his picture coming in, so I'm not sure why there is a change in position on that."

"I don't think it is necessary," repeated the judge. "I'm going to exclude it. Anything else?" There was one more matter, and it also involved photography. Anthony Youso, the next witness for the prosecution, did not want his picture taken.

Tony Youso couldn't remember very much about anything, nor did he want to. He'd spent a good year distancing himself from the St. Pierres and the infamous bucket, both physically and emotionally. Under Carl Hultman's guidance, and after a careful review of his sworn statement, Youso testified. Speaking so softly that he was almost inaudible, Youso haltingly answered the prosecutor's questions.

The courtesy David Murdach displayed concerning Youso's travel arrangements vanished during cross-examination. "Isn't it true that you almost killed somebody in an accident May 18, 1984? Do you remember running into the house claiming that you thought you killed somebody?"

"I don't know," answered Youso. "I don't remember anything about the accident except that I didn't hit another car; the car hit me. I remember going through a green light and looking over to my left, and that was it. I went to the hospital and had a CAT scan done. They released me and my mom took me home. The doctors just told me to be cautious with myself. If it had been serious, I probably would have been told."

Following the accident, police originally charged Youso with "hit and run." The nature of his head injury validated his innocence, placing blame on the other driver. All charges against Youso regarding the traffic incident were dropped.

Murdach questioned Youso relentlessly, demanding he accurately recount conversations had with Paul St. Pierre. "It's been a year and I've just been trying to forget this, so I really don't know. To tell you the truth," Youso replied, "I have a very short memory span. It's hard for me to remember things."

"Isn't it true, Mr. Youso, that you told Mr. Paul St. Pierre to go up and cut the head off the body? Isn't it true that you're the one who suggested cutting the head off the body so they couldn't find the bullet?"

"I don't know," said Youso repeatedly. "I don't

know if I did or if I didn't. If I did, I don't know. I'm not sure." When Murdach asked him why he couldn't remember, Youso became more irritated and less defensive. "How would you feel if you were going through this? You try to forget as much as you can! I didn't kill nobody!

"Yes, sir, I disposed of evidence in this case," admitted Youso. "What are you going to do when your life might be in danger, or your family's life?" Enough was enough. The questioning stopped and an exasperated Anthony Youso stepped down from the witness stand.

Youso turned his back on David Murdach, squared his shoulders, and walked out of the Pierce County Courthouse.

"I don't think Youso should've walked on those criminal charges, or been treated so lightly even though he didn't actually do the murder," commented Roy Kissler several years later. "I don't recall all that he was involved in, but if he were involved in digging up somebody that's been murdered, and if he helped decapitate him, put his head in the bucket, then Tony Youso got off easy—he 'walked' on the whole thing. Walked on the charges, walked right out of sight, too."

"I think Youso really agonized over the whole thing," said a more sympathetic Marty Webb. "It was much more devastating to him to be involved in something like that than it was for Paul St. Pierre. That's probably because Tony had some brain cells that still worked, while Paul was a few clowns short of a circus. Shrinks were checking him out all the time, and I believe the doctors finally determined that he was 'terminally uptight and dangerous as hell.'"

The official diagnosis by learned psychologists and psychiatrists was couched in more professional parlance than Ms. Webb's colloquial rendering, and that was the primary purpose of Dr. Tappin's testimony. Before the doctor took the stand, Murdach asked Judge Steiner if Paul St. Pierre could be excused from the room.

"We could have him sitting on the bench out in the hall, Your Honor," said Murdach, and kindly offered his mathematical equation for the redistribution of courtroom guards. If Paul St. Pierre voluntarily waited outside while his doctor explained the depths of his depravity, delusions, and dangerousness, St. Pierre would be waiving his constitutional right to attend any and all proceedings. Judge Steiner saw numerous problems in that eventuality.

"I would prefer for him not to be here," reiterated Murdach. "If the court is afraid of his competency to waive his right to sit here, then I think we should look into competency more. If he is incompetent now, he shouldn't be here."

Steiner emphatically disagreed. "I think he should stay here," the judge ruled. "Bring in the jury."

David Murdach insisted his client was not guilty by reason of insanity. To verify Paul St. Pierre's tragic mental condition, Murdach enlisted several respected and accomplished mental health professionals, including Dr. Charles Tappin. Jurors were somewhat mystified when Tappin gave defense testimony in the middle of the prosecution's presentation.

"Under normal circumstances, the defense would not call witnesses or present evidence prior to the state resting its case," explained Murdach. "For the record, and so the jury understands, Dr. Tappin is being called out of order. We would normally wait until the conclusion of the state's case to present any evidence whatsoever. But in an effort to let him keep his time commitments to go to Europe, and the length of this trial, counsel has consented, and we've agreed, to have him testify now rather than later."

Tappin previously provided pretrial reports to the court concerning St. Pierre's competency to stand trial. Determination of diminished mental capacity, however, was another medical and legal matter altogether. Per Murdach's request, Dr. Tappin conducted extensive testing, interviews, and evaluations of Paul St. Pierre's mental condition.

David Murdach knew that Dr. Tappin's prestigious professional credentials, coupled with the physician's pleasant, self-effacing manner, would make a profound and positive impression upon the jurors. A graduate of the University of Kiel in Germany, Charles Tappin opened a private practice in Seattle, Washington, following his psychiatry residency at the University of Washington.

"I am a private practicing psychiatrist at Fairfax Hospital, as well as Cabrini Hospital, in Seattle," said Dr. Tappin. "I am also on the instruction staff at the University of Washington, and considered an associate staff member at Harborview Hospital," he added. Dr. Tappin, a member of the American Psychiatric Association, is board certified in psychiatry, and the published author of works dealing with forensic medicine in psychiatry. There was no way the jurors could doubt his diagnosis.

"What kind of examinations did you perform on Paul St. Pierre in connection with my request to determine whether or not he suffers from mental illness?" asked Murdach.

Dr. Tappin smoothly explained that the examination usually takes the form of a lengthy interview. "One goes into the history of the individual and his adjustment to life, to school, to work, and to his relationship with individuals," answered the doctor. "I also had at my disposal information from various sources dating back to the time he was in school. As a rule," he explained, "we try to get as much data as possible. I think psychiatric evaluation entails talking with the individual for quite a considerable length of time.

"Mr. St. Pierre suffers from what we call a paranoid personality illness. This diagnosis has been substantiated by all of the examiners who have seen him," testified Tappin. "We all agree that he suffers from a rather severe mental illness. He would like to see himself as being a big individual and therefore he has attempted to fortify himself by surrounding himself with dangerous weapons."

David Murdach repeatedly asked Dr. Tappin if Paul St. Pierre's condition was truly a mental illness. "Oh, yes," Tappin repeatedly said, "it's a mental illness." Further, Tappin described St. Pierre's condition as "extreme."

The main point Murdach wanted Tappin to communicate was that Paul St. Pierre was incapable of forming rational judgment, especially under the influence of LSD and alcohol. If his client was not able to form the conscious intent of murder, Paul St. Pierre could be considered not guilty of aggravated first-degree murder.

"As a result of your examination of Mr. Paul St. Pierre," asked David Murdach, "do you have an opinion within a reasonable certainty whether or not Mr. Paul St. Pierre would be capable of consciously forming an intent to murder or kill Mr. John Achord?"

"Yes, I have," responded Dr. Tappin. "Paul St. Pierre is suffering from a chronic paranoid condition, and having taken alcohol and LSD was not in a position to process in a rational manner what was going on around him, and therefore was unable to form any rational judgment with respect to his responses toward the individual concerned. In the formation of intention to harm someone, I feel it is necessary that the individual be in control of his intellectual and cognitive capacities."

When David Murdach inquired as to his client's mental condition during the grave site decapitation of John Achord, the extremity of Paul St. Pierre's mental illness baffled even the imminent Dr. Tappin. "Despite my psychiatric expertise," he admitted, "I am bewildered by the bizarreness of this whole incident, and really question to what degree this individual is disturbed. This is a disturbance beyond paranoia. It comes closer to a severe mental illness, more toward a schizophrenic type of thing."

Carl Hultman's cross-examination targeted the concept of "intent"—the rational process of which, according to Tappin, Paul St. Pierre was bereft. Hultman continually used the word "intent" in the colloquial meaning. In describing St. Pierre's shooting of Achord, Hultman asked Tappin if this took place because St. Pierre imagined Achord was a threat. "So he intended to stop whatever threat he saw, didn't he?" asked Hultman.

"Oh, yes. He told me that he feared for his own life. In order to protect himself, he reacted in this manner," said Tappin, referring to Paul St. Pierre's shooting of John Achord. The doctor also testified that Paul told him that it was Andrew Webb who handed him the knife to stab Achord in the back.

"Mr. St. Pierre was aware that the individual appeared to still be alive. To use his own words," said Dr. Tappin, "there were gurgling sounds and he described to me in extremely sick terms what he saw of [the] brain coming out of the individual's head, and sometimes he used terms which did not seem to really coincide with the pathologists' findings. I'm aware of the fact that there was no brain damage to Mr. Achord from the gunshot. That's why I'm saying his description of this whole thing to me, it seems almost as though he was experiencing some sort of visual hallucinations at the time. He spoke of brain coming out of the back of the individual's head and so on. Then he was handed this knife and proceeded to finish him off."

"So Paul St. Pierre intended to kill Mr. Achord when he shot him?"

"He intended to protect himself," responded Tappin, "when he shot John Achord." Hultman immediately pounced on the doctor's use of "intended."

"So," asked the prosecutor, a hint of triumph in his voice, "he *intended* to shoot him to protect himself?" Dr. Tappin remained unruffled, and quickly clarified his response. "Even though one can consider this an intent to protect oneself, the process was not a rational one. It was an instantaneous response to a delusion."

Hultman kept at it, repeatedly forming his question so that Tappin's answer would confirm the prosecution's use of, or definition of, "intend." Another technique Hultman employed was to stop Tappin's answers before the doctor was done answering, especially if the doctor was attempting to explain or clarify his response. Judge Steiner finally intervened. "You're going to have to allow him time to answer," admonished the judge, "or you're going to send him off to Europe with a stutter!"

"I object to the use of the word 'intend,'" complained Murdach, noticing Hultman's technique. Tappin, who also was becoming aggravated, spoke up. "I would not like to get involved in the semantics of the word 'intend,' or 'intention.' It is obvious from a layman's standpoint that he intended to kill this person.

From a psychiatric standpoint, we would avoid the use of the word 'intention' because it connotes that there was a rationally involved process that resulted in this killing." The process was a disturbed one, insisted Tappin, not a rational one. Therefore, it was not a true intention because it was irrational, and "intention" is a rational process. "He is more prone," said Tappin of Paul St. Pierre, "to attack in an aggressive way than the average individual."

"He's dangerous, isn't he?" Before Murdach could call out an objection, Dr. Tappin answered, "Oh, yes." The trial screeched to a halt and Steiner excused the jury. David Murdach demanded a mistrial. Once again, the proceedings were precariously teetering on the brink of total collapse.

The court had previously approved Murdach's pre-trial motion prohibiting any questions delving into Paul St. Pierre's possible "future dangerousness." In David Murdach's estimation, Carl Hultman had breached the court order. "The prosecutor *did* breach the order," he insisted forcefully. "Now the issue of present dangerousness is opened and the jury can speculate, 'If he's dangerous now, he's going to be dangerous in the future.' Mr. Hultman, perhaps cleverly, asked about present dangerousness to get into the issue of future dangerousness. A mistrial should be declared because of that."

"The state is not being 'clever,' " said Hultman, "when it notices that Mr. Murdach brings out through his own examination of Dr. Tappin, over and over again, that his client is an individual who reacts with hostility toward people who, in reality, do not represent hostility toward him. He reacts with physical violence. I'm aware of the court's ruling," he argued, "and I didn't ask any question that dealt with the future. I asked if he was dangerous—the answer is so obvious that it didn't really need to be asked. I didn't go into any future dangerousness."

"Don't ask anybody a question," Steiner warned Hultman, "that relates to the possible inference of future dangerousness." The prosecutor said he hadn't asked that "yet," and Steiner expressed judicial concern. "There is a basis of alleged appeal with respect to any argument to the jury as to the dangerousness of the defendant or defendants. Stay away from future dangerousness and present dangerousness."

"In addition," continued Murdach, unloading his second complaint, "the court has allowed the prosecutor to introduce all the evidence in the Damon Wells homicide." By doing so, reasoned Murdach, Hultman was essentially asking the court and jury to try the Wells homicide case all over again. "If the motion for a mistrial is not granted, we ask that the evidence and testimony regarding the Damon Wells incident up to this point be stricken, and the jury admonished not to consider it."

"I have admitted it," said Steiner of the Wells evidence, and ruled against a mistrial. "I don't know whether that ruling is going to stand on appeal or not, but that's the judgment of the court."

The state called Detective Robert Yerbury, who, as he did in the previous trial, began by answering essential questions of fact. "In the early morning hours of June nineteenth," asked Hultman, "did you encounter Christopher St. Pierre?"

Yerbury recounted the tale of St. Pierre's final exit from Ericson's, his cooperative revelations of evidence, guidance to grave sites, and the conditions under which Christopher St. Pierre gave his sworn statement.

"We went over the conversations of the day and what had occurred. When the written statement was ultimately given by Chris, it was given by him verbalizing to a secretary who typed it as he spoke." Detective Yerbury confirmed that the statement was not his own impression of the defendant's words, but an accurate word-for-word statement typed while St. Pierre dictated.

Carl Hultman handed Yerbury a copy of the statement, and asked him to identify it, then read it aloud. " 'I hereby make the following statement free and voluntary,' " Robert Yerbury began, and the jury sat spellbound, growing progressively more repulsed by the ghoulish nature of St. Pierre's nightmare narrative.

Yerbury's monologue remained uninterrupted through the murder of Wells and Achord, the decapitation, and attempts to destroy or hide evidence.

"Now, Detective," asked Carl Hultman, "did you obtain a search warrant for the residence of Tony Youso's brother, Martin Youso, in order to determine if you could find the ax?"

John Ladenburg quickly asked for the jury to be excused. He had a motion for the court's consideration that, due to Hultman's obvious testimonial trajectory, required an immediate ruling.

"I believe the prosecutor intends to introduce the ax into evidence," Ladenburg told Steiner. "We ask that the ax be excluded because it would be unduly inflammatory and prejudicial. The decapitation of John Achord is an established fact, and neither defense attorney disputes it. I see nothing the ax can add, other than a gruesome artifact in this case."

Steiner asked Hultman if the ax was necessary to prove the prosecution's case. "We won't know what is necessary to prove our case until the verdict is announced," he replied. "This case involves the jury's ability to fully interpret the deliberations and the totality with which Christopher St. Pierre joined in what

Paul St. Pierre was doing. The evidence of what they did to the head of the victim relates to both of them.

"The fact of the matter," argued Carl Hultman, "is that murders are gruesome. This may be one of the more horrible crimes. Unfortunately, the defense isn't going to be spared from some of the horror and gruesomeness they created."

"For the record," interjected David Murdach, "we join in the objection. I would ask at this time that the prosecution be precluded from bringing any other instruments in connection with this case, namely, the bucket which Mr. Hultman perhaps jokingly mentioned he was going to attempt to introduce. We can't just have Mr. Hultman bring these items to court in a sack, and then bring them out one at a time and try to have them admitted as evidence. . . ."

Murdach's grab-bag scenario disturbed Judge Steiner. "Is it the prosecution's intention to bring in the bucket," he asked, "or anything else, so we know about it in advance?" The bucket wasn't on the prosecution's exhibits list, but Paul St. Pierre's Gerber knife was. "I think anybody looking at it would see it is a dagger instrument which you can't think of any other purpose it might have other than sticking it in humans," said Hultman assertively. "I think it's important to see that knife, and for the jurors to understand the depth of the stab wounds." Steiner denied the photo of John Achord and the ax used to decapitate him, but allowed the alleged murder weapons. The jury was reseated, and the judge recited the following instruction: "Out-of-court statements by one of the St. Pierre brothers cannot be used as evidence against the other."

The instruction's timing was perfectly appropriate. Hultman next requested Detective Yerbury to read aloud selected excerpts from the sworn statement of

Paul St. Pierre. While Yerbury intoned the elder St.
Pierre brother's confessional narrative, David Murdach's mind was preoccupied by the possibility that
the use of his client's statement, considering the circumstances under which it was obtained, might still
be improper despite the court ruling in favor of its
admission into evidence.

➤ Deputy Prosecutor Chris Quinn-Brintnall, Murdach
recalled, had been recently subjected to an investigation by the Washington State Bar Association, the im-
petus being that she granted permission for Yerbury
and Price to take Paul St. Pierre's statement without
informing his lawyer. If the investigation determined
that there were legal violations beyond, or including,
ethical violations, the entire statement could be tossed
out, and the jury advised to forget all about it. Prior
to today's testimony, Murdach requested full disclosure
of the material Quinn-Brintnall provided the Bar Association for their investigation. So far, nothing had
been delivered.

Yerbury's disquieting testimony, followed by further
"Isn't it true that . . ." questions from each defense
counsel, concluded in synchronicity with Judge Steiner's quick glance at the courtroom clock. The time-
piece confirmed high noon in Pierce County. When
court reconvened following lunch, Hultman moved his
witnesses along with swift precision. First up, Identification Technician Douglas Walker explained how police recovered Paul St. Pierre's hidden .45-caliber
handgun; then Sergeant Parkhurst took the stand to
confirm quickly Walker's testimony. As a prelude to
Medical Examiner Emanuel Lacsina's testimony, Parkhurst recounted the successful recovery of Achord's
head from the Puyallup River. Dr. Lacsina's imperative,
authoritative, and disturbingly detailed discussion of
John Achord's autopsy consumed the rest of the day.

"The decapitated body of John Achord demonstrated the presence of ten stab wounds to the back of the chest and the abdomen. These were all deep stab wounds. In addition," testified Lacsina, "there were two superficial stab wounds at the back of the neck. The deepest wound was approximately five inches. All of the stab wounds inflicted on the body of John Achord were all inflicted while he was still alive." The jury heard in no uncertain terms that John Achord died because of the stab wounds, not the bullet wound. During cross-examination by David Murdach, Lacsina acknowledged that a gunshot's concussion could be fatal. A wound such as Achord's, he further confirmed, could possibly cause death if left unattended.

The prosecution's case neared completion. There were four brief testimonies scheduled for the morning of July 23; then the state would rest. "I doubt Hultman got much rest the night of July twenty-second," said news commentator Chet Rogers. "The anticipation of his first witness's testimony probably had him tossing and turning. I bet he met the milkman at the door." That was no milkman on Pierce County's porch the following morn, and the distinctive clanking sound came not from quarts of milk and pints of cream, but from leg irons, waist chains, and handcuffs restraining Hultman's first scheduled witness—Mr. Andrew K. Webb.

"Do you remember when you and I met in the Pierce County Jail in December of 1984?" To Carl Hultman's dismay, Andrew Webb gave reply. Murdach continued, and attempted asking if Webb recalled telling him that the suggestion to dispose of Achord's body was made the day after the murder. Murdach became tongue-tied; the question was incomprehensible.

"I don't even understand that question," said Webb. The court suggested a mini-conference between Webb and his attorney, Larry Nichols. Following his lawyer's advice, Webb relapsed into silence.

Delaying the unavoidable argument for Webb's plea-bargain statement being admitted as evidence, Hultman called Tacoma Police identification technicians to the stand for quick testimony regarding evidence recovery and identification.

The state's final witness and most effective testimony would be Detective Robert Yerbury reading aloud from Webb's elaborate, damning plea-bargain statement. The defense fought against it, citing Webb's unreliability, history of mental and behavioral problems, and the self-serving nature of the statement itself. Murdach and Ladenburg also argued that Webb's refusal to cooperate with the prosecution didn't mean that Mr. Webb was "unavailable." None of these arguments were new to Hultman. He staunchly defended the prosecution's position, utilizing the unique nature of the case, Webb's self-incriminating confession, and various legal precedents as his primary armaments against Ladenburg's and Murdach's combined assault.

"I think it is a difficult, difficult decision," said Judge Steiner. "It's one I have great difficulty making. My ruling is the same. He is unavailable. It's against penal interest. It is reasonably trustworthy. There are indicia of reliability. There are corroborating circumstances and evidence. My ruling is the same as Judge Stone's."

"I'm going to rest when Detective Yerbury is done," stated Hultman. "But I have one other matter." He then reoffered the portrait of John Achord as a plaintiff's exhibit. "It is the only picture that the jury would have in any fashion that depicts John Achord. The photograph isn't gruesome. It simply shows the jury that there was a victim here, a pleasant human being." The motion was denied, as the photo was not necessary to prove Achord was a human being, nor was it required to prove death or the cause of death.

The state called Detective Robert Yerbury who read aloud admitted murderer Andrew Webb's judiciously edited plea-bargain statement. Yerbury's deadpan recitation invested Webb's disturbing narrative of death and dementia with an eerie, perhaps accurate, aura of cold, unemotional distance.

Immediately following Yerbury, the state rested. Then John Ladenburg injected the proceedings with a renewed sense of live drama. "We move for the court to dismiss the case against Chris St. Pierre," announced Ladenburg, who had every reason to so move, and solid reasoning behind the motion.

Carl Hultman looked to his left, then to his right, as if anticipating the arrival of divine intervention. He turned expectantly to Judge Steiner, silently entreating against immediate irrevocable judicial acquiescence. Ladenburg, however, wasn't done speaking. He'd made the motion, and in two short, well-pitched sentences, he could knock the proverbial ball out of the park. Christopher St. Pierre, already sentenced to life in the Wells case, couldn't slide home, but he could stay far afield of the hangman's noose.

"All of the stuff we've heard," said Ladenburg emphatically, "*all* of it gets down to one thing: Andrew

Webb's statement that was just read by Detective Yerbury. There is no evidence! There is *nothing* in this statement or anybody else's statement that proves the charge beyond a reasonable doubt! Hence, we move for dismissal of the case against Christopher St. Pierre."

"Motion denied," said the judge. Then, after a momentary pause, Steiner prompted the well-prepared attorney to present his official opening statement.

"I'm going to give you an overview of what we expect to prove in this case," Ladenburg began. "As in all criminal cases, part is proven through witnesses, part is proven through direct evidence, and part of it is evidentiary things that may be read to you, or documents given to you. At the end, we'll give a closing statement and try to make you see what we see in the evidence to convince you, hopefully, of what the evidence shows."

The previous trial revealed Carl Hultman's portrayal of the St. Pierre brothers as two men acting in concert, even referring to them as "one" as if they were mirror-image twins of evil. Ladenburg knew his first challenge was to firmly establish the individual identity of Chris St. Pierre, and the singular nature of the charges against him. "The individuals are not the same, and you're not to look at them the same," he said. "When I speak, I only speak as to what is being shown or proven to you in regard to Chris St. Pierre.

"One of the things you are going to have to do in this case," he explained, "and it really is the crux of the case, is to determine the credibility of Andrew Webb, who you saw here earlier today and [who] refused to testify."

Experienced attorneys followed the Achord trial with intense interest, not only because the alleged crimes and the court rulings were controversial and

unusual, but because the courtroom combatants—
Hultman, Murdach, and Ladenburg—were all of exceptional skill and excellent reputation.

John Ladenburg's opening statement was exemplary in structure, and perfectly pitched to capture and maintain the interest of his primary audience: the twelve jurors, who held his client's life in their hands. When Ladenburg announced the names of his first two witnesses on behalf of Christopher St. Pierre, jurors and spectators looked at each other in sincere surprise. Ladenburg's witnesses for the defense included attorney David Murdach and Deputy Prosecutor Carl Hultman.

It is quite unusual, admitted Ladenburg, to have a witness testify when that witness is also one of the attorneys on the case. "The reason we're going to have to do that is because Mr. Webb refuses to testify. I'm going to have to put Mr. Murdach on the stand because back in November or December of last year, Mr. David Murdach met with Andrew Webb. He asked him questions about the statement—the one you heard Detective Yerbury read aloud at the end of Mr. Hultman's presentation."

Ladenburg zeroed in on what could be the most crucial evidence that his client was innocent of first-degree aggravated murder in the death of John Achord. The prosecution continually asserted that Chris St. Pierre, seeing that Achord was still alive, urged, commanded, convinced, and/or encouraged his brother to kill Achord on the spot to further cover up the murder of Damon Wells. Andrew Webb told David Murdach that those remarks were not made while John Achord was bleeding on the dining room floor. In truth, those remarks were not made until the next day.

If this forthcoming testimony raised reasonable doubt in jurors' minds, Christopher St. Pierre could be spared a possible death sentence. "That is going to be crucial evidence in this case. If you believe Mr. Murdach that Webb said that, then there are no *aggravating circumstances* of this murder."

Ladenburg explained that Carl Hultman was going to testify as a defense witness. During an interview similar to that of David Murdach's, Webb told Hultman that his statement, "Paul and Chris stabbed Wells in the back," was not true at all, and that he put the blame on the St. Pierres "out of vengeance."

The bizarre assault by Andrew Webb and Randy Nolan on the school-age kids and their hysterical mother became courtroom knowledge, as did the possible twenty-year sentence faced by Webb if Damon Wells complained to the cops about the Salmon Beach beatings. "There was only one gentleman," said Ladenburg, "who had prison hanging over his head the very next month if that fact came to light—Andrew Webb. It was Andrew Webb who chased down Damon Wells and slit his throat to keep him from talking."

Webb wasn't sentenced the following month as originally scheduled, Ladenburg explained. He was still facing a possible twenty-year prison sentence when he walked into Paul St. Pierre's house and saw John Achord in a pool of blood.

"We also expect to show," the defense continued, "that the reason Chris St. Pierre didn't know that Mr. Achord was then stabbed in the back was because he was out of the room when it happened."

Mark Perez, Ladenburg said, would confirm that Chris, appalled by his brother's deadly behavior, left the scene and went into Mark Perez's bedroom. While Chris was expressing his dismay to Perez, Paul repeatedly stabbed John Achord.

"Christopher St. Pierre may take the stand in his own defense later this afternoon," said John Ladenburg. "It may be a horrible thing to say, that Chris was afraid of his own brother, but Chris will have to admit it to you. He was afraid of Paul and afraid of Andrew Webb, and he was convinced that if he told the police anything, then eventually they would kill him."

"Chris will tell you the bad things along with the good things. He will tell you everything just as he did to the police department. 'I came to tell you to clear it up, to prove I wasn't involved in these two murders.' He was, however, involved in the kidnapping and assault that resulted in murder, and he was sentenced to life in prison. He will tell you that," said Ladenburg.

"I think when you have heard the testimony of the two attorneys, when you have heard the testimony of Christopher St. Pierre, you will be convinced that Christopher St. Pierre has already been found guilty of what he was guilty of. He is already being punished. But in the second murder," Ladenburg said dramatically, "Christopher St. Pierre was not guilty of murder, not guilty of covering up the first murder, not guilty of doing anything in this case. If you listen carefully to the testimony, you should vote not guilty as to Christopher St. Pierre."

His opening remarks closed, the court thanked him, and John Ladenburg called David Murdach to testify about his December 18, 1984, interview with Andrew Webb. "Did Mr. Webb give you any statements that contradict in any way the statement that was read for the jury today as to the Wells killing?"

"Yes," Murdach said, "he admitted he didn't actually see a knife in Paul St. Pierre's hand, and he did not see Paul St. Pierre stabbing Damon Wells. He further stated that Damon Wells was not forced or kidnapped or threatened to go for a ride."

Ladenburg then pursued similar questions regard-

ing any comments Andrew Webb made about the
Achord case that contradicted what the jury heard in
court. "Maybe I can just state the whole scenario as
we went along—I had my tape recorder with me during the whole interview because I went to the jail to
see him to discuss his possible future testimony."

Carl Hultman interrupted Murdach and Ladenburg
with an objection. "It's not fair," he complained to
the judge. "What's happening here is the two defense
attorneys are allowed to pick or choose what one or
both of them perceive to be contradicting statements.
I have no way of knowing if there are other contradictory statements that may in fact hurt their clients."

Steiner agreed, and advised Ladenburg to rephrase
his question so Murdach would not be subjectively de-
termining what was contradictory. This posed no problem for Ladenburg. He simply posed the question
inversely. "Mr. Murdach, during your conversation
with Mr. Webb, did he confirm the statement made
today in the courtroom that Chris St. Pierre on the
night of the Achord killing said that we should bury
the body because if we don't, they'll find out about
Damon Wells? Did he confirm that was true?"

"No, and this is from my notes, that the comment
or discussion amongst them did not take place on the
night of Mr. Achord's death, but the following day."

To make sure the jury got the point, Ladenburg
asked the same question in different form. "From
what Mr. Webb said to you, is it true that on the night
of the Achord killing there was no comment as to covering up the prior homicide of Damon Wells?"

"That conversation took place the following day,"
Murdach replied, "not on the night of the homicide."
The witness managed to repeat that information three
times in his one response.

Having made that fact perfectly clear, Ladenburg

had no further questions; Hultman had only one in cross-examination; then Judge Steiner asked, "Mr. Murdach, because you're a witness, do you wish Mr. Ladenburg to ask you your questions, or do you wish to ask yourself any questions?"

"I would like to ask myself a couple more questions that are pertinent to Paul St. Pierre," said Murdach. Hultman objected, was overruled, and Murdach read aloud from his notes. " 'Mr. Webb said that Paul and Cory were high on acid, that there was an eight-foot circle of blood on the floor, that Paul showed him a piece of metal, and it looked like self-defense. He said that you don't see things right when you are high on acid. Paul sees the metal and it scared him. Paul misunderstood and shot him.' That's all I have," said Murdach. Ladenburg said that he didn't have any other questions, and Carl Hultman had no further questions, either. Murdach left the witness stand and returned to the defense table. Carl Hultman sighed with resignation. He knew what was coming.

"I call Mr. Carl Hultman to the stand," said Ladenburg. He retained his serious decorum despite deriving a measure of professional pleasure in the irony of the prosecuting attorney testifying for the defense. Hultman didn't bother objecting. He walked over, sat down, was duly sworn, and prepared to answer honestly the questions posed by John Ladenburg on behalf of Christopher St. Pierre.

Ladenburg asked, "Is it correct that Mr. Webb told you that there were inaccuracies in his statement given to the police in July of 1984?" Hultman agreed, and when asked for a sample inaccuracy, he acknowledged that Andrew Webb said that Chris and Paul St. Pierre really didn't stab Damon Wells. Webb took full responsibility for the knife wounds. That was all Ladenburg wanted from Hultman, and the prosecutor had no questions for himself.

Christopher St. Pierre was not obligated to say a word. To differentiate his client from the uncooperative Mr. Webb, and to demonstrate Chris St. Pierre's attitude of full disclosure, John Ladenburg called him to the witness stand. Glancing nervously at the twelve people who could send him to the gallows, Christopher St. Pierre swore to tell the truth, the whole truth, and nothing but the truth.

"I was really drunk," admitted Chris St. Pierre about the night Damon Wells was murdered. "Me and Andrew had been drinking at the tavern even before we got to the house. We had four cases of beer and we had been drinking for a period of maybe a half hour. I found Paul and Damon in the bathroom, arguing. Paul started hitting Damon. I was drunk and being rowdy; I started hitting him, too. Then Andrew came in and started hitting Damon, really beating him up bad. He was hitting and kicking him."

Ladenburg's questions led Christopher St. Pierre through the evening's events in chronological order, faithfully following the precise structure and content of his sworn statement to the Tacoma Police. He told the jury how Andrew Webb chased Wells at Salmon Beach, tackled him, and slit his throat. When Damon Wells stopped breathing, Webb threw the knife into Damon Wells's back, removed it, and threw it again.

Questioned about discovering John Achord on the dining room floor, Paul St. Pierre standing over the bloody body, brandishing his .45, Christopher answered in clear detail. "I went into shock. I started saying to Paul, 'What the hell are you doing? What the hell is going on?' I just asked him that over and over again. I was shouting it at him," added Chris, explaining that the *Rambo* movie *First Blood* was blaring loudly from the television. Andrew Webb was shouting as well, said Chris St. Pierre. " 'Goddamn it, Paul. I can't believe this,' " yelled Andrew Webb. " 'I'm already facing twenty years. I killed one guy, and now you kill this guy. I can't believe this.' "

"When you saw Mr. Achord," asked Ladenburg, "did it appear to you that he was alive?" The witness answered in the negative. "Did he make any breathing sounds or did he make any movements?" Again, St. Pierre said he heard and saw no signs of life from John Achord. "When you asked Paul what he was doing, what did he say?" Chris testified that Paul said that Achord had come at him with a knife, or threatened him in some manner. "Paul pulled out his gun and told him to cool out, but the guy wouldn't. The guy just came at him or something and then Paul shot him."

Ladenburg asked if Chris St. Pierre saw any knife in the room, or anything that Achord could have had as a weapon. "Yes, on the floor was a single-bladed folding pocketknife, brown handle, about eight inches long, opened."

"Bullshit! Bullshit! Bullshit!" The jury's attention quickly shifted from the witness stand to the spectator gallery. Larry Achord, the victim's brother, stood spewing a torrent of outrage and insults toward Chris St. Pierre. Achord's outburst was accompanied by additional derisive remarks and insults spontaneously offered by Achord's friends and relatives.

"Officer Dillon," said the judge sternly, "take the gentleman out, please." The upset sibling of the deceased was immediately escorted from the Pierce County courtroom by uniformed security.

Aggravated, Judge Gary Steiner requested the jury to step out for a minute. This incident resonated with import and implications far beyond merely altering the courtroom's staid and officious atmosphere. There are laws, precedents, and policies regarding outburst in the courtroom. Steiner knew those laws, precedents, and policies. So did John Ladenburg. "We move for a mistrial on the basis of misconduct of a spectator in the courtroom," said Ladenburg. Judge Steiner wasn't surprised.

"The jury heard all of this," said Ladenburg. "All of the jurors looked in the direction of the spectators. It was a direct comment on Mr. St. Pierre's testimony by people whom we are not allowed to cross-examine, and who are not participants in the case, and who are not witnesses to the crime scene or anything else."

"I think it obviously directly influences the jury's opinion of Mr. St. Pierre's testimony. It's a very unfortunate incident, but one we can do nothing about at this point, and it's certainly going to influence the jury's opinion."

Steiner's exemplary courtroom courtesy and decorum now began to show aggravation and displeasure leading to dramatically expressed anger from the bench. "I'm going to have to invoke powers of contempt to put people in jail if this conduct continues! Aside from the jury question," snapped Steiner, aiming his justifiable ire at spectators who augmented Larry Achord's outburst with impolite remarks of their own. "You're destroying the efficacy of this trial, and all the money associated with it! The gallery is instructed not to make any kind of commotion, not to demonstrate emotion, not to say anything during the progress of the trial!"

Ladenburg demanding a mistrial because one spectator yelled "Bullshit" was not an extreme response. In truth, he was no more eager to start the trial all over again than Hultman or Steiner. Had he not moved for a mistrial, however, he could have been open to charges of ineffective counsel. "I don't want to try this case over again, but I don't want my client convicted on the basis of statements made by spectators. This isn't a three-ring circus. I think the court has no choice now but to grant a mistrial."

David Murdach spoke up, saying, "We would join in the motion and simply repeat that at the beginning of this case there were obviously problems with the spectator gallery with respect to certain comments being made."

Carl Hultman acknowledged the sensitivity of the situation, and asked the court to not declare a mistrial. "The court can cure this problem, and it is a problem. I think the individual that was escorted out of the courtroom is one of the deceased's brothers. It's understandable, it's human, and it's regrettable, but I think the court can cure it by an instruction." Hultman proposed that the judge simply tell the jurors to disregard the outburst.

"The motion for a mistrial is denied," said Judge Steiner. A new instruction for the present jury, he decided, was preferable to a future trial with a new jury.

John Ladenburg discerned something peculiar about Achord's sudden outpouring of disruptive anger. Upon reflection, he realized that there was nothing new, unexpected, or surprising about Chris St. Pierre's testimony that could spark spontaneous, unrehearsed outrage.

"I think the comments just made in the courtroom were intentional," admitted Ladenburg, the idea becoming more solidified as he spoke. "In fact, I can see no other way around. The evidence that Mr. St. Pierre said he 'saw a knife' has been in his statement, in the police report, and has been referred to in this courtroom in numerous hearings a number of times over this last year. This isn't anything that just suddenly surprised everyone. The Achords and all of their fam-

Eighteen

"They have been mumbling in the background that they are going to get me," David Murdach revealed to Judge Gary Steiner the following morning. "I would like some testimony taken from these people as to what has been going on. . . ."

Judge Steiner had no intention of taking testimony from the spectators, but every intention of taking the spectators to task. "If there is any outbursts, whether it be vocal or it be visual, [it] will result in personal penalty from the court to the person who is doing so," he dramatically announced. "There should be no discussion in the audience, no veiled threats, no gestures, no facial expressions. The conduct of this trial is one the administration of which is justice, and I won't permit it. If anybody violates the order, they will first be excused from the court for the balance of the trial. The other option is to clear the courtroom entirely. The third thing is personal penalty, including contempt and jail.

"If there is a mistrial resulting, the cost of the mistrial will be directed to the person causing the mistrial," he said, echoing the words of Judge Thomas Sauriol. "The cost of this trial is well into the hundreds of thousands of dollars. Bring on the jury so I can instruct them.

"Good morning, ladies and gentlemen," Steiner said. "The outburst by the spectator had nothing to do with the trial. You should not allow any outside influence to interfere with your decision. It is your duty to try the case solely upon the evidence heard from the witness stand and the exhibits admitted into evidence and under the law as given to you by the court."

John Ladenburg resumed his direct examination of Christopher St. Pierre exactly where he had left off. "When you entered the house, what did you see?" The witness recounted the same essential testimony as he did prior to the previous day's outburst. Ladenburg then asked for details about his interaction with Mark Perez.

"I went into Mark Perez's room. He was just waking up. He sat up in bed and was squinting his eyes, clearing his eyes. I started to ask him if he heard anything and started just telling him to stay in his room and not come out because I didn't want him to get involved in this or see what was going on. I was in there for a short thirty seconds. Andrew Webb came in and he started saying the same type of things to Mark, 'Just stay in your room; don't come out; you don't want to see what's going on.' Then Paul came up to Mark Perez's door and said something, but I don't remember what he said. Andrew told him to leave.

"We went back into the living room, into the dining room area," testified Chris St. Pierre. "Paul was there. He was starting to cut the carpet up around the body and folding it up over the body. We helped him roll the body up and finish cutting up the other side of the carpet."

"At that time," asked Ladenburg, "did you see any

knife wounds in Mr. Achord, and if you had seen knife wounds, would you have told the police about it on the nineteenth of June when you made your statement to them?"

Chris St. Pierre assured him that he most certainly would have told the police about knife wounds had he known about them. After all, he led the police to the body. If he knew there were knife wounds, he would also know those wounds would be revealed once the body was recovered.

"After we rolled up the body in the carpet, Paul, Andrew, and I carried it out to Andrew's car," he said, continuing his testimony. "We placed it in the backseat. We were going to go bury the body, you know."

Ladenburg knew the story all too well, and all the different versions. The defense strategy was direct and clearly supported. Chris was the "cooperative defendant"—he helped the police, directed them to evidence and the bodies, and told them everything he knew. Andrew Webb, whose plea-bargain statement was the only "evidence" loosely linking Chris St. Pierre to the killing of John Achord, was the "uncooperative defendant." He was the unreliable opposite of Chris St. Pierre. He refused to testify, admitted his statement was false, and took full responsibility for the murder of Damon Wells. Paul St. Pierre was the "insane defendant"—the one for whom murder was an accomplishment worth bragging about, and everyone else was perceived as a possible enemy, potential victim, or both.

Chris St. Pierre's testimony, Ladenburg reasoned, would demonstrate his willingness and honesty, differentiate him from the unwilling and dishonest Andrew Webb, and definitely raise reasonable doubt about the prosecution's charge of aggravated first-degree murder. The entire "aggravated" aspect of the charge re-

volved around Andrew Webb's assertion that Chris St.
Pierre encouraged his brother to kill Achord to cover
up the Wells homicide. Chris testified that he thought
John Achord was dead from the .45 head shot, he
never heard Achord breathing, never saw him move,
was convinced that Paul had killed him with the .45,
and that Andrew Webb never once suggested calling
the police or ambulance.

"Andrew said that you told him that the police
should not be called because Paul was high on acid
and the police would not believe him," said Murdach,
"and that you said that if the police came snooping
around they might find out about Damon Wells. Did
you ever say that?"

"No, I never heard anything like that," responded
Chris St. Pierre. When Webb's latest revised version
was recounted, the narrative in which Chris's comments about covering up the Wells murder took place
the next day, St. Pierre said even that was untrue. "As
a matter of fact, if Andrew said it was the next day,
that's impossible because I didn't see Andrew for three
days afterward. Paul and Andrew were working together at the bakery, they might have had some discussion like that, but nothing like that was ever said
in my presence."

David Murdach began his cross-examination asking
for clarification about the genesis of the decapitation
concept, an idea originated by Tony Youso. "The next
day, Paul was discussing what had happened with Tony
Youso. Paul was still concerned about the bullet being
in the man's head. Tony Youso suggested that he remove the head. Once Paul got the idea into his head
himself, he said, 'Yeah, I better do it, I guess.' At that
time, Paul gave Tony and I some money and told him
to go get some cement and stuff."

Murdach wanted one more point made clear to the

jury, and he asked the question with practiced precision. "From your testimony, I understand you to say that you do not recall any conversation whatsoever about any discussion about calling the police?"

St. Pierre answered, "No."

"Is that because," asked Murdach, "you didn't hear it? Were you present during the entire time that Andrew and Paul were together by the body of John Achord?" Chris St. Pierre had already testified that he went into Mark Perez's room, but Murdach wanted to make sure the jury had it drilled into their heads so they would never forget it.

"So I understand what you said," restated Murdach, "you left the room for a period of time and if there was a conversation between Paul and Andrew, you were not in their presence?"

"I was not in their presence," confirmed Chris St. Pierre. Murdach had no further questions, but prosecutor Carl Hultman had plenty of questions designed to elicit testimony that would hopefully reveal Christopher St. Pierre as a disgusting, repellent, heartless murderer. He wanted to paint him as a man devoid of compassion, who willingly participated in the kidnapping and killing of Damon Wells, concealed the crime, encouraged the murder of John Achord, participated in the gruesome decapitation of Achord's corpse, concealed those crimes as well, and only revealed information after he was in police custody.

"Chris, I believe you said that there wasn't any conversation that you ever heard about being concerned about the police finding out about Damon Wells's murder," said Hultman. Again, St. Pierre stated that he never heard such a conversation. "But you were afraid of being found out, weren't you?"

"If I was so afraid of being found out, I wouldn't have gone and told the police everything like I did," replied St. Pierre strongly. It was then that Hultman moved in. "In your statement, you say that Detective Price came by your house three weeks after Damon's death. You knew the police understood and realized that your house was the last place Damon was seen alive. You knew that, didn't you?" The witness agreed.

"So you knew sometime in March of 1984, two months before John Achord was killed, that the police knew Damon Wells had not been seen alive since he came to your house. Therefore, you people would be logical suspects. You knew that, didn't you? Detective Price came to your house and asked about Damon Wells. You lied to him about that, didn't you? That's because you were afraid of being found out, isn't it?"

"I was afraid," admitted St. Pierre. "I was afraid that if I told what Andrew had done and stuff, if he could get at me, he would kill me." Hultman questioned if that was the only source of St. Pierre's fear, asking if he felt guilty about what he had done. "I didn't feel guilty of murder; I didn't kill anybody," responded St. Pierre.

Carl Hultman elicited testimony concerning the witness's previous murder conviction in the Wells trial, his life sentence plus an additional thirty years for the kidnapping and assault. "That's the kidnapping you say was a voluntary trip by Damon Wells, is that correct? Do you want to think about it for a minute? Are you sure that's what it was? A voluntary trip? Damon went voluntarily with you and your brother and Andrew Webb?"

"Yes," said Christopher St. Pierre.

"The jury didn't believe you last time," said Hultman with a hint of sarcasm, "did they?" Both defense counsels voiced objections sustained by Judge Steiner. David Murdach then asked that the jury be excused. Once the jurors went out, Murdach went ballistic.

"This is prosecutorial misconduct," he said vehemently. "The jury should be admonished to disregard that last question and admonished to disregard any comments further along this line."

The reason for Murdach's outrage was that Carl Hultman was trying to get Chris St. Pierre to mention that he didn't take the stand in his own behalf during the Wells trial. "The prosecutor knows that neither Paul nor Chris testified in the previous trial. This is nothing more than an attempt to get into evidence that Christopher St. Pierre didn't take the stand."

"He exercised his Fifth Amendment privilege," added John Ladenburg. "The case is presently on appeal. If it is retried, he may exercise that privilege again. I don't think the prosecutor should be allowed to do this."

The judge agreed; the jury would be instructed to disregard the question. Hultman then told the court that he intended to ask the same question again, except change the wording slightly.

"I move for a mistrial," said Murdach.

"Your motion is denied," said Steiner. "Bring in the jury."

Carl Hultman asked for a brief delay. He wanted another intended line of questioning approved. "I intend to ask him to describe Damon Wells's physical size inasmuch as he's asserted that Damon went voluntarily. I think his size, relative to Andrew Webb and the St. Pierre brothers, is a matter which relates to a question of how anybody would believe his claim that Damon went voluntarily. I think that's an absurd statement! I think the jury is entitled to know that Damon Wells was very, very small—five feet tall and [about] one hundred five pounds. We are looking at the witness's credibility, and I think the jury is entitled to examine his credibility on this matter."

Judge Steiner ruled otherwise. "The fact of the conviction of kidnapping speaks for itself. You are retrying the first case." The prosecutor argued that the witness was not testifying honestly or accurately. "I don't think it is relevant at all," said Steiner. The jurors returned, and he advised them to disregard the previous question and the answer.

Hultman, however, refused to abandon the Wells incident. He continued questioning Chris St. Pierre about his violent contributions to Damon Wells's final hours. "Yes" was the reply, again and again, as the prosecutor asked, "Did you beat Damon Wells in the bathroom? Did you beat him again in the car? Did you beat him still more at the beach?"

And finally: "Did you think there was anything wrong with what happened to Damon Wells?" The only answer was affirmative, giving Hultman the opening he was waiting for. "Then why did you stand there for five to ten minutes waiting for him to bleed to death?"

"What was I supposed to do? Was I supposed to run off yelling for help? What was I supposed to do? I stood there in shock," said St. Pierre. "There was nothing I could do."

"Except hide the evidence of the crime?"

"That's true," admitted St. Pierre. "I did participate in covering up the evidence." Hultman asked about building a fire and burning their clothes. "I didn't do that. I didn't burn my clothes. I did burn my boots." The prosecutor selected a particularly disturbing portion of Christopher St. Pierre's original sworn statement, and read it aloud: " 'We took showers to wash away the blood.' "

"Is that right?" asked Hultman. "Did you shower to wash away the blood?"

"I didn't have to take a shower," St. Pierre said. "I

could have just washed my hands. I had some blood on my hands." The witness's remark, a simple statement of physical fact, was too similar to an expression indicating undeniable guilt for Hultman to resist.

"Did you have . . . blood on your hands?" he asked slowly. St. Pierre answered yes. "Interesting comment," Hultman murmured. Murdach instantly objected.

"Objection sustained," ruled the judge. "That remark will be stricken. The jury is instructed to disregard it."

Instructing a jury to disregard a remark is often the same as asking them to not think about green elephants. Once the remark is made, or the question asked, the impression has been made. Lawyers, of course, know this. It is precisely for this reason that they often risk a sustained objection—they know that it is impossible to disregard 100 percent a remark that one is told to disregard.

With tension and temperature rising in the Pierce County courtroom, the prosecution questioned Chris St. Pierre's firm assertion that he never saw Paul St. Pierre stab John Achord, nor did he notice the wounds. "When you came into the room, you walked by the body; I assume you looked at it?" asked Carl Hultman.

"I tried not to, but I looked at it. I just went into shock, like it was unbelievable. I mean, you leave the house for a half hour or something and come back and there's a guy lying on the floor here, shot in the head, blood all over the place."

Christopher St. Pierre held steadfast in his claim that he was out of the room, speaking with Mark Perez, when Paul St. Pierre stabbed John Achord. "The first I knew of the stab wounds at all was after the autopsy was performed," he repeatedly said. "That's when I first heard about the stab wounds; I never saw Paul stab him; I never saw the wounds."

"That stabbing would have had to have happened in that thirty seconds when you were in Mark Perez's room, all twelve stab wounds would had to have happened in that thirty seconds that were outside your presence, wouldn't it?"

"I never saw it happen; I never heard it happen! When I came back into the room, Paul was already cutting the carpet up around the body. I had a pretty good idea what he was going to do with the body, what he wanted to do with the body."

It was the state's contention that Chris St. Pierre encouraged the murder of John Achord to conceal the murder of Damon Wells. Hence, Carl Hultman continually linked the two events during his cross-examination. "Why didn't you call the police? Is it because you were afraid that they wouldn't believe Paul because he was high on acid?"

"I didn't care if they believed Paul or not. I wasn't the one who shot the guy," St. Pierre replied. He acknowledged that the police were not called. This was the introduction Carl Hultman wanted to trigger his next barrage of interrelated questions. "On the night John Achord was killed, the police didn't know where Damon's body was, did they? They didn't know anything about it yet, did they? They didn't know your actual involvement or what anybody had done to Damon Wells, did they?" Each question was answered negatively. "You didn't want them to know about it, did you?"

"I came forward and told that stuff had gone too far," said Chris St. Pierre. "It had to be stopped!"

"Nobody is disagreeing with that," Hultman said, and delivered the remark as if it were a punch line. He cast a glance at John Ladenburg and perceived the defense counsel's preobjection body language. The unspoken was easily deciphered and just as easily ignored. Carl Hultman would abandon this line of questioning only by court ruling.

"What we are talking about is your state of mind when John Achord was murdered," explained Hultman to St. Pierre. "You were afraid about being found out about Damon Wells; that's why he was murdered, too, isn't it?"

Ladenburg's anticipated objection found voice before his client could answer. "I think this is the fourth time this question has been asked. I don't see any point in Mr. Hultman continuing to ask the same question over and over again in this trial."

"I'm trying to get at the truth, Your Honor," pleaded Hultman. The judge permitted the prosecutor to continue.

"That's why he was murdered, isn't it?" reiterated Hultman. "So the police would not find out about Damon Wells, isn't that true?"

"I don't know why Paul killed him," said St. Pierre. "You'll have to ask him. I don't know what transpired. I wasn't there. I can't tell you."

What St. Pierre could tell and confirm under oath was that at no time after discovering the body of John Achord did he even consider calling the police. Despite numerous opportunities to distance himself from the murder and burial, he fully participated in every aspect of the transporting of the body, the burial, preparation for the decapitation, and the delivery of Achord's severed head to the Puyallup River Bridge.

"When the decision was made to decapitate John Achord's body, you went and got the cement with Youso. Who made you do that?"

"Paul told me to do it, and I was just listening to him," answered Chris St. Pierre, admitting that while he could have gone to the police, he went instead to help his brother remove John Achord's head. "Paul dug the body up. I helped him get the body out of the grave. Then I went back and got the bucket and cement, mixed up some cement. Paul went back into the brush. I was by the road. He was about thirty feet back by the grave site and proceeded to remove John Achord's head. He chopped it off with an ax. He came out of the brush carrying John Achord's head. He came over and placed the head in the bucket of cement; we brought it back to the house, removed the lid, and saw that the cement had set up. Paul placed it in the garage. Then he asked Tony and I to get rid of it."

Hultman provided a thoughtful pause sufficient for whatever ghoulish images occupied the jurors' minds to sink in before commenting, "You people spent a lot of time moving bodies and stuff at night, didn't you?"

"Objection," declared Ladenburg; "Sustained," ruled the judge. Carl Hultman was past any objection, sustained or overruled; he was already asking Chris St. Pierre for an important clarification regarding his stance of innocence in the murder of John Achord. "So your claim is that you just happened to be an unfortunate guy in the wrong place at the wrong time all the time, is that kind of what your claim is here?"

"I was caught in the middle of a lot of stuff. I was afraid for my life. I didn't know what to do. I told the police repeatedly when I gave my statement that for turning these guys in, I was most likely going to be killed."

"You told them that you were afraid," countered Hultman, "that you were going to be *convicted of murder!* You told the police that, didn't you?"

"No, I said, 'I'll probably be *charged* with the murder.'"

"That's all," stated Hultman. He was done with Christopher St. Pierre. John Ladenburg, however, was entitled to redirect examination—an immediate opportunity to punch holes in Hultman's portrayal of his client's motives and involvement in the death of John Achord.

"Didn't you also tell Detective Yerbury and Price that the reason you came forward was to prove you weren't involved in these two murders?" St. Pierre confirmed Ladenburg's assertion. "Mr. Hultman numerous times asked you whether or not you wanted to have John Achord killed in order to cover up Damon Wells's murder. Who was it that murdered Damon Wells? Who was it who slit Damon Wells's throat and stabbed him in the back? Who was it who handed Paul a knife and told him to kill John Achord that night?" Each question elicited the same two-word answer: "Andrew Webb."

Ladenburg, asking the last question of Christopher St. Pierre, made sure the jury's final thought was the unmistakable guilt and complicity of Andrew Webb—the man who refused to cooperate, and the only man implicating his client in the murder of John Achord.

The case on behalf of Chris St. Pierre had one more witness whose testimony was anticipated as exceptionally brief—Mark Perez would simply confirm three things. First, Andrew Webb had a knife-throwing set. Second, Chris St. Pierre was not the kind of person who would stand up to his brother Paul or Andrew Webb. Third, the night Damon Wells was beaten in the bathroom, Chris was in the living room talking with Perez most of the time. Whatever transpired in the bathroom with Damon Wells happened primarily with Andrew and Paul, not Chris St. Pierre.

"At this time, Your Honor," said John Ladenburg, "I would like to have the admission of Exhibit D two-twenty-three—an excerpt of testimony given by Andrew Webb on April 17, 1984."

Judge Steiner allowed Ladenburg to read aloud the entire transcript of Andrew Webb's testimony as to why he refused to testify against the St. Pierres. The jury listened carefully, and heard with perfect clarity, Webb's admission that he originally intended to testify "out of vengeance" and "to look good in the public eye."

The defense of Christopher St. Pierre rested. David Murdach, attorney for the one defendant pleading not guilty by reason of insanity, assured the jury that they wouldn't have to go through all those witnesses again. "I am not going to duplicate what has already been presented. I will simply call new and fresh material for you to consider," he said in his opening statement. "You've already heard Dr. Tappin's testimony, and we'll offer the testimony of Dr. Lloyd, staff psychiatrist with Western State Hospital. You might wonder what Western State Hospital has to do with this entire matter.

"During the course of these proceedings," explained Murdach, "my client, Paul St. Pierre, was diagnosed with a paranoid disorder and an almost borderline personality with respect to having psychotic interludes. Because of those impressions, he was found to be incompetent to proceed. When a person is classified 'incompetent,' " Murdach explained, "they send them to a mental hospital, where they are again tested to determine if they are competent, or not competent, to stand trial." Murdach told the jury that the combined testimonies of the doctors Tappin, Muscatel, and Lloyd would explain the fact of mental illness.

"There will be no question after the testimony is

unfolded that my client has a mental illness, a mental defect, paranoid personality, borderline psychotic, and that illness hindered his ability to form the requisite intent on the night of this particular killing."

Following the medical experts who evaluated Paul St. Pierre, Murdach would call Michael Comte, the man who supervised the psychological evaluation on Andrew Webb. "You'll be able to find out what kind of person Andrew Webb is through the eyes of Dr. Comte," he advised the jury. "Then we will call Ms. Gerri Woolf, a probation officer from Pierce County, who will also talk about Andrew Webb and the difficulties he was experiencing from a legal standpoint when this incident occurred. Realizing that we are unable to cross-examine Andrew Webb because his statement was merely read to you, far different than what Christopher St. Pierre underwent, the rigorous cross-examination by the prosecutor. We can't cross-examine Mr. Andrew Webb, we can only . . ."

Carl Hultman, aggravated, objected. "I think counsel has made his point. I think he's arguing." The judge permitted it, and Murdach continued exactly where he left off. ". . . put in these things to show what kind of person Andrew Webb was, and what was going on in his life at the time these incidents occurred."

The jury would hear testimony from pathologist Dr. Cordova establishing that even if Achord was stabbed twelve times, he was already dead from the gunshot. Mr. Donaldson would testify that he saw a man whom he believed to be John Achord acting bizarre and drug-crazed the night of the Rush concert.

"I believe from the evidence you will receive here, you'll far better understand what was going on in everybody's mind," said Murdach. "The mind," and the condition of Paul St. Pierre's on the night Achord was killed, was the essence of Murdach's defense. He immediately called Dr. Lloyd to the witness stand. Lloyd, staff psychiatrist at the mentally ill offender unit of Western State Hospital, confirmed that he examined and diagnosed Paul St. Pierre, and that his findings were the same as Dr. Tappin and Dr. Muscatel. "He is so tenuously controlled," said Lloyd, "that psychosis is highly possible at any time." The basic unchanged diagnosis, said Lloyd, was a "paranoid personality."

Ladenburg had no questions, but Carl Hultman made sure the jury knew that only three days after Dr. Lloyd admitted Paul St. Pierre for an intended ninety-day stay, the patient was discharged.

"He was discharged in three days by other doctors," said Dr. Lloyd, making his disapproval clear. "He wasn't discharged by me."

"And was he found competent by these other doctors?"

"I believe that's what they said," Lloyd answered, and that was all Hultman wanted the jury to know. David Murdach, entitled to redirect examination, said, "Just one final question. You didn't render an opinion that he should be released?"

"No, I was taken off the case," said Dr. Lloyd. When asked why he was suddenly removed, he replied, "You'll have to ask Mr. Griffies, the prosecuting attorney, about that."

Carl Hultman and Judge Steiner were momentarily taken aback, and in their moment of inaction, Murdach launched a series of questions, which, if answered as he expected, would be damning to the prosecution's case.

"Why would you be taken off the case if you saw him when he's admitted to Western State Hospital? What was going on as to why you should be suddenly taken off the case?"

The answer Murdach sought, and the one Dr. Lloyd would potentially provide, was that the chief prosecutor of Pierce County, William Griffies, manipulated the entire process, including the removal of Lloyd, an immediate reversal in diagnosis, and a three-day discharge making sure the brothers would be tried "as one."

"I'm going to object," said Hultman. "I don't think that's a germane issue in this case." The trial, should Judge Steiner overrule the objection, could take a sudden digression, diverting the jury from first-degree aggravated murder to suspicious and/or spurious allegations of prosecutorial misconduct.

Judge Steiner thought it over, then turned to Dr. Lloyd. "Can you answer the question 'Why were you taken off the case?' from personal knowledge?" As all Lloyd had was conjecture and opinion, his testimony came to an abrupt conclusion. Dr. Proctor was waiting in the wings, as was Mr. Alfred Donaldson. Donaldson's testimony would be brief compared to Proctor's; Murdach called him to the stand first.

"I was on my way to purchase a ticket for the Rush concert," testified Donaldson. "This person walked up toward me, muttering total nothingness, very confused as to who he was and where he was. Fifteen minutes later, I ran into him again. He was asking how to find a ticket or something. The ticket office was right in front of him. About forty-five minutes later, he was out leaning against the fence, screaming at the top of his lungs. He was very incoherent. He was talking to himself, spouting off things, screaming, yelling about things that were not in existence around him."

Murdach showed Donaldson a Missing Persons poster featuring John Achord. According to Donaldson, when he saw the poster two days after the concert, he called the Tacoma Police Department. If Donaldson's portrayal of Achord was believable, then Paul St. Pierre's feeling threatened, and acting in what he saw as self-defense, was certainly favorable toward his client.

Dr. Charles Proctor, the clinical psychologist employed at Western State Hospital who participated in the short examination and evaluation of Paul St. Pierre, was quickly sworn in.

"Had you met with him prior to that evaluation when you saw him at Western State Hospital?" Murdach asked.

Proctor replied that he had never seen Paul St. Pierre except one time before writing the report. He further confirmed that the removal of Dr. Lloyd was "unusual"; the evaluation session lasted only forty-five minutes; no tests were conducted; St. Pierre was diagnosed as having mental illness and was deemed competent to stand trial.

☛John Ladenburg had a few questions for Dr. Proctor, and posed them politely. First, he established that when Dr. Lloyd examined Paul St. Pierre, the patient was not on any antipsychotic medication. When Dr. Proctor and Dr. Allison saw him for those forty-five minutes, St. Pierre was medicated. "You see him when he's on the medication that is supposed to reduce that psychosis. Is it surprising then that you don't see the psychosis?"

Proctor acknowledged that the effect of the medication was a reasonable explanation for Paul St. Pierre not manifesting the same behavioral symptoms as he did when examined by Dr. Lloyd. Ladenburg then made sure that the jury knew that the medical definition of competency is different from the legal definition of the same word. "Did you ever do any testing whatsoever to determine whether or not he met the legal definition of diminished capacity or of complete capacity? Did you do any questioning or testing as to that idea at all?"

"I wasn't asked for that," said Dr. Proctor. "I would have to have been given the legal mental-capacity requirement, the specific intent requirement in order to answer that question. I wasn't asked to do any tests, so I didn't do any." Proctor made it clear that his evaluation was not conducted with the question of legal competency in mind.

Hultman's cross-examination was surprisingly brief, during which he asked the doctor to explain the term "defense mechanism of projection," a phrase first brought to the jury's attention by the earlier testimony of Dr. Tappin.

"The term projection refers to the person saying to himself, 'Other people must be like me, I am a tough character, and so other people are tough characters, and I've got to protect myself from them.' Most paranoid personalities exhibit the tendency to 'hit them back' first in a defensive sense. They are ready to protect themselves before a real threat even exists."

"As we have said," summarized Carl Hultman, "they project that kind of aggressive, hostile attitude into the other person, and believe it's coming from the other person, when it's really their feelings toward that person?" Dr. Proctor agreed with Hultman's analysis, and validated that definition of "the defense mechanism of projection."

Proctor stepped down, and David Murdach asked that the jury step out. The next witness, Gerri Woolf, was also important to Ladenburg and disturbing to Hultman. Woolf was from the Adult Probation and Parole Office. A previous "client" of hers, following his arrests for assault, was Andrew Webb.

"What we want to get to," explained Ladenburg, "is Officer Woolf's almost prophetic prediction about the future behavior of Andrew Webb." This prediction arose from the four-page presentence report prepared by Woolf, following Webb's conviction in the three assault cases.

"Another issue, too," Ladenburg added, "is that Andrew Webb obviously lied to his probation officer during the course of that report. He held back all information about his involvement in other criminal activity. These murders occurred during a time when he was in contact with Ms. Woolf, and misleading the court."

Officer Woolf's testimony would establish Andrew Webb as a violent, dangerous liar. Judge Steiner wanted to know how Murdach and Ladenburg planned to get this information before the jury. "Because Andrew Webb is not on the stand," he inquired, "are you going to ask her about his believability or credibility based on the statements he made to her, whether or not those were lies?"

"Right," replied Ladenburg.

"Wrong," objected Hultman. "That's not the way opinion evidence is admitted in this state. Specific instances of fabrication are specifically not admissible in this state. There's no rule of evidence that would permit that admission."

Judge Steiner, however, saw the dog-door-sized loophole through which Murdach and Ladenburg were pushing their argument. If this evidence concerned Andrew Webb's motive or intent in hiding the material facts, then it was admissible. "Is that where we are going here?"

That was exactly where the defense was going. Ladenburg explained, "Mr. Webb admitted having assaulted the victim, and admitted that he slapped the victim, but denied sticking the rifle barrel into Shane's mouth. That incident was witnessed by a police officer.

Webb later denied that to the police, and lied to the police. I think that's important to show he was not truthful in his first case and that he lied." Ladenburg offered Officer Bahr's police report to Steiner as validation of Webb's dishonesty.

"In addition," continued Ladenburg, "Mr. Webb denied all use of drugs and narcotics to Officer Woolf. On the date of Achord's murder, prior to his interview with Officer Woolf, Andrew Webb states that he was using LSD. If Mr. Webb would take the stand, I would ask him, 'Did you tell your probation officer that you didn't use drugs during this period?' He would say yes or no. Then I would be able to show Gerri Woolf and say that he lied about that. He did tell his probation officer he was using drugs, and in fact, he told the police during the statement that he was using LSD."

The judge could see the relationship to the present incident, and the loophole became larger. "In addition to that," Ladenburg said, "the history of Andrew Webb is extremely violent. I think we have the right to portray him as he actually is, and to show how spontaneous his violence is and how heinous the acts are."

Steiner thought it over, and despite the possibility of some "shaky ground," he decided to permit Officer Woolf to testify about Andrew Webb's truthfulness or lying, based upon her investigation, "particularly those that are related to this crime," he said. "I think the question is whether she can, on the basis of her investigation, render an opinion about whether or not he was truthful with her. I think that's a valid question. Bring in the jury."

" 'You motherfucker,' " said Officer Woolf, reading aloud from the police report, " 'tell me where the guns are or I'll blow your fucking head off.' " She confirmed that Andrew Webb denied, despite the eyewitness account of Officer Bahr, that this incident ever took place. She also told jurors that the court sentenced Webb on the assault charges after Damon Wells was killed, but before Andrew Webb was arrested for murder.

"You may step down," said Steiner to Woolf, then turned toward the waiting witness, Dr. Juan Cordova, a physician and surgeon specializing in pathology. In the previous twenty-five years, Cordova had performed up to 800 autopsies on behalf of the Pierce County coroner. He had also conducted autopsies for hospitals when a patient died while a resident.

David Murdach asked Dr. Cordova if he performed an autopsy on the recovered head of John Achord. "I examined the head," Cordova explained, "but there was not an autopsy conducted on the head itself."

After a few preliminary foundation questions, Murdach told Dr. Cordova that there was a debate as to whether John Achord's death resulted from the gunshot wound or the stab wounds. "Based on your examination of the head, and Mr. Achord's shirt, do you have any opinion as to what caused death, or are you able to tell?"

"Well, the examination of the head didn't help me. There is a large pool of blood. There's a head wound with a bullet. There is no blood on the shirt even after the stabbing, so my assumption is—my conclusion is, that the wound to the head was fatal, as far as bleeding out."

On cross-examination, Carl Hultman asked why there was a difference between the witness's conclusion and that of Dr. Lacsina's, also a respected and qualified pathologist. "I have the right to disagree with his statement," commented Dr. Cordova politely, "because it depends on the amount of blood in the person." A discussion of wounds, hemorrhaging, and the influence of the body's position on blood seepage, whether the body was faceup or facedown, occupied many more minutes of testimony. Hultman kept trying to maneuver Cordova into revising his conclusion; all such efforts proved ineffectual and were punctuated by numerous objections from almost everyone except the jurors and spectators. Dr. Cordova was finally allowed to step down, and Judge Steiner informed the jury that they would get a four-day break.

"What we have decided to do," said the judge, "is not have you come in tomorrow or Friday." The witnesses originally scheduled for Thursday and Friday would be moved to Monday, and the entire trial would wrap up with less strain upon the already weary jurors.

"I wish I had been in the courtroom that next Monday," Andrew Webb's ex-wife lamented several years later. "I never knew about the mental tests, diagnoses, explanations, or anything about why my husband was the way he was. Of course, I had been so brainwashed that I thought I was nuts and he was fine. He's a violent murderer, a wife strangler, and . . . Oh, yeah: there's a rumor that he and Paul St. Pierre might have been one of the Green River Killers."

This allegation, buttressed by nothing more substantial than speculation and coincidence, offended even Marty Webb. "I thought it was a horrible thing to say about a member of the family," she said. "This was no secret, whispered rumor. It was blabbed all over to family and friends. Personally, I think it's a bunch of crap. But as for Paul St. Pierre being a likely suspect, I wouldn't be surprised."

"I always thought it was likely that Paul St. Pierre could have been one of the Green River Killers," said Gail Webb. "Paul had a motorcycle, and he used to cruise that Sea-Tac strip all the time. Plus, he had the military training that was part of the profile, and that Green River area was where Paul and Andrew used to hang out, drop acid, get drunk, and that sort of thing. When Paul was arrested, the killings stopped. That might only be a coincidence, but it makes me wonder. One thing I know for sure is that both Andrew and Paul enjoyed hitting and punching people. They liked the way it felt to hit someone. They used to go out to bars looking on purpose to get into a fight so they could beat up someone. They were both really into violence. That's a documented fact."

Knowledge of Andrew Webb's undisputed and fully documented history of violent break-ins, beatings, threats, and irrational life-threatening behavior was something attorneys Ladenburg and Murdach considered imperative to the jury's deliberations. They should have known that Andrew Webb, despite his "Head of the Class" academic achievements in Tacoma's public schools, was seriously severed from acceptable civilized behavior.

"From the neck up, Uncle Andrew was cut off from reality," said his nephew, Travis. "I don't know if the jury heard about the talking dead beaver skulls and the invisible Vikings, but I'm sure that when Mr. Comte testified about how screwy and unreliable Andrew is, he told about when Grandma parked the car on his head."

"The back tire ran over his head," testified Michael Comte. "Actually, one of the tires went over his face, breaking a bone in the jaw. That was not the only head injury he sustained in his childhood. At age seven he came home from school and complained to his parents that his head hurt. Apparently, he experienced a concussion with subsequent memory loss."

Based on this information, Comte suspected that Andrew Webb had some type of brain damage. In 1983, Comte requested that the court mandate a complete mental screening for Webb, the request was granted, and the results were shared with the Achord trial jury.

"The state has to object," insisted Carl Hultman. "This evidence is being allowed in terms of how it impacts the credibility of Andrew Webb, not on his violence of why he may have been involved in a murder. The murder speaks for itself."

Judge Steiner allowed Murdach to continue. Comte explained how he and Dr. Peterson conducted their intensive and extensive evaluations, and then testified as to his impression of Andrew Webb. " 'I want it and I want it now, and I'll do anything to get it, regardless of who stands in my way,' that was the essential attitude of Mr. Webb," said Comte.

"Why," asked David Murdach, "was Andrew Webb placed in the moderate-risk category, especially considering the violence of the assaults?" Comte answered that the strong family support, including that of estranged wife Anne Webb, was the deciding factor. "However," he added, "I felt he had to be contained. I recommended to the court that he be placed in a work-release facility so his movements could be monitored, and that he be required to abstain from alcohol and drugs and that his abstention be verified through urinalysis and breathalyzers."

Murdach knew that the jury, above all, needed to grasp the chronology of events following Comte's evaluations. Careful consideration of Webb's mental and legal situations at that time was imperative. They needed the full picture of Webb's irrational personality, his proclivity toward sudden, life-threatening violence, and a jail sentence beginning in only two days. Webb had to be seen as unreliable, dishonest, and self-serving for the jury to disregard the plea-bargain statement—the only thing linking Christopher St. Pierre to the murder of John Achord.

Murdach continually repeated the dates and sequence of events, which are summarized as follows: April 11 and April 30, 1984, Andrew Webb submitted to the court-mandated psychological evaluations and testing. The results and Webb's interim behavior would determine whether or not he went to prison. Less than thirty days later, May 18, he helped the St. Pierres dispose of John Achord's body.

Because Webb had no apparent criminal history, he received on June 7 a deferred 10-year sentence for the assaults, 700 hours of community service, and 30 days in the Pierce County Jail commencing on June 11. On June 9, Paul St. Pierre shot Andrew Webb, and that was when the story of the murders began to unfold. On June 21, Andrew Webb was arrested for murder, and had remained behind bars ever since that date. He had never served any sentence or been punished for the serious felony assaults that he committed in 1983.

Following Comte's explanation of Webb's antisocial and distressing personality problems, Murdach presented the testimony given by Jeffery Gross, one of Paul St. Pierre's former attorneys, during the Wells trial. The jury heard another example of Webb's contradictory statements and further indications of his unreliability.

The final witness for Paul St. Pierre was Michael ("Mike") Compton, a resident of the Shelton, Washington, Correction Center. He refuted Gordon Gibson's testimony for the prosecution. Compton testified that the conversation between Paul St. Pierre and Gibson, during which St. Pierre bragged about the homicides, never took place. It was, he asserted, a complete fabrication. "Your Honor," said David Murdach, "the defense for Mr. Paul St. Pierre rests."

Prosecutor Carl Hultman was entitled to call last-

minute witnesses to refute testimony for the defense.
"Our expert rebuttal witness is scheduled for one-
thirty," he said. "I guess I could call Mrs. Bitney at
this time." Opal Bitney, John Achord's mother, would
refute the allegations that her son was out of his mind
on drugs, wailing like an animal, and conversing with
the nonexistent. Her son, she would insist, did not
smoke, drink, or use drugs of any kind. Everything
had been progressing smoothly toward closing arguments; then Carl Hultman announced the "secret
identity" of his last-minute "expert witness."

"The trial was close to completion," recalled newsman Chet Rogers, "and suddenly there was a major
battle that put the whole proceeding in serious question. We didn't know if there was going to be a mistrial, the charges dismissed, or what was going to
happen. It was Hultman's last-minute expert witness
that made the situation a real cliff-hanger."

Nineteen

"I move to exclude this rebuttal witness," said David Murdach forcefully, and a few minutes later, he followed with: "I seek to dismiss this case!"

Judge Gary Steiner, hearing the first remark, gave the defense counsel a raised eyebrow. It is not necessary for the prosecution to reveal the identity of rebuttal expert witnesses to the defense. Murdach knew this. He also knew the proposed witness, and the proposed witness knew him. Their relationship, although limited to brief professional interaction, was characterized by antipathy. "He and I don't get along very well," said Murdach. It was a profound understatement; as in truth, one refused to speak to the other.

The proposed witness was Dr. Donald F. Allison, the retired osteopath turned psychiatrist who had replaced Dr. Lloyd for Western State Hospital's quick competency determination of Paul St. Pierre. It was not Dr. Allison's identity or personality that formed grounds for legal objection—it was the simple fact that Dr. Allison, to the best of David Murdach's knowledge, had never been requested to provide a professional opinion on the topic of diminished capacity. As previously mentioned, "competency" and "diminished capacity" are two separate issues entirely.

"And if he was requested to offer such an opinion, or perform such an evaluation, then I seek to dismiss this case," stated Murdach, "for the failure of the state to furnish me with that information." He had strong basis for both objection and dismissal. Steiner took Murdach's reasoning very seriously. The prosecution was required to provide the defense with the names of any individuals having information relevant to the issues involved. If Allison had relevant information, this should have been disclosed long ago. Likewise, if Allison didn't have information on that topic, there was no reason for him to testify. Either way, Murdach's bark was equal to his argument's legal bite.

"I have no objection to Dr. Allison testifying about his investigation into my client's competency, his diagnosis of paranoid personality, and so forth. But then we get into the other area—diminished capacity to commit the crime. Dr. Allison doesn't know anything about the facts of this case. My client never discussed this case with him in the manner he did with Dr. Tappin. Dr. Allison never reviewed the psychiatric data; he never read the police reports; he didn't read Dr. Tappin's report; he didn't read Dr. Muscatel's report; he didn't read Dr. Proctor's report; he didn't even read his own report!" (Murdach was referring to the competency report that listed Proctor and Allison as coauthors. Allison acknowledged that Proctor prepared it, and Allison's secretary read it to him over the phone prior to signing it on his behalf). "And . . . and . . . he doesn't read the newspaper, either," said Murdach, sputtering to a stop.

"I understand your objection," Judge Steiner said. "There is a lack of foundation. I am going to overrule your objection, but I'm going to do it in the presence of the jury. You can object at that time. I want you to spend time now," Steiner told Murdach, "talking to

Dr. Allison in preparation for his one-thirty testimony."

"I previously subpoenaed him to bring his notes to my office," lamented Murdach, "and he didn't bring them, and I'm sure he will not discuss it with me on the telephone. He won't respond to my phone calls."

"David," admonished Hultman, "you can't subpoena anybody to your office. The only power of subpoena is to subpoena him to court proceedings. I don't think you can subpoena anybody to your office."

"Oh, yeah, you do it all the time," countered Murdach. As he was correct, Hultman didn't continue the dialogue. Allison took the witness stand at one-thirty. Questioned by the prosecution, he summarily dismissed the defense's claim of diminished capacity as "ridiculous." Under cross-examination by an aggressive and sarcastic David Murdach, Allison acknowledged that he had heard that the superintendent of Western State Hospital chewed out Dr. Lloyd.

"Did you see anything in the hospital chart that would show that Dr. Lloyd was doing anything wrong with Mr. Paul St. Pierre?" asked Murdach.

"Yes," replied Allison, "Dr. Lloyd called him incompetent and he put him on medication."

"That's the problem, isn't it? He called him incompetent and that's the error he made?"

"That's one of them."

"So you were called in on the case to declare him competent," asserted Murdach. "Isn't that correct?"

"To tidy up the mess, I think, is a better word," said Dr. Allison pleasantly. "Paul St. Pierre was never incompetent." The doctor then stunned the courtroom by flatly stating that diminished capacity was in this case "far-fetched and ridiculous," and David Murdach's use of it in defending Paul St. Pierre was "a smoke screen."

"You're blaming me for bringing a smoke screen in front of the jury, is that correct?" asked Murdach incredulously. He then inquired of Allison's opinion of the diagnostic reference book *DSM-III,* which, by law, Allison must consult. "It was written by a bunch of out-of-work psychologists," he said, adding that the authors "didn't know what they were talking about."

Murdach pinned his hopes of reasonable doubt about the accuracy of Allison's contradiction of Tappin's opinion on the following questions: "Are you board certified as a psychiatrist? Have you ever been board certified as a psychiatrist? Have you ever been a member of a hospital staff—other than Western State—as a psychiatrist?"

The answers were all negative, leaving the jury to choose between the impressive credentials of Dr. Charles Tappin, and the independent opinion of Dr. Allison—an opinion based upon his extensive experience working in the "Criminally Insane Unit" at Western State Hospital since 1973. In that capacity, Dr. Allison filed up to sixty reports per month to various judges on the sanity of individuals facing criminal charges. There was no disputing his experience, or the conviction of his beliefs. With Allison's unique testimony, the case wound to a close. Judge Steiner set aside the following day, Tuesday, for the preparation of final jury instructions, advising jurors that they would be sequestered when they returned Wednesday for the attorneys' closing arguments and for the jury deliberations.

"The most publicized and controversial murder trial in Pierce County history is coming to its climax," intoned newscaster Chet Rogers. "The prosecution and the defense both insist upon justice—each, however, defines that justice differently."

The prosecution envisioned final justice meted out

by the designated executioner at the Washington State Prison. For David Murdach, justice was recognizing that Paul St. Pierre's mental illness, by the laws of the United States of America, made him not guilty by reason of insanity. For John Ladenburg, justice was validation of his firm and unalterable belief that the state's use of Andrew Webb's plea-bargain statement as testimonial evidence against Christopher St. Pierre was a horrific and inexcusable violation of the law, ethics, and the United States Constitution.

The jury would hear each version of justice detailed, explained, and pleaded during the trial's closing arguments. The first to speak, and most emotionally so, was Carl Hultman.

"Ladies and gentlemen, the defendants in this case are murderers. They are killers. There isn't any other way to describe them." With these words, Hultman commenced his closing argument on Wednesday. "They killed Damon Wells, and then they killed John Achord. Worse than that, they killed John Achord to cover up, or keep secret, the killing of Damon Wells.

"The evidence in this case is overwhelming," he insisted. "It's beyond any question. The standard of proof doesn't rise that high." The standard to which he referred, he reminded them, is simply: "Does the state sustain its burden of proof beyond a reasonable doubt?" From the state's perspective, the answer was an absolute affirmative.

The prosecutor paused momentarily, then presented two disquieting displays: the Gerber knife and Paul St. Pierre's .45-caliber handgun. "The state has proved beyond a reasonable doubt that Paul St. Pierre shot John Achord in the face with a forty-five semiautomatic. He admits it himself. The state has proved that Paul St. Pierre, being aware that John Achord was still alive, and at the suggestion of Christopher St. Pierre, stabbed John Achord in the back with that knife."

"Take a look at that knife," Hultman requested. "That's Paul St. Pierre's Gerber knife—the one he called his fighting knife. That's the knife that killed Damon Wells. That's the knife that killed John Achord. That's the fighting knife of Paul St. Pierre."

Jurors' eyes went back and forth between the murder weapon and the accused murderer. Despite the stifling heat and muggy humidity, the courtroom's emotional atmosphere was ice; Paul St. Pierre sat frozen and expressionless. "The evidence is overwhelmingly conclusive that Paul St. Pierre is guilty of this crime, aggravated murder in the first degree. But what about Christopher St. Pierre? That's a fair question. There isn't any evidence that he had his hands on the knife," Hultman acknowledged. "He was an accomplice, and an accomplice is as guilty as the person doing the crime. It's time to start thinking of these two acting as one. They acted as one with Damon Wells; they acted as one with John Achord."

The prosecutor skillfully backed up his "two as one" theory with a well-structured and expertly delivered explanation. "When Chris St. Pierre's attorney tells you his client wasn't part of it, remember that he ran after Damon Wells. He yelled at Damon Wells to shut up. He stabbed Damon Wells in the back. He helped bury him." Hultman continually referenced the St. Pierres as if they were one entity, encouraging the jury to regard them as "twins" who "acted as one."

The only primary source material damning Christopher St. Pierre was the plea-bargaining statement of Andrew Webb. Hultman acknowledged that this singular evidence against the younger brother required "a little more evaluation. Christopher St. Pierre doesn't come out and admit it frankly like Paul does. The death of Damon Wells is evidence in this case primarily because we are alleging that John Achord was murdered to keep that secret. That comes from Andrew Webb's statement: . . . and Chris said we can't get him help. We're going to have to get rid of him, take him up and bury him," the prosecutor paraphrased, "the police are liable to investigate. They won't believe Paul anyway. They are liable to find out about Damon Wells."

Hultman reminded jurors of the undisputed truth that Christopher St. Pierre fully participated in the grisly fate of John Achord. "Did he ever tell the police that he did what he did because he was afraid? No, never. He never said that to the police. He was part of it because he desperately didn't want to be found out for what he had done to Damon Wells. The only way to keep it secret was to get rid of John Achord."

There were two reasons why Carl Hultman continued referencing Damon Wells's brutal death. "It was the motive for killing John Achord," Hultman insisted, "and it tells you something about this defendant; the choirboy here with the blue tie, Chris St. Pierre. Is he that innocent-looking boy that you see sitting there, who just happened to be in the wrong place at the wrong time?"

"Chris St. Pierre, an innocent lad in bad company? That's a complete crock of shit. In fact," Ben Webb later commented, "Chris always said that 'dead is dead'—once someone is dead, it doesn't matter what you do to the body because he can't feel it, he's not alive, he's not there at all. It's just an empty body. It may be disrespectful and impolite to mistreat a human body, but it doesn't hurt the dead person at all because dead is dead. It was the same with Damon Wells as it was for John Achord. Once that poor Wells kid was dead, what difference did it make to Andrew, Paul, and Chris what they did to his dead body?"

"The beating, kidnapping, the murdering; throwing the body off into the bushes," Hultman recounted, "going out and getting it the next day, taking it up and burying it, bragging to people that they buried it so good it wouldn't be found for ten years. That's Chris talking! Is he the choirboy that sits there?"

David Murdach, although not Christopher St. Pierre's lawyer, objected to the "choirboy" characterization. "It's argument, not evidence," said Steiner. Hultman couldn't resist taking another potshot at the St. Pierres. "I don't have any evidence that he really is a choirboy," he said with obvious sarcasm, "so you can disregard that."

"I object," Murdach again complained, hoping for at least some commentary from Judge Steiner, if not a firm reprimand for Hultman. "I won't comment," said Steiner, and Carl Hultman continued.

"Chris St. Pierre is a scared, scared young man. He's a cowardly young man who is afraid of what he did. You can bet it haunts him. It haunts him because he didn't go to the police. Don't let Mr. Ladenburg lead you to believe that Chris is a Good Samaritan who went to the police because of what his brother did, or what Andrew Webb was doing. He just happened to get caught, so he took the opportunity to spill his guts—to describe events as thoroughly as he could without implicating himself, and without implicating his brother." Hultman mocked the assertion that Chris St. Pierre didn't know Achord had been stabbed to death, and reminded the jury of an obscene absurdity: "Guess who else didn't talk about the stab wounds? Paul St. Pierre. What a surprise! Maybe that's because he didn't know about them, either. Of course, that's absurd. If anybody knew the stab wounds were going to be discovered, it's Paul. Why didn't he mention it? Because he would be confessing to premeditated first-degree murder. He stabbed him in the back to end his life."

Refocusing on John Achord's tragic demise, Hultman referenced Dr. Tappin's testimony about the defendant's mental condition. "Paul St. Pierre was a man with violence on his mind. He had his gun out, brandishing it. John Achord can't tell us whether he pulled out his pocketknife, or for what reason. He can't tell us because Paul St. Pierre shot him in the face. That's the paranoia that Dr. Tappin talks about. That's not self-defense. That's not legal. There isn't any defense in the world available for that crime."

Paul St. Pierre was indeed a paranoid personality, agreed Hultman. "The questions you have to answer [are]: Why did Paul kill John Achord by stabbing him in the back? Paul St. Pierre kills people because in his paranoid mind they are a threat to him. Why was Damon Wells killed? The same reason why Achord was killed—Paul thinks he's in danger because he misjudges situations. It is not a rational process by which he makes these decisions to shoot people in the face or stab them in the back."

Lest the jury think the prosecution was offering Paul St. Pierre some mental illness excuse, Hultman immediately said, "Just because he can't control his impulses to kill, and just because he doesn't have good judgment, it's no excuse for what he's done. It's no excuse at all. But killing John Achord to prevent disclosure of Damon Wells's murder was not an act of paranoia," he declared. "It was just plain fear. There is another word for that—cowardice."

The primary character defect of both St. Pierres was, in Hultman's opinion, despicable cowardice.

"That's the constant theme in this case, and it is the constant theme because it started with the way Damon Wells was brutally beat by three good-sized young men. The way they slashed his throat, stabbed him in the back, and watched him bleed to death. It's not paranoia. It's cowardice. They were afraid of being found out. Not paranoia—fear of facing what they did, fear of facing the punishment for this most horrid crime.

"Cowards. That is the only word for them," he said, projecting blatant disgust, "except in this instance there is one other word—murderers." Anticipating Ladenburg's closing arguments, the prosecutor then asked jurors to seriously question the defense's assertion that Chris St. Pierre never knew that John Achord was still breathing. "Andrew Webb said Achord was making a horrible gurgling sound. He was making a horrible breathing sound out of his throat—does that sound to you like something that's barely audible?

"You know as well as anyone that John Achord was alive on the floor, seriously wounded, no question about that. Seriously wounded. Anybody shot in the face with a forty-five is going to be hurt, but he was not dead. He was breathing. They knew he was breathing. Paul admitted to the doctor that he knew John Achord was breathing. That's when he killed John Achord. Is that self-defense? Is it self-defense to stab a man who is so seriously injured with a severe head wound, he's laying on the floor, he's making horrible gurgling noises? Is it self-defense to take this dagger and stab him at least ten times in the back? Mr. Murdach is going to explain to you how that is self-defense, I'm sure. I wish him luck.

"Ladies and gentlemen," he concluded, "they killed John Achord to hide what they had done to him and to keep the police from finding out what they had done to Damon Wells. They are calculating killers. Return us a verdict of guilty as charged."

Hultman stopped speaking, returned to his table, and sat down. The courtroom was dead quiet until Steiner's voice of authority cracked the silent wall. "It's time for lunch," said the judge, and court recessed until 1:00 P.M.

When court reconvened, John Ladenburg stood and addressed the jury. His presentation was flawlessly constructed, and built upon a firm foundation of American law. He focused the jury's collective attention upon their sworn duty, independent judgment, matters of evidence versus inference, and established every logical reason why Chris St. Pierre deserved exoneration, not execution. In short, Ladenburg summoned his full range of admirable professional abilities to the singular task of ripping Hultman's negative portrayal and damning emotional argument into tattered shreds of empty rhetoric.

"I approach argument a little differently than Mr. Hultman," acknowledged Ladenburg. "This is a very serious case, and I can't possibly go through everything that occurred during the trial. I can only try to highlight areas that I think are the most important."

In direct contrast to Hultman's gut-level, go-for-the-throat style, Ladenburg ingratiated himself with the jury by seemingly confiding in them. "I may forget something. There is a danger as an attorney that you live with a case for over a year, and there is really so much evidence in your favor, well . . . I think, 'It's so obvious the jury can't miss it. I'm not going to have to harp on that.' I don't want to bore you to tears," he said almost apologetically, "but after all, Chris is on trial for his life here. I don't want to do anything that would damage or destroy his ability to get a fair trial."

"Ladenburg is so damn affable," remarked Marty Webb later, "the jurors practically wanted to take him home and cook him dinner. 'This supernice guy is doing his best to keep his choirboy client from being wrongfully convicted'—I mean, you could almost hear them thinking that as he gave his argument."

"The most important thing to think about," Ladenburg told the jury, was the entire issue of persuasion: Who is trying to persuade them? What are they supposed to be persuaded about? How do they get persuaded? The answers to those three questions form the very crux of American criminal law, and Ladenburg made sure the jury knew those answers by heart.

"First of all, we have the concept of reasonable doubt. The reason everybody keeps mentioning it is because it is the whole concept of criminal law in our country. It is also what each of you has sworn to uphold. You have sworn," he reminded them, "that you will assure yourself beyond a reasonable doubt that those elements of the crime have been proven in this courtroom, that you will not assume anything."

Jurors slowly nodded in affirmation, aware of the seriousness of the case, and the ominous responsibility of their forthcoming deliberations. This is exactly the response Ladenburg rightfully anticipated. He quietly took aim and fired his first salvo at the prosecution's argument. "Mr. Hultman said, 'Look through the instructions and draw inferences.' Ask Mr. Hultman to read you the instruction that says you may draw an inference in a criminal case. There is no such instruction. It says it must be *proven as fact beyond a reasonable* doubt.

"There are no inferences to draw," said Ladenburg in a more authoritative tone. "There are no assumptions allowed in criminal law. This case against Chris St. Pierre is full of so many assumptions that no reasonable person could find him guilty beyond a reasonable doubt. It is not possible."

If jurors harbored doubts about reasonable doubt, Ladenburg quickly dispelled them by offering the concept's concrete definition. "A reasonable doubt is one for which a reason exists." Simple. If you have a doubt, and you have a reason for that doubt, you have "reasonable doubt."

"A lack of evidence can give you reasonable doubt," he said, and offered a relevant example. "One of the most glaring ones in this case is Andrew Webb's testimony that was presented to you by a written document made in the course of a plea bargain. Then you found out that he made several other statements contradicting that one. Mr. Webb refused to testify. There is a lack of evidence there because there was never an opportunity to cross-examine Andrew Webb."

Ladenburg referenced the tough and demanding cross-examinations they'd seen during the trial, especially that of Chris St. Pierre. "Imagine, if you will, what might have happened if I'd had the chance to cross-examine Andrew Webb on the stand, to cross-examine him about all the contradictory things in his different statements. Imagine what we might have found out."

As for the prosecution's "two as one" portrayal of the St. Pierres, Ladenburg again buttressed his rebuttal with the American legal standard that mere presence at a crime scene does not make someone an accomplice. "You know what else doesn't make you an accomplice of a crime? Being somebody's brother," said Ladenburg. "We don't convict people for being the brother of someone in this country. We convict

you for what you do—for your guilty mind, not someone else's.

"One of the dangers of this case that I warned you
about earlier," Ladenburg said, "was that the prosecution is going to try to tie Chris to his brother so
close that you won't separate the evidence one from
another. Mr. Hultman called them twins, trying to get
you, in your mind, to wrap these two so close that you
won't separate the evidence, that you won't do your
job as jurors."

Chris St. Pierre's previous conviction in the Wells
case could possibly poison any juror's objectivity.
Ladenburg faced that problem head-on, recounting
the Wells case's original chronology, his client's initial
cooperation with authorities, and Andrew Webb's slip-
pery relationship with the Pierce County prosecutor.

"What I don't want you to do is assume that Chris
is automatically guilty of something in this case because of his conviction in the Wells case. Remember
what Chris said to Detective Yerbury when he told
them everything in the Wells case: 'I decided to tell
you all this information to prove that I wasn't involved
in these two murders.' He had no idea that he could
be convicted of the murder of Damon Wells simply
because he was a participant in an assault where another participant killed somebody. Who was that other
participant? Andrew Webb.

"Andrew Webb killed Damon Wells," Ladenburg
stated. "Chris was there and got convicted of murder
for it. There was just one person standing there who
was facing two ten-year prison sentences if anybody
knew about what they did to Damon Wells. Not Chris.
Not Paul. Andrew Webb. The same Andrew Webb who
becomes violent when he thinks people have stolen
anything from him, and becomes even more violent
when he is on alcohol. Who was it that tackled Damon

Wells? Andrew Webb. Who immediately took a knife and slit his throat? Andrew Webb.

"What happened here," said Ladenburg, "was that Andrew Webb, violent, aggressive person that he was, murdered someone before Chris's and Paul's eyes. Then, after Andrew Webb sat there in the pokey for a month, he thought up his story to tell the police and cut a deal. He did. He very cleverly did. I think he may have pulled the wool over some people's eyes here in Pierce County.

"He very neatly got everyone involved—Paul and Chris—by saying, 'Then the St. Pierres each stabbed him once in the back.' Now, however, Andrew Webb tells Mr. Hultman that isn't true. Instead, Webb now admits that *he* threw the knife into Damon Wells's back. Do you think Andrew Webb is saying that just as a favor to the St. Pierres? I hardly think so in light of the fact that Christ St. Pierre is the one that led them to all the evidence and led Andrew Webb to jail to begin with. I hardly think so when Andrew Webb said under oath that one of the reasons he made his original plea-bargain statement was out of vengeance. Why did he have vengeance? Because Chris led them to all the evidence; it resulted in them being charge; it resulted in them facing the death penalty. Andrew Webb made up this statement and got the St. Pierres involved in this thing, and it is not a statement you can believe beyond a reasonable doubt."

As his closing argument's purpose was not the exoneration of Christopher St. Pierre in the Wells homicide, Ladenburg swiftly transitioned to the night John Achord was shot and stabbed. A consistent factor in both homicides, he asserted, was the murderous and duplicitous presence of Andrew Webb.

"Who on the night John Achord was shot had a motive to cover this up? Chris, who believed he was not criminally involved in the Damon Wells killing, but only involved in an assault, or Andrew Webb who not only killed Damon Wells, but was involved in another first-degree assault and was still awaiting sentencing for it? In May, when John Achord was killed, Webb was still awaiting sentencing on those felonies. It was Andrew Webb who had the motive to want to keep things covered up. It was Andrew Webb who had the motive to cover things up, not Chris St. Pierre."

• Throughout the trial, Ladenburg not only gave his client the obligatory "best defense," he vociferously assaulted the very concept that any defendant could be subject to conviction based upon "testimony" given by a "witness" who could not be confronted, questioned, or cross-examined. Ladenburg, and Connelly before him, were drop-jawed with amazement that such an apparent violation of the United States Constitution would be allowed in an American court of law.

Allowed, however, it was. And that meant Ladenburg had to assault the statement's reliability from every possible angle. It also meant that were his client convicted, the odds of reversal upon appeal to a higher court were greatly in his favor.

"You are asked to convict Chris St. Pierre in this case on Andrew Webb's testimony alone," Ladenburg said to the jury. "The law says you should act with great caution. You should not find the defendant guilty upon such testimony alone unless you are satisfied beyond a reasonable doubt of its truth. You can't be convinced of anything Andrew Webb said in this case beyond a reasonable doubt. It just can't be done.

"The first reason you can't believe Webb's plea-bargain statement beyond a reasonable doubt," argued Ladenburg, "is Carl Hultman. I think Carl is a reliable person. He said that Webb told him there

were inaccuracies in that statement." Again and
again, Ladenburg assaulted any shred of reliability
in Webb's plea-bargain statement. Having placed the
entire issue of statements in the forefront of the
jury's collective conscience, he then turned their attention to the statement of Paul St. Pierre.

"Remember, there is an instruction from the court
that says there is one thing you cannot consider with
regard to Chris St. Pierre, and that is anything Paul
said to anybody. Paul's statement that he made to the
police, the statements he made to anybody else. All of
those things that Paul said are absolutely not evidence
against Chris. That's the law. So what are you left with?
You're left with two things: what Chris said about what
happened, and what Andrew Webb said about what
happened."

No matter whose statement the jury believed, Chris
St. Pierre's active participation in the decapitation and
burial of John Achord was beyond dispute. Ladenburg
didn't deny his client's involvement in that ghoulish
and reprehensible behavior. Rather, Ladenburg was
defending Chris St. Pierre against a charge of premeditated murder. "Going out and decapitating the
body is not the crime charged here. It is some other
criminal activity," he acknowledged, "but it's not aggravated murder. It's not murder of any kind. When
you are deliberating as a jury, don't let someone tell
you that Chris's involvement in events that occurred
afterward means that he's guilty of a crime that took
place earlier." A crime, it was often noted, that Chris
believed transpired before he even walked in the door.

His client, John Ladenburg insisted, entered the
residence and saw what he believed was the dead body
of John Achord sprawled on the dining room floor.
Chris saying, "Let's bury the body," the defense reasoned, didn't mean "Let's kill him." Even if the jurors

believed every contradictory word of Andrew Webb's recanted statement beyond a reasonable doubt, what Webb said about Christopher St. Pierre did not prove his client guilty of murder.

The horrific nature of the case, the unsettling, gruesome details, and the often nitpicky nature of thorough cross-examination could wear down the jurors' patience. Eager to "get it over with," a jury might rush to judgment for the sake of their own collective comfort. Not a pleasant thought, but one that trial attorneys must seriously consider and occasionally address.

"You all promised me that you would uphold your oath as jurors, and that you would not compromise to reach a verdict, not just cave in," said Ladenburg, "not say, well, 'This crime is too awful. I don't want to think about it. I just want to go home. I think Paul did something wrong and so therefore Chris did.' Do one of those things that are clearly prohibited in the law, and you will not be able to live with yourself. You will not be able to sleep at night. I think you are the kind of people that want to do the best job you can and uphold the law. That's what we ask you to do."

The law to which he referred precluded relying upon assumptions as proof of guilt. Ladenburg returned to that theme for his well-crafted conclusion. "If you are to convict Chris St. Pierre, there are many things you have to assume. Remember that you are not allowed to assume anything. They have to be facts, not assumptions."

"First of all," he elaborated, "you have to assume Mr. Webb's statement is accurate—that he was a reliable witness—then you have to assume that Chris knew John Achord was still alive. What's the next thing we better assume? You've got to assume Chris said, 'Let's cover up the killing of Damon Wells,' although Webb was the one who actually slit the throat, and the only one with reason to fear Damon going to the police."

Jurors must also assume, Ladenburg advised them, that Chris meant "Let's kill him" when he said, "Let's bury him." And lastly, Ladenburg told the jury that they must assume that Paul stabbed Achord to death only because Chris made that remark, "and not on any other motive such as his own paranoid delusions.

"When Mr. Hultman gets another chance to stand up and shoot down everything I said, or attempts to, I will be very interested to see him tell you why you have to assume all those things. I don't think he's talked to you about the facts. He tried to say that if you can convict Paul, you can convict Chris. That's not the law; that's not the case. He would have you believe that Andrew Webb can be relied upon as proof beyond a reasonable doubt, and that you can't believe Chris St. Pierre."

Ladenburg then offered a unique approach to the Webb and St. Pierre statements, asking the jury to imagine "the tables were turned, and that I was defending Andrew Webb and Chris St. Pierre was the main prosecution witness. I think Mr. Hultman would be jumping up and down about the consistency of Chris St. Pierre—from day one, he told the same story. He never deviated. He told the same story on the stand as he told all along, but my client Andrew Webb has told different stories and changed his mind and lied. Imagine the shoe on the other foot."

Chris St. Pierre potentially faced being found guilty of any of four charges in Achord's death: aggravated murder, premeditated murder, second-degree murder, or manslaughter. "Chris is not guilty," said Ladenburg, "because the only way he can be involved in any one of those is if he's an accomplice. I'm convinced you will come back with a verdict of not guilty for Chris

St. Pierre. I threw so much at you for your consideration in such a short time," concluded the defense, "I know you are going to take time during deliberations to do an honest and good job."

That was John Ladenburg's last word. For Chris St. Pierre, it was now up to twelve King County residents bused down daily to Pierce County. "We'll take a fifteen-minute recess," said Judge Steiner. "We will then hear from Mr. Murdach."

David Murdach—the only qualified attorney with a window of opportunity to defend Paul St. Pierre, the lawyer who respectfully requested that he not be assigned the case, the defender whose client didn't want him—would argue on behalf of Paul St. Pierre.

"It's difficult," David Murdach acknowledged. "I have a client who admits to taking a person's life. I've got a client who's suspicious of me, of the psychiatrists, and globally suspicious of everybody."

"Suspicious enough to kill," Wesley Webb later commented. "I think the way Paul was suspicious of everyone, and the sense of power he got from killing, I bet he would have just kept killing one person after another as long as he could. And the whole time he'd be thinking that he was protecting himself."

Paul St. Pierre's only protection from being hanged by the neck until dead was the final argument on his behalf by someone that he never trusted to begin with—David Murdach.

"My client is a demented individual," stated Murdach. "Dr. Tappin said that Paul St. Pierre suffers from what we call a paranoid personality illness. I admit it has been difficult trying to fit Mr. St. Pierre into the diagnostic manual for psychiatric illness. He is border-line schizophrenic, psychotic . . . There can be a lot of intellectual discussion amongst psychiatrists as to how to classify him, but they all agree that he suffers from a rather severe mental illness.

"This is important," said Murdach, "a paranoid individual is an individual who has difficulty interpreting what is happening around him. In most instances, the interpretation is fear of being persecuted." Paul St. Pierre's perception of the world, explained Murdach, "is one in which he feels there is hostility constantly surrounding him." Indeed, a primary symptom of St. Pierre's mental condition was "a readiness to counter-attack at any threat that is perceived."

"I'm up here acting on behalf of my client, and he even distrusts me. He distrusts everyone. He distrusted the psychiatrists. Dr. Tappin said that Paul St. Pierre sees everyone as a threat—he even thought Dr. Tappin was part of a conspiracy against him. Dr. Tappin said, 'I feel that he comes frighteningly close to the edge—given enough stressful situations, Mr. Paul St. Pierre can become psychotic.'

"Quite frankly," Murdach said, "this case cries out for the sickness which my client is affected with. It cries out for an extreme analysis of what disorder was going through my client's brain at that time. Here is a man who is so paranoid that he goes out and he decapitates a dead man's head! Can you imagine anyone in their right mind doing something like that?

"I have a client who cut off the head of a dead man so they wouldn't find the bullet," acknowledged Murdach. "I have a client who is sick. He's been sick since before the case started. He is sick now. He's on medication. He's been sick throughout these proceedings. He was sick and out at Western State Hospital until the psychiatrist that was treating him was dismissed by the Pierce County Prosecutor's Office. They took the treating psychiatrist, Dr. Lloyd, off the case for no reason and put on Dr. Allison. They put on the retired Dr. Allison to find the man competent. Then take this man from the hospital to the courtroom for trial."

David Murdach's final argument was long, detailed, tiring, and required two fifteen-minute stretch breaks. The length and detail were not due to excessive or needless prolixity. Jurors needed to understand how Paul St. Pierre could be "not guilty" of murder or manslaughter despite having undeniably killed John Achord. The reason, Murdach explained, was that Paul St. Pierre was incapable of forming purposeful intent. Suffering from undeniable mental illness, St. Pierre was further deranged by the mind-altering effects of alcohol and LSD.

"The state is required to prove," said Murdach, "that the defendant acted with premeditated intent, intentionally or knowingly or recklessly—the state must prove beyond a reasonable doubt that the defendant did not have a mental disorder that was interfering with his ability to form the requisite intent."

No acts committed by a person in a voluntary state of intoxication are less criminal simply because the person is intoxicated. "A drunk is equally culpable as a person that's not drunk," Murdach acknowledged, "but so far we have talked about mental disorder, mental defect, intoxication, and drug use—all of these are present in this case. It's not as if we are selecting one from a multiple-choice list. All of these are present in this case. All of them apply."

The issue of self-defense also came under close examination. If jurors didn't believe Paul St. Pierre suffered from diminished capacity, there was still the burden on the state to convince them that there was no self-defense. "The state must prove the absence of self-defense beyond a reasonable doubt," he reminded the jurors. "Put yourself in the shoes of Paul St. Pierre in this circumstance. Imagine a person operating under the influence of LSD, intoxicated, and [who] also has a mental disorder. It's difficult for us to imagine exactly what was going through his mind. All the objective facts in this case say that Mr. Achord had some sort of weapon and was coming toward Mr. St. Pierre.

"We have to deal with both issues in this case," explained Murdach accurately, "diminished capacity and self-defense. The provision that the state must prove the absence of self-defense applicable to first-degree manslaughter, second-degree murder, first-degree murder, and aggravated first-degree murder—it is in all four. It's a complete defense to all the crimes charged."

As the old courtroom saying goes: "The evidence was uncomfortable, and so were the seats." By 2:45 P.M., jurors were dripping with perspiration, clock-watching with anticipation, and nearly fainting from the heat.

"It's hot in here," said Murdach, and no one objected. "It's stuffy in here," he added. Carl Hultman didn't interrupt. "Because of the largeness of the spectator gathering, and ourselves, it's very uncomfortable in here." Judge Steiner seemed to momentarily meditate upon "ourselves" and "largeness." His Honor was very hot under his black robe and was valiantly fighting the torpor created by the oppressive courtroom atmosphere.

Although David Murdach represented Paul St. Pierre, he took time to speak on behalf of Paul's younger brother. "There was a statement by my client that he felt that Chris was in the wrong place at the wrong time. When you look at all the facts here, the truth of that statement is borne out. We have a brother—Chris St. Pierre—who is on trial for a murder he didn't commit. He walked into a room in which a body was laying on the floor. That killing was done by a man who had a severe personality disorder—a mental illness by everyone's admission. The truth in this case is that my client was a severely disturbed individual then, and now. There is no getting around the fact that my client was mentally ill and sick. He did not have the prerequisite intent in each one of these crimes. That's the law—follow the law whether you agree or disagree with that concept.

"We don't punish people out of retribution," concluded Murdach, "we look at each case individually. We don't treat a mentally ill person by sending them to the gallows."

"Thank you, Mr. Murdach," said Judge Steiner. "Mr. Hultman, I'm going to give the jury about five minutes to stretch their legs before we go into rebuttal argument."

Carl Hultman spent the stretch break reviewing his notes, mentally rehearsing the elements of evidence and emotion most favorable to the prosecution. In this final address to the jurors, who desperately wanted to go home, Hultman would verbally assault the combined arguments of Ladenburg and Murdach.

Court reconvened with Judge Steiner saying, "Ladies and gentlemen, rebuttal argument on behalf of the state; Carl Hultman." The prosecutor stood and approached the jury.

"I'm going to be brief," he began. "You ought to retire and bring back the verdict that the evidence commands. Bring back guilty as charged." Obligated to refute the defense's arguments, and do so beyond a reasonable doubt, Hultman took them on one at a time. "With respect to the issue of diminished capacity—just keep this in mind: there isn't any evidence at all that Paul St. Pierre satisfied any test of insanity or not guilty by reason of insanity."

Having a "paranoid personality" wasn't sufficient to

free St. Pierre from intent and responsibility, reasoned Hultman. "Dr. Tappin testified that anybody that would do these things, probably all of them that were involved in this, have some of the same sorts of problems. Use your own common sense. People who go around burying bodies and cutting off heads are bound to be bizarre people, but that doesn't diminish their responsibility for the crime."

Hultman continued his point-by-point rebuttal, attacking Murdach's argument that Paul St. Pierre's mental problems precluded him from forming intent. "What did Dr. Tappin say about Paul St. Pierre? He said he *intentionally* shot John Achord. What did Paul St. Pierre tell Dr. Tappin the *reason* was for stabbing John Achord? It was to kill him! That's not diminished capacity. That's not even close. Paul St. Pierre killed John Achord *on purpose*. He *intended* to shoot him. When Mr. Achord wasn't dead, he stabbed him until he was dead."

Ladenburg's admonitions against regarding assumptions as evidence were countered by reading aloud from Instruction #8: " 'Circumstantial evidence consists of proof of facts or circumstances which, according to common experience, *permit a reasonable inference* that other facts existed or exist.' "

"You're entitled to examine the evidence as a whole," said Hultman, "the way these defendants lived, what they did to Damon Wells—they are totally lacking in conscience. Another pervasive factor common to both murders is an obsessive concern with concealing evidence. They didn't just kill Damon Wells and throw him off in the bushes—they burned their clothes; they cleaned other clothes; they washed the carpet; then they went back the next day and hauled the body off into the woods. They are obsessed with secrecy; that's a fact from which you are entitled to start making inferences."

The first inference Hultman wanted them to make concerned the reliability and veracity of Andrew Webb. "Start making inferences that tell you that there is credibility to what Andrew Webb says," he suggested. What Webb said and Hultman endorsed was that John Achord was killed to further conceal the murder of Damon Wells. "When they tell you that there is nothing to corroborate Andrew Webb's testimony, remember that Paul's own words to his psychiatrist corroborate what Andrew Webb said. Paul admitted that he thought this man was still alive. He was breathing. Paul thought he was alive and stabbed him. He said so, and Andrew Webb said the same thing. This person was still alive."

As he did earlier, Carl Hultman portrayed the stabbing death of John Achord as a concerted action of the St. Pierre brothers. While Achord was "laying there gurgling away on the floor," explained the prosecutor, "Chris St. Pierre said, 'We are going to have to bury him.' Andrew Webb says, 'But he's still alive.' Paul says, 'I know how to take care of that.' That's a concert of action between Paul and Chris. They knew what they wanted to do. They knew what they had to do.

"The defense tells you Andrew Webb is not a believable guy," said Hultman mockingly. "I suggest to you it's a smoke screen. The evidence has cleared the way. There's no fog anymore. You don't need Andrew Webb alone because you've got Paul St. Pierre speaking to Dr. Tappin. Dr. Tappin said—"

Ladenburg interrupted Hultman midsentence with a strenuous objection. "Your Honor, I object! Counsel is aware that statements made by Paul St. Pierre have been directed as 'no evidence.' He's trying to lead the jury to believe that they can use that against Chris St. Pierre—"

It was Hultman's turn to interrupt. "I haven't gotten there, and I'm not going there."

Judge Steiner sighed and simply said, "All right." Hultman, whatever his original intent, only mentioned that there was a "discussion" before Paul St. Pierre stabbed John Achord. "Isn't that what Andrew Webb told you? Isn't that exactly what he told you?

"Ladies and gentlemen," said Hultman with dramatic finality, "the evidence is overwhelming. There is only one verdict you can bring. We live in a civilized society. The rules that we are supposed to live by in this society apply to everyone. They apply to Paul St. Pierre even if he does have a distorted mind. They apply to Chris St. Pierre even if he's too afraid to do the right thing. Ladies and gentlemen, bring back that verdict of guilty."

Judge Steiner gave the obligatory "Thank you very much, counsel" before turning his attention to the alternate jurors. "You are discharged with this instruction: You cannot discuss this matter with anyone until the case is totally and completely finished. You can have no contact with this jury.

"I'm advising the people and spectators," continued the judge, "that they are to have no contact with the alternate jurors or with the jury. Please do not hang around the outside of the courtroom or the County-City Building or in a place of proximity to where the jury is likely to appear, or anyplace where they are eating. Try to avoid all contact."

The jury would now begin a period of complete sequestration. "You cannot have any contact with the outside world," explained Judge Steiner, "no radio, no television, no newspaper. Your deliberations should take place only in the deliberation room. You're not to discuss the case in your hotel rooms or anywhere else. You are to have no contact with anybody from outside. You are not," he again emphasized, "to discuss this case with anyone else nor discuss it amongst yourselves except in the jury deliberation room."

Having endured all day Wednesday, July 31, 1985, listening to closing arguments, the jury of nine women and three men deliberated one hour before retiring to the solitude of their hotel rooms. With no fore-knowledge of when deliberations would conclude, the families of victims and defendants, attorneys, court personnel, and representatives of the press kept an anticipatory vigil throughout Thursday, August 1.

"The jurors reached their decision," recalled Detective Yerbury, "and we were all informed that the verdicts would be announced Friday afternoon, August 2, in the courtroom of Pierce County Superior Court Judge D. Gary Steiner."

The crowded courtroom's principal players and the onlookers waited in high anxiety. The forthcoming legal determinations, the culmination of over a year's worth of continuances and court proceedings, could be condemnations, absolutions, or a combination of both.

Paul and Christopher St. Pierre's parents and siblings were noticeable in their absence, but two female friends arrived to show emotional support. When Judge Steiner read the verdicts aloud, the two women broke into uncontrollable sobs and ran from the courtroom. The Achord family held hands, some weeping quietly; a family friend gave Carl Hultman the thumbs-up sign.

Both brothers were found guilty of first-degree aggravated murder. Paul St. Pierre's only reaction was to glance up at the ceiling; Chris St. Pierre sat bolt upright, then whispered frantically to his attorney. For the second time in twelve months, the St. Pierre brothers faced the distinct possibility of death by hanging.

"I'm so happy it's over," said Opal Bitney, mother of John Achord. "I'm sad for all of us, including [the St. Pierre family], but I'm happy at the verdict." Damon Wells's great-grandmother, Ann Robertson, sat with the Achord family throughout the trial. "At least I know where Damon is, and he won't be hurt anymore," she said. "He is resting in peace."

Judge Steiner intended commencing the sentencing phase on Monday morning, giving jurors the entire weekend off. When Ladenburg and Murdach strongly pressed for continued jury sequestration, Steiner ruled that the new proceedings would begin immediately.

"This verdict will obviously be appealed," asserted John Ladenburg forcefully. As if to demonstrate his determination, and validate his defense arguments, the following morning, Saturday, August 3, he and David Murdach launched combined strategies to overturn the convictions and rescue their clients from the gallows.

Twenty

The sentencing phase, at the outset, followed a predictable course. Mitigating circumstances intended to prompt leniency toward the St. Pierres were presented in an orderly and timely fashion. George and Carmella St. Pierre, the defendants' siblings, a priest, and a schoolteacher with positive memories of Chris St. Pierre spoke on the brothers' behalf. Even Mark Ericson and his father, Bill, testified that Christopher St. Pierre was a valued employee, a likable sort, and a good person. Once these obligatory and unsurprising testimonies were presented, Murdach and Ladenburg went into full-force legal action.

"Your Honor," began David Murdach, "we have an additional exhibit which I propose we introduce, and that is the judgment and sentence of Andrew Webb where he pled guilty to first-degree murder. This exhibit has never been proposed so far in this trial. There was testimony from one of the police officers, but the jurors have never seen the actual document."

Hultman objected. "I don't believe it's relevant." The judge marked the judgment and sentence of Andrew Webb as Exhibit D1-9. "That's admitted," Steiner said. "Now we have two other exhibits, is that correct? Why don't we take those up?"

The two other exhibits Murdach and Ladenburg had included a motion calling for an arrest of judgment and/or a new trial. If Steiner granted the motion, the convictions of Paul and Christopher St. Pierre would be reduced to nothing more than huge stacks of trial transcripts.

"This document," Murdach announced, "lists some of the errors which we claim were committed during the first case involving the St. Pierres." The other document was "a statement to the Washington State Supreme Court enumerating several additional errors which we claim were brought out in the first case."

"The state objects," said Hultman wearily. "They make major and grand assertions about misconduct, and it's not for this jury's consideration." Judge Steiner ignored the objection; Hultman objected more strenuously. "Your Honor, they start arguing about misconduct of the prosecution, including misconduct of the prosecution in destroying evidence!" The "destroyed evidence" was Paul St. Pierre's car—the vehicle towed, stored, and sold by Pierce County. "This court has ruled that the evidence wasn't destroyed. How can the court permit the jury to see a document that alleges that without anybody explaining?"

"Let me tell you my reasoning," responded Judge Steiner. "The question of what is relevant rests in this case purely within the province of the jury. The special sentencing procedure says that the jury explicitly has a right to determine what mitigating factors are relevant."

"No," Hultman snapped, "that isn't the law—"

"In my judgment," said Judge Steiner firmly, "it's out of abundance of caution that I'm going to put it in."

Hultman wasn't giving up or giving in. "Your Honor, now they're going to introduce the documents that they are submitting to the Supreme Court as issues on appeal in the other trial! And that's going to be admitted?"

"Yes," affirmed the judge, "it is admitted." Hultman, incredulous, sat down. The jury returned, court reconvened, and Father Bill Bichsel of Saint Nell's parish, the second priest speaking on behalf of the St. Pierres, took the witness stand.

"I also work with people coming out of Western State Hospital, people with emotional or mental health problems," said Father Bichsel, who had been another occasional visitor of the St. Pierres during their pretrial incarceration. He, too, noticed Paul St. Pierre's paranoia and hypervigilance. Father Bichsel opposed the death sentence, and over Carl Hultman's overruled objections, he explained his reasoning. "The deaths of John Achord and Damon Wells are deeply sorrowful things, and they are tragic. At the same time, I feel that the death penalty is a very vindictive thing. It's a very punitive thing. It no more cures the evils that we struggle with in our society than working for peace while building weapons of destruction. I do not believe the death penalty can be justified. I have my own deep convictions about that. I'd like to say in regard to Chris St. Pierre," he added, "I think Chris's only involvement was being there after the deaths took place, using bad judgment or whatever it is, but I believe that was his major sort of involvement."

Detective Robert Yerbury was now a familiar face to the twelve jurors holding the power of life or death over Paul and Chris St. Pierre. Called as a prosecution witness, Yerbury's integrity and professional knowledge were also utilized effectively by the defense. Un-

der Ladenburg's questioning, Yerbury acknowledged
that police would never have found the knife, the gun,
the bodies, or anything else had it not been for Christopher St. Pierre. He also verified that the defendant
spent from 9:00 A.M. until 11:00 P.M cooperating with
the police.

During David Murdach's cross-examination, Yerbury confirmed the precise sequence of the various
defendants' sworn statements. "Chris gave his statement, Paul gave his statement, and then Andrew Webb
plea-bargained and gave a statement," recounted Murdach. "Does that sound right to you?"

"I wouldn't argue with that," agreed Yerbury. "I'm
sure that is exactly what it was." The detective easily
acknowledged that both Paul and Chris stated emphatically that Andrew Webb chased down Damon
Wells, pulled his head back, and sliced his throat.

"From those statements, obviously, there were two
witnesses that witnessed a crime, saw that Damon Wells
was murdered, and the person that committed the
murder was Andrew Webb. Isn't that correct?" asked
Murdach. Yerbury again agreed.

"Then along comes Andrew Webb and he makes a
statement against these two gentlemen and then a
choice was made, a plea bargain was made, and Andrew Webb pled guilty to first-degree murder with the
possibility of parole?" Yerbury confirmed Murdach's
accurate portrayal. "That decision was made in the
prosecutor's office; you didn't have anything to do
with that?"

"No, I didn't have anything to do with that," said
Yerbury, and he was allowed to step down.

Murdach and Ladenburg, together and separately,
continually reminded the jury of Andrew Webb's manipulations, multiple statements, recantations, mental
instability, and unreliability. Andrew Webb, they essen-

tially claimed, got away with murder. In doing so, he placed the necks of Paul and Christopher St. Pierre in a noose that was rightfully his. Of all mitigating circumstance calling for leniency, contemplation of Mr. Andrew Webb was the most compelling argument.

Carl Hultman, of course, completely disagreed. The state wanted the St. Pierre brothers hanged. That was the purpose of Hultman's final address before the jury, and it was no surprise that he called for the gallows. Perhaps the only surprise was the honest intensity of his emotion. It was as if the entire community's pent-up outrage erupted during his argument.

"There are just no mitigating circumstances to warrant leniency," insisted Hultman in his final presentation. "Who made Chris St. Pierre go out and get that cement? Paul didn't make him do that. Who went out when John Achord was to be buried? Chris—he drove himself out in a separate car. Luckily, he had, because Andrew went into a ditch and they had to move the body from one car to the other. What a bizarre scene that must have been.

"Think of the standard of conduct that these two individuals have for themselves," he continued. "When it came down to the question of the gun being traced, they couldn't just take that gun and drop it in the Puyallup River. They did what they did—it was horrid—digging up John Achord's remains and beheading him. The testimony in this case is just awful. It's horrid what they did to these two victims, and the pain of the families of those victims."

David Murdach had previously called the defendants' mother, Carmella St. Pierre, to plead for her sons' lives. Hultman used her touching appeal for leniency to the state's advantage. "We don't need to call Mrs. Bitney, the mother of John Achord, who got that picture on Mother's Day, the week before he was killed by these guys," he said. "We don't need to call her to testify that she loved him and wished they hadn't killed him. We don't need to call Mrs. Wells, Damon's mother, to tell you the same thing about him.

"You're not a lynch mob, and you're not reacting like a lynch mob," he assured them. "You're instructed to measure and weigh the circumstances. You are to determine whether the circumstances mitigate sufficiently against the charges for which these defendants are now convicted in this case.

"You've convicted these defendants of murdering John Achord in order to cover up the murder of Damon Wells. Two murders. Two murders! What mitigates against that? You've had the evidence. You've heard my arguments before. What have you heard today as mitigating circumstances that balance against the way they descended upon Damon Wells, beat him mercilessly in that bathroom, dragged him out to Salmon Beach, and slashed his throat?

"They're hostile. They're mean. They hurt people. They don't obey the rules of society," snapped Hultman, spitting out unpleasant appellatives as if the words themselves soured his tongue. "What did they do to John Achord? He's shot in the face; then they had to stab him! Paul had to stab him in the back to kill him. Two deep stab wounds, each capable of producing death—as Damon Wells received—wasn't enough that night. What does Paul do? He puts twelve of them in this man's back. What did you hear today that mitigates against that?

"I mean, my God, you don't even hear an assertion of being repelled by what they were doing from either of them. Nothing! They cut off the head of poor John Achord so Paul could keep his gun! We heard a lot of short testimony this morning from people caring about Paul and Chris—family members, a priest—but you know what you didn't hear? Did any of these witnesses say that they ever heard Paul and Chris acknowledge that what they did was wrong? Where did you ever hear them say that they were sorry for what they did to John Achord and Damon Wells?

"Your judgment is somewhat difficult, but it's clear," said Hultman in conclusion, "there are no sufficient circumstances here to warrant leniency. Thank you."

Judge Steiner immediately called upon David Murdach. He cut to the heart of the issue in his opening paragraph. "This part of the proceedings is most difficult for an attorney—having the responsibility of trying to address twelve people to decide whether your client lives or dies.

"If you were to sentence these defendants to death, and that sentence is carried out, and Andrew Webb comes up and says, 'It wasn't true. It didn't happen that way. I lied a third or fourth time,' do you want that responsibility?"

Murdach then subjected jurors to a vivid depiction of the conditions at the Washington State Penitentiary. He described Paul St. Pierre being repeatedly beaten and raped by unruly motorcycle gangs, as well as making references to the stench from open toilets that permeated the sweat-soaked bedding upon which inmates sweltered in Walla Walla's unrelenting 100+ degree heat. Life in prison was a repetitive, noisy, painful, excruciating punishment exceeding the pangs of death itself.

"If you sentence him to death, are you comfortable enough with your decision that you would attend the execution," asked Murdach. "Death is decisive and not retrievable. To execute Paul, you would have to decide that he has no right to exist. Death is final. There is no appeal." Murdach then reminded the jury that the prosecution must prove beyond a reasonable doubt that there is a lack of mitigating circumstances. "The defense does not have to prove any mitigating factors. The state must prove a lack of it." The state, Murdach insisted, had proved absolutely nothing regarding a lack of mitigating circumstances. "And your only verdict," he concluded, "can be the decision that Paul St. Pierre should receive life in prison without possibility of parole. This is not a lesser punishment, but a very serious long-lasting sentence that will be forever imposed on Mr. Paul St. Pierre. Thank you very much."

After a short recess, John Ladenburg made his final plea for mercy on behalf of Christopher St. Pierre. "Mr. Hultman glided rather quickly through the purpose of this hearing and the instructions that the judge has given you. Really, he stood here and brought up the most horrible things he could think of, and asked for vengeance and nothing more."

Countering Hultman's emotional outrage, Ladenburg calmly quoted the first lines of Instruction No. 3: " *'The defendant is presumed to merit leniency.'* I think Mr. Hultman didn't talk about that because the defendant does not have to prove the existence of any mitigating circumstances, nor the sufficiency of the mitigating circumstances. Mr. Hultman said, 'Well, I see there are some mitigating circumstances,' but now he says, 'They're not *sufficient* mitigating circumstances.' " Ladenburg reminded the jury that the defendants could be sentenced to life in prison without any mitigating circumstances being proved by the defense. In fact, the defense didn't have to prove anything—the burden of proof was on the prosecution.

One of the eight recognized examples of mitigating circumstances is extreme mental illness. "Paul is an extremely sick person," acknowledged Ladenburg. As for his own client, Christopher St. Pierre, the law also states that another mitigating circumstance is if the defendant's participation in a murder committed by another person was relatively minor. In other words, if Christopher St. Pierre was not the man with the gun or the knife—were he not the prime mover—that qualifies as mitigating circumstance.

Once again, Andrew Webb's special circumstances were highlighted when Ladenburg said, "The man who committed the first murder is going to be released probably in twelve years, and Chris may never get out for the rest of his life, or he may be put to death.

"The decision here is really the choice between two horrible futures—the future of waiting on death row for a hangman's noose, or a future of sitting in the state prison for the rest of your life.

"We are above retribution for a crime. It does no good to bring forward the pain and anguish of the various families involved here. It does no good to drag that up and throw it out to the jury. It's a horrible circumstance, but it is not one of the facts for making decisions in this case.

"These men will be punished for the rest of their lives. They will virtually have no lives. I ask you not to put Chris to death."

If the jurors were impressed, Hultman remained untouched. "This murder is far more heinous and serious than any other murder. Paul St. Pierre's illness is that he's obsessed with guns and weapons. He strikes out at innocent people, who bear him no ill will, at random, [and] with great violence, death—he kills because he suspects other people. That's his illness. He values his gun to the point—and Chris shares this value with him—to the point of going up and beheading John Achord."

Hultman, in his final rebuttal, asked the jury to take a good look at Paul St. Pierre. "Look at the face, and look at those eyes—after shooting John Achord, he went into Mr. Perez's room and said, 'Come on, Mark, you ought to come out and see this.' What kind of illness is this? His illness doesn't cut against a severe penalty."

Damon Wells and John Achord were two totally innocent young men whose lives were snuffed out, Hultman told them. He again directed the jury's gaze to the defendants. "They did it. They did it for no good reason other than violence. They seem to like violence. They seem to glory in it. The only thing they are sorry about is that they got caught."

There would be no more arguments, rebuttals, evidence, or pleadings. The trial and verdict were over. Only deliberation on sentencing remained. "You may now retire to deliberate your verdict," said Judge Steiner. "The verdict forms, instructions, and exhibits will be brought to you."

In less than two hours, the jury from King County reached their final decisions in the life-or-death matter of Paul and Christopher St. Pierre.

August 5, 1985

Paul St. Pierre, for the first time in months, actually smiled. His brother and he would not be hanged. The sentence: life in prison with no possibility of parole. The jury's verdict was binding, and Judge Steiner would make it formal on September 6. St. Pierre thanked David Murdach for his fine defense, and Murdach promptly submitted a bill to the Department of Assigned Counsel for 300.25 hours at $40 per hour. Between May 20 and August 5, 1985, David Murdach had earned every cent of that $12,465.38. He had a sick client who didn't trust him, a dreadful crime of incredible emotional content, and a prosecutor's office, in his opinion, continually crossing the lines of professional ethics. The case was ugly, tragic, and took an emotional toll on the attorneys, judges, witnesses, and jurors.

"It was a horrible crime. It was an awful crime," commented juror Helen Hammond. "It was a crime no one could imagine that a human being could commit. We felt that anybody who would do something like that is not normal. The majority seemed to think that [Paul St. Pierre] had a mental disturbance. That was the mitigating circumstance that kept the jury from imposing the death penalty."

Opal Bitney, mother of John Achord, regretted that his killer would not be punished by the hangman's noose. "I don't know how gruesome a murder has to be before they give them the death penalty," she said sadly.

According to juror Michael Spilila, there were two or three jurors who were adamantly for the death penalty, and an equal number against it. "Since we had to have a unanimous verdict, there was no point going any further."

William Griffies, the Pierce County prosecutor, expressed pleasure with the trial's final outcome. When a jury decides either the death penalty or life in prison with no parole, he said, "You have obtained the ultimate deterrent—the defendant will never be able to offend again." A strong advocate of the death penalty, Griffies acknowledged the higher costs of a death penalty case. "But that doesn't mean that we should not have a death penalty. We definitely should. I think society wants it. Recent polls show, I think, seventy to eighty percent are in favor of the death penalty."

On September 6, 1985, Judge D. Gary Steiner issued

the formal sentencing of life in prison without parole. Griffies, as chief prosecutor, celebrated his office's victory over Murdach and Ladenburg. The state won the verdicts, but Murdach and Ladenburg saved their clients' necks. One week after the formal sentencing, September 11, everyone was back in the courtroom. The issue at hand was John Achord's head.

September 11, 1985

The medical examiner's office retained the head of John Achord and his clothing for over a year. The state asked that the head be turned over to either the funeral home or John Achord's relatives, but David Murdach, after consulting his client, objected to any physical evidence being destroyed or moved from its current location.

The defense's reasoning was neither complex nor unnecessarily adversarial. Dr. Cordova had performed an independent examination of the head and then testified for the defense. If the head and shirt were removed from evidence, and should something happen to Dr. Cordova, the defense would have neither witness nor evidence for another pathologist to examine.

Individuals unfamiliar with the American legal system may question the defense's need for witnesses or evidence when the defendants were already convicted and sentenced. If the cases suffered from significant errors in legal procedure, erroneous rulings by the court, or violations of the United States Constitution, the convictions could be overturned, the defendant(s) freed, or new trials granted.

"The question is," summarized the judge, "in the

event of a new trial, how would you present defense
testimony with respect to a pathological report?"

"That's the problem," confirmed Murdach. Ladenburg didn't mind releasing the remains. "We only objected to the clothing being destroyed."

The medical examiner's office wanted both items removed from the freezer. If Murdach or Ladenburg
wanted further examination of either item, "they can
still have them done, but they ought to have them done
right away and then the items can be removed, and the
remains of John Achord can be properly taken care of."

At length, after continued discussions of the freezer,
the shirt, and Mr. Achord's head, David Murdach
turned cranky. "If the prosecutor's office wants to destroy evidence," he said heatedly, "they can do what
they bloody want with these two items!" Murdach
warned Hultman that such destruction could be contrary to his client's rights.

"I think you're missing the point, Dave," said Carl
Hultman. "We're giving you the opportunity—"

"Let me finish," Murdach's voice slashed through
Hultman's attempted explanation. He then directly
addressed the judge. "If he wants to do whatever he
wants to do, he doesn't have to seek this court's permission. He doesn't need your permission. He's asking
you to sanction his moves and I don't think that's appropriate.

"The way this thing is being presented to you,"
stressed Murdach, "you would think that the freezer
is eight inches by ten inches. I've been in the freezer!
It is huge. They roll bodies into it. There's no problem. That shirt is probably bundled up in some
butcher paper in a corner of the freezer!"

Hultman, his patience exceeding that of his courtroom adversary, suggested that Murdach take a mo-

ment to actually read the medical examiner's memo.
The defense counsel snatched it up off the table.

"This memo states, *'We're extremely short of freezer
space. We need to clean it out and make it available for body
storage. Achord's head and several items of clothing belonging
to Mr. Achord are taking up that part.'* I know of no other
item that they're keeping other than the shirt. We
don't want the pants. If they have the pants, we don't
want them. We just want the shirt. That shirt with the
stab wounds and the presence of blood!"

The judge swiveled his head toward Hultman's corner and awaited the responsive volley. He didn't have
to wait long. "There isn't any contest about the stab
wounds—he's got twelve stab wounds! The fact is that
the evidence is there. The shirt has been available
since June 19, 1984, and we're now at September 11,
1985!" Hultman addressed his next comments to the
court. "If defense counsel has any concept of representing his client, or that this is an issue that has some
relevance to his client's future representation, he
ought to take steps now to do whatever else he thinks
needs to be done on that shirt, and we'll give him
three or four weeks if necessary. But," said the prosecutor sternly, "he is on notice that we want to get rid
of it for the reasons stated by the medical examiner's
office."

When enough was too much, the judge made comment. "The court appreciates the courtesy and caution of the medical examiner and the prosecutor in
presenting the matter to the court," he said. "The
court will order that the shirt not be destroyed, but
be maintained in refrigeration for a period not to ex-
ceed thirty days to allow defense counsel, if they wish,
any further examination. As for the head, just maintain it for a period of thirty days to allow further examination."

"I see a problem here," said John Ladenburg. "I think we're going to have to ask for some chemical analysis of the shirt to protect our clients' rights, and we may have an objection from the Department of Assigned Counsel paying for those tests when, in fact, no trial is scheduled in this matter." The court kindly authorized payment of reasonable costs; the judge then looked down at the two silent St. Pierres, convicted killers whose only audible contribution to the afternoon's proceedings was the occasional metallic clatter of waist chains, handcuffs, and leg irons.

Paul and Christopher St. Pierre, the court was informed, remained indefinite residents of the Pierce County Jail because The Department of Corrections refused to transport them to the state penitentiary, or other correctional facility, until the proper paperwork was completed.

"In this instance," commented Hultman, "they're pretty noneffective. Normally, these reports are prepared for the purpose of advising the parole board with respect to minimum term options." For the St. Pierres, the minimum term was until death.

For Paul St. Pierre, gone were delusions of adequacy, let alone grandiosity. Violent outbursts and overt attempts at intimidation earned him only enforced isolation. St. Pierre's mental and emotional condition deteriorated exponentially in twenty-four-hour segments. Strong in body, weak in mind, and life threatening in attitude, his mental illnesses manifested themselves in argumentative outbursts alternating with downward spirals of depression.

The impassioned courtroom discussions of his mental condition and possible future behavior were now irrelevant rhetoric reduced to officially stamped trial transcripts stored away in cardboard boxes somewhere in the Pierce County Courthouse. The best perceptions of medical experts converged on one inescapable reality: Paul St. Pierre's future was all used up.

On Sunday, October 13, 1985, Paul St. Pierre entered the Intensive Management Program at the Washington State Corrections Center in Shelton, Washington. The term "intensive management" precisely describes this specialized unit's purpose and function—every individual is closely monitored, and never alone, at least not longer than fifteen minutes. According to Veltry Johnson of the Corrections Department in the state capital, St. Pierre was under "close observation."

On October 14, 1985, Paul St. Pierre committed another act of senseless violence. While there was never an official version of events released to the public, the predominant story is that St. Pierre shoved feces-filled toilet paper down his throat. For many, such behavior by Paul St. Pierre was not surprising.

The Mason County Medic 1 Team administered cardiopulmonary resuscitation, but their valiant efforts failed. Paul St. Pierre, transported by ambulance to Mason County General Hospital, was pronounced dead within the hour. His strange death, announced Veltry Johnson, had "the appearance of suicide."

"I don't believe he committed suicide," commented Mark Ericson several years later. "You see, I think Paul could have handled life in jail. It was Chris that I was more worried about. I heard that Paul had marks on his body that the coroners overlooked. He supposedly beat up a guard, and that was the real reason that he was in that Intensive Management Unit."

Roy Kissler also doesn't believe the "suicide by toilet paper" allegations. "I just have never heard of anybody committing suicide that way. To my understanding, I thought he got into a physical conflict with a guard right after he got up there. He was in solitary at that point in time. There's something weird about his death. He was in solitary lockup by himself while they did their evaluation, so he's not in any of the other population. The guards are the only ones that I think have access to him. So much of what we hear is rumor and hearsay. Even the stories we all know about Paul get confused and changed. For example," Kissler explained, "there was a guy named Mikey Green. And Paul showed him the corpse of a black guy that he had shot out in Spanaway, in a mobile home. Had him in the back room. Blanket over the corpse. And Mike was there and Paul said, 'Come on. I want to show you something.' Shows it to him and said, 'Tell anybody about it and that's what you're going to look like.' That just messed with the kid's head big time. Then one day I hear the story being told, except it isn't about Paul and Green, it's about Paul and someone else. Not that it's a big difference, but which of the two stories of the same event are true? I mean, that's what the big deal was about the statements during the trials—which statement, which version, is true? Or, which parts are true? So I really doubt if I've heard the whole story of everything that Paul St. Pierre did in his short, sad life. Just in what I've heard, there is the possibility of at least a half a dozen murders. Even with all that—even him being a murderer and out of his mind—and despite me having thought of putting a bullet in him myself at one point, it was still a tragedy for his family when he died, especially to die in a gross way like that."

Paul St. Pierre's funeral was both traditionally reverent and understandably uncomfortable. Mark Ericson, Chris St. Pierre's former employer, attended the somber event. "I didn't stay long. I went to the funeral out of respect for Mr. and Mrs. St. Pierre. Were it not for them, I wouldn't have gone. Chris was there, escorted and handcuffed, to pay his last respects. I

Twenty-one

Paul St. Pierre's death aborted his appeal, but Chris St. Pierre's appeal moved ahead. On June 17, 1986, John Ladenburg requested the court appoint a cocounsel to assist him in the appeal's preparation. "The appearance of fairness," said Ladenburg, "may be violated if cocounsel is not appointed." Fairness became a serious consideration, recalled newsman Chet Rogers, "because John Ladenburg had officially become a candidate for Pierce County prosecuting attorney. He was running against Bill Griffies in the next election." The court appointed Bertha Fitzer as cocounsel on July 21, 1986.

In the first week of November 1986, Bill Griffies was voted out of the prosecutor's office. Chief Deputy Prosecutor Chris Quinn-Brintnall and Carl Hultman now worked under Chief Prosecutor John Ladenburg. Christopher St. Pierre understood the problem of having the chief prosecuting attorney involved with his appeal and strongly requested that John Ladenburg no longer be involved. The Pierce County Prosecutor's Office agreed.

"I probably wouldn't have handled the appeal personally even if I hadn't won the election," Ladenburg later commented. "At that point in my career, I wasn't

doing many appeals. The excellent defense attorney
Bertha Fitzer was first assigned as cocounsel; then she
assumed full representation. She appealed Chris St.
Pierre's conviction to the state supreme court."

Although there was a precise time frame for filing
the appeal, the appellate court allowed Fitzer an
added measure of grace. "That's because I was pregnant with my son," recalled Fitzer. "That's one reason
I remember it so well."

Her brief on behalf of Christopher St. Pierre cited
numerous reasons why his convictions should be overturned, and/or a new trial granted. "Chris St. Pierre
did not murder either of the two victims," stated Fitzer
factually. "Nonetheless, based on the statements of Andrew Webb, who pled guilty and then refused to testify,
Chris St. Pierre must spend the remainder of his life
in prison. His brother Paul also gave statements to the
police. Admission of these statements assured that
Chris St. Pierre would be convicted. Yet, Chris had no
opportunity to test the truthfulness of these statements
by cross-examination. Because admission of these
statements violated Chris St. Pierre's right to confront
witnesses against him, and for other reasons, Chris St.
Pierre's convictions must be reversed."

Among the other reasons cited for consideration by
the state supreme court were:

1. Violation of his right to a speedy trial.
2. The improper refusal to sever his case from
Paul St. Pierre's.
3. Appearing before the jurors in leg irons
tainted his right to an impartial jury.
4. Admission of Andrew Webb's plea-bargain
statement was improper.
5. Admission of Paul St. Pierre's statement was
improper.

6. The prosecutor's conduct, before and during the trials, was reprehensible and improper.

7. Evidence of the decapitation of John Achord, which occurred days after the murder, should not have been admitted.

8. Evidence relating to the manner in which Damon Wells was killed was not admissible against Chris St. Pierre.

9. The spectator outburst of "Bullshit!" during his testimony denied him a fair trial.

10. The judge should not have allowed the prosecutor to amend the information in a capital case immediately prior to the case going to the jury.

11. There was not sufficient evidence to convict Chris St. Pierre of aggravated murder.

"Chris St. Pierre, Paul St. Pierre, and Andrew Webb were the only three people present when Damon Wells and John Achord were killed," said Fitzer. "Each gave statements about the events, but only Chris St. Pierre chose to testify." In doing so, St. Pierre was subjected to rigorous cross-examination by Carl Hultman. Neither Andrew Webb nor Paul St. Pierre's testimony—the sworn statement—were subject to cross-examination.

The United States Constitution provides that "in all criminal prosecutions, the accused shall enjoy the right . . . to be confronted with the witnesses against him." The constitution of Washington State contains an equivalent, and perhaps stronger statement: "The accused shall have the right to meet the witnesses against him face-to-face."

"One cannot imagine a more explicit requirement than face-to-face confrontation," noted Fitzer. This requirement assures three fundamental safeguards: one, it insures that the witness will give his statement under oath; two, it forces the witness to submit to cross-examination; three, cross-examination permits the jury to observe the demeanor of the witness, thus aiding in assessing his credibility.

Perhaps the most disturbing aspect of the Wells and Achord trials, in Fitzer's opinion, was the behavior of the Pierce County Prosecutor's Office. "Repeatedly publicizing the case, baiting the witness, making sarcastic comments during the defendant's cross-examination, commenting on the defendant's right to remain silent, and drawing from evidence in the Wells trial to prejudice the jury in the Achord trial" were among reasons Fitzer cited in requesting the supreme court's intervention.

"Hultman, and his former boss, William Griffies," she said to the state supreme court, "seem to measure their devotion to duty, like the prowess of the savage, by the number of their victims. This attitude is not only unseemly in a prosecutor, it is impermissible."

The Washington State Supreme Court upheld Chris St. Pierre's conviction for the murder of Damon Wells. "Admitting the statements from Paul St. Pierre and Andrew Webb did not deny Christopher St. Pierre his Sixth Amendment right of confrontation," wrote the supreme court, "since Christopher St. Pierre's own statements established his guilt for this crime."

Judge Waldo F. Stone, the man who had presided over the Wells trial, was perfectly pleased with the court's decision. "Nothing has occurred in the last five years to alter my previous recommendation of life in prison without parole. The defendant participated in two brutal murders. The only mitigating factor was the fact that the defendant's brother was the prime instigator and this defendant played more of a follower role."

On July 26, 1989, the Washington State Supreme

Court ruled in favor of Christopher St. Pierre, reversing his conviction in the murder of John Achord. "Andrew Webb's statement pertaining to Christopher's alleged involvement in the slaying of John Achord did not have sufficient indicia of reliability," wrote the supreme court, "and its admission in that case improperly denied Christopher St. Pierre his Sixth Amendment right to confrontation. The conviction for aggravated murder is reversed."

The supreme court's ruling was perhaps more a victory for the American Constitution than for Christopher St. Pierre. His conviction and life sentence for the murder of Damon Wells remained irrevocable. So did the heart condition with which he was born and the multiple sclerosis that revealed itself during his incarceration.

When the latter disease became increasingly manifest, Carmella and George St. Pierre retained attorney David Zuckerman on their son's behalf. "Chris has heart problems, and he also has multiple sclerosis," confirmed Zuckerman. "That's part of the reason that the family is so eager to litigate these issues over his precise release date, because, you know, they want him to get out while he can still walk."

By the time Zuckerman began representing Christopher St. Pierre, any attacks on the convictions had run their course. "We're looking into the legitimacy of the sentence that the parole board gave him. You see, there are certain things that are unique to Chris's case and certain things that are common to everyone under parole jurisdiction. Back when Chris was convicted, everyone convicted of a felony murder—if they had been good—got a parole hearing after thirteen years and four months. Then, in 1989, they changed the rules on everybody. We don't have a parole system anymore. We have determinate sentences, which I think is a much . . . a far superior system to the parole system, that everyone gets a definite sentence based on certain tables and guidelines. So then the question is: what do we do with guys like Chris St. Pierre who committed their crimes back at the time when we had a parole system?"

According to David Zuckerman, they gave them the worst of all worlds. "The minimum term gets recalculated under the sentencing reformat. It is much, much longer than thirteen years four months for almost everybody, and then you still don't get out. When you've done that lengthier term, you're still just a parole prisoner at the whim of the board. Even after you've done this lengthy minimum term, the board can still keep you in prison."

This controversial policy of indeterminate incarceration was taken to the state supreme court and was upheld 5 to 4. Then it went to federal court, and the federal court judge threw it out. "But then it went up to the Ninth Circuit Court of Appeals, and two out of three of the judges on that panel upheld it." Christopher St. Pierre's sentence remained indefinite, indeterminate, and subject to extension, termination, or neither.

While in prison, Christopher St. Pierre drafted a letter of apology to the family of Damon Wells. Forbidden to contact the Wells family directly, he asked David Zuckerman to track down the victim's mother and/or siblings. Zuckerman's efforts also were to no avail. The undelivered letter written by Christopher St. Pierre on November 15, 1998, reads as follows:

I want to begin this letter by first saying how sincerely sorry I am for my actions that contributed to your son's death. There hasn't been a day in my life since that evening, nearly fifteen years ago, that I haven't thought about it, regretted it, and wished that none of it had ever happened. I often look back and try to understand how the events of that evening escalated to the point where Damon was killed.

I am not attempting to excuse my actions or the role I played in this senseless crime, but I swear I honestly never expected or intended this to occur. Still I know that is probably little or no consolation to you. How can it be, compared to the enormity of the pain, anguish, suffering and loss I have caused you and your family? I realize that this changed the course of your life and that of your family life forever. Again, I am so sorry for this and would do anything I could if it were possible to change it.

You're probably wondering why I'm writing and expressing this now. Well, I talked with and listened to a woman whose daughter had been murdered, and the man responsible had never apologized. This further compounded the trauma and suffering because she wanted to at least hear the man say he was sorry and take responsibility. I know why I did a very similar thing to you and your family. At the time of my trial, I was thinking of nearly no one but myself. I was fixated on the plea-bargain the prosecutors made with Andrew Webb, who I saw as the worst offender. With some time to think things over in prison, my perspective changed. But I still said nothing because I could not even find words that could be adequate to reconcile or lessen the damage I have done to you, your family and my family as well. I know even now what I am saying is not enough to express the level of remorse, sorrow and shame I feel for what I did, but I feel that I should at least try.

I am sending this to you through an attorney, who may use an investigator to try to find you. Both of them are under instructions not to reveal your address or phone number to me or my family. If you wish to respond to this letter you can do so through the attorney. Whether you respond with anger, hatred, outrage—or perhaps forgiveness—I'm willing to listen.

Sincerely & respectfully,
Christopher St. Pierre

David Zuckerman expressed understandable amazement at Andrew Webb, and the unorthodox arrangement made with him by previous Pierce County prosecutor Bill Griffies. "Chris was actually the first one through the door, and most of the prosecutors that I'm used to dealing with will value that. If one defendant comes in and gives a complete confession, and fully cooperates before he even has a lawyer, and before he's even pushing for any kind of deal for himself, that is something that typically they want to encourage and reward. It sends a message that "this is the way we want people to behave—this is what gets rewarded.

"In this particular case," elaborated Zuckerman, "they punished that behavior, and rewarded the guy—Andrew Webb—who wouldn't say a word until his lawyer made some cushy deal for him. What kind of message does that send? It sends the message 'Don't tell the truth, don't confess, don't cooperate with the police, but make sure that you get everything you pos-

sibly can, and get it promised to you first before you
say anything.' "

John Ladenburg, Christopher St. Pierre's former
defense lawyer, issued an official statement concerning
the Webb incident, and did so in his new capacity as
Pierce County's chief prosecutor. This admission of error was read aloud at a special hearing in the state
capital in December 1999.

"The purpose of that hearing," said Anne Webb,
"was to decide if Andrew could leave prison early, you
know, for being so wonderful, spiritual, and reformed.
My former father-in-law, Lowell Webb, gave a real impassioned plea, saying how much his son had changed
since 1984."

"I see a wonderful change in a person, and it's a
pleasure to go and hear him talk," Lowell Webb said
to the clemency board. "I can understand why people
who have been discipled by him have changed so dras-
tically and have become better citizens because of that,
and I believe he would be a greater blessing on the
outside than he is on the inside."

Andrew Webb, according to his father, was a beloved
son with whom he was pleased. Lowell saw Andrew as
one who transcended his former identity as cold-
blooded killer and was now a fountain of spirituality.
His son was a man whose love changed lives, redi-
rected destinies, and showered spiritual blessings upon
the discipled and undiscipled alike.

From a more practical standpoint, Andrew Webb
could help his father live out his final days in relative
ease. "I've had surgery just recently myself," said Lowell Webb, "and they found colon cancer, and it's been
quite a challenge here."

News of Lowell's colon cancer was equally challenging for his children. "When Mom died," said Gail, "I
felt a sense of release for her. I was happy that she

would find peace at last. The news about Dad being ill devastated me. I cried and cried more over his cancer than about Mom passing away."

"I have other children," Lowell Webb told the clemency board, "but they have families, and it's difficult for them to break away from their family and help. So that's why I believe that Andrew would be so much greater benefit on the outside than he will be on the inside under the conditions that he would be a great asset to me."

Don Garrett, volunteer chaplain for fourteen years at the Washington State Prison, also spoke on behalf of Andrew Webb. "I've known Andrew Webb only in prison," he told the clemency board. "I don't know anything about him before that. I can tell you I've never met a finer young man. I have sons that are older than he, and I wish that they were like him. I've watched this young man grow in those surroundings, terrible surroundings, but I've watched him grow to be a terrific young man. I could go on, and I could sit here for the next two days talking about Andrew Webb. You won't find a finer young man. I would give him anything that I have. I would give him my checkbook, my car keys, and you name it. As I said, I don't know what he did before, but I know what he is now. He's a fine, upstanding young man with high integrity."

The most emotional and dramatic entreaty for clemency came from Pepper Black, Andrew Webb's new girlfriend. "I'm very closely and intimately involved with Andrew," she confessed. "He is a man of character and honor and integrity. Andrew murdered someone, he killed someone, and that's a matter of record, and Andrew's taken full responsibility for that. He's never denied it. Andrew is reminded of what he did every single day of his life, and Andrew has paid for that. He's paid fifteen years. He's taken responsibility for this and he feels horrible about it. Andrew gave me my sanity back," Black declared, but didn't elaborate. "Andrew reaches past the walls of the prison and he impacts and influences people's lives in a way that just amazes me. I realize that Damon's family is here, and I know that they're hurting, and I cannot imagine being where they are today. But I speak for Andrew in saying that an apology, and I'm sorry, will never take the pain away from them, will never remove that hurt, will never remove that loss, and it won't bring Damon back. But who Andrew is and what he will do and who he's become will make an incredible difference in honor of that."

The families of Damon Wells and John Achord remained unimpressed by Black's unstinting praise for the marvelous character and personality of Andrew Webb. "God only knows what manner of nonsense Andrew fed her, what lies she's swallowed, or what shallow duplicity she's accepted as spiritual depth," said Anne Webb. "What really amazed me more than poor Pepper Black falling for his crap was the Walla Walla prosecutor almost wetting his pants over what a fine chap this Andrew Webb had become."

Gabriel Acosta, the chief deputy prosecutor for Walla Walla County, spoke glowingly of the convicted killer. "He has done whatever he can within the system to make himself a better person. I understand that for the last several years the prison has been recommending that he be paroled, and that he's rehabilitated. I have no hesitation as a prosecutor," Acosta asserted, "in saying that he is a changed person from the murderer that he was. I don't say this lightly because of my position."

When Acosta completed his heartfelt endorsement of clemency for Andrew Webb, Gerald Costello spoke.

Costello, administrative assistant to the chief prosecutor of Pierce County, did not share fellow prosecutor Acosta's rosy view of Webb's character. Speaking boldly and authoritatively, Costello held nothing back. He revealed Webb's numerous manipulations and deceptions, beginning with Nellie Sanford's night of terror.

"They caught him on the spot, retrieved the weapons, and he was facing trial," explained Costello. "In January of 1984, before he killed Mr. Wells, he pled guilty to two counts of second-degree assault, and he was out on bond, and sentencing was put off until later in 1984. While out on bond, he murdered Mr. Wells. Then, on May eighteenth, he helped the St. Pierres dispose of John Achord's body, who had just been murdered. On June twenty-first, he was arrested for murder, and he's remained incarcerated ever since."

Costello then hit home his primary point: "He has never served any sentence. He has never been punished for the serious felony assaults that he committed in 1983." It seemed as if his emphatic statement had difficulty penetrating the clemency board's consciousness. He reiterated it several times until it gradually sank in. "He has escaped to this day any punishment for those felony assaults, and the story continues, of course. He strikes this plea bargain with the state of Washington. Now, bearing in mind, of course, that he was involved in two different homicides, and as the board is well aware, he strikes a plea bargain, and it was a mistake. I'm here to acknowledge publicly that it was a mistake for the Pierce County Prosecutor's Office to trust Mr. Webb to testify, and to give him the benefit of his bargain before he testified. It is a lesson that we have lived with to this day, and it is talked about in our office to this day. We will never do that again."

Costello reminded the board that Webb "violated his bargain, a solemn bargain with the state. Integrity has been discussed. It's been said that Mr. Webb has great integrity, but he clearly did not. In the face of a court order that he testify, he ignored that court order and wouldn't do it.

"Mr. Webb was the beneficiary of his own manipulations and of the state's stupidity," said Costello, "and yet those who receive the detriment are the Achord family and the Wells family, and there's never been justice for the Achord family at all. The jury convicted based on the written statement of Mr. Webb that was introduced into evidence. The supreme court reversed those convictions, and there will never be justice for the Achords, and I lay that at the feet of Mr. Webb.

"The way that we see it in our office is that he has already received a significant, substantial amount of leniency based on charges not being pursued that could have been pursued, and based on his own manipulations in receiving that leniency. The state views it this way," concluded Mr. Costello, "that to this day Mr. Webb has not suffered punishment for felony assault, which had been ordered by the court. Number two, he has received the benefit of his bargain, and the state has not, the people have not. Most importantly, no justice for Mr. Achord's murder. To those who suggest that we should only focus on the present, on what kind of a person Mr. Webb is today, I say that Mr. Webb's actions have resulted in a situation where justice will never, never be fully served. He should not receive clemency. He's already received more benefit from the state of Washington than he was legally and morally entitled to receive."

Damon Wells's brother Sean agreed completely with Costello. Speaking tremulously, Sean Wells bravely revealed his own pain, and that of his entire family. "In the last fifteen years, I've chosen not to deal with it," he said. "I just buried all my feelings and my hurts, and when my mom told me that Andrew Webb was going up for a clemency hearing, I didn't know what to do. And just to hear all the stuff that Webb has done, and to serve only thirteen years or fifteen years or even twenty years is not right. It just ain't right!"

Referring to Lowell Webb's entreaty on behalf of his son, Wells said, "His father gets to see him three days a week. We don't get to see Damon ever at all. I just hope that you guys just consider the Wellses and the Achords." Sean Wells then held up Andrew Webb's statements. "This is the first time I've got to look at this. . . . He tries to make my brother out to be a criminal! 'Was the victim known to you?' 'I knew Damon indirectly. I had prior knowledge that he had burglarized my friend's house.' That ain't right! That ain't right! Here he's turning everything around. And it says here on his letter asking for clemency: 'I was denied parole for no reason.' No reason? He killed my brother! They talk about how good he is. The chaplain says he gets to watch him grow. Well, my mom and dad watched Damon grow until he was twenty years old. That's it. He also said that he doesn't know a finer young man," stated Sean Wells. "Well, you're looking at a finer young man. In my opinion, I don't think Andrew Webb should walk the face of the earth again as a free person, and breathe the same air as we breathe, or be around our children. I just ask you, please," he begged in conclusion, "just don't consider letting him out."

Brandon Wells also spoke, adding his plea to that of his brother. "I can't see letting a murderer out, a vicious murderer. If he's doing so good in there, and helping out in there, then maybe he should stay in there and continue to do what he's doing in there, because he's not going to be doing no good out here."

Gail Webb agreed, although she didn't share this opinion with the clemency board or her siblings. "If Andrew was doing so well in prison, and doing so much good for the Lord, then he was right where he was supposed to be. Let him stay there and do some good, because God only knows what Andrew would be doing on the outside."

The clemency hearing brought Gail back together with her sisters and brothers. It was there that she asked pointed personal questions concerning her siblings' alleged incestuous relationships. "I questioned my younger sisters about Andrew or one of my other brothers doing things with them, and she confirmed it. Figures. I have one brother who, if you ask me, still has a problem with inappropriate touching of women, and another I bet would freely acknowledge being a sex addict. I hate to say it, but it's true—despite our mother's love and efforts to protect us, and not solely because of Dad's beatings and hollering, we all grew up in a maelstrom of domestic violence and abuse. This is very ironic because our folks honestly loved us, and honestly loved the Lord. A lot of pain and misery came from the children drinking alcohol and taking other drugs, too. Andrew and I were once really close. We could communicate on a deep level on any topic. Then, when the beer became a lifestyle instead of an occasional beverage, and LSD didn't mean Luke, Samuel, and David, then it was as if someone drilled a hole in his head, removed his common sense, then sucked the sense of shame right out of his heart."

"My son was shot in the head," said Opal Bitney. The clemency board, unfamiliar with details of the

Achord case, sat silently spellbound as she told the dreadful tale. "He lay conscious, unconscious I pray, on the St. Pierres' floor, till they all three—Webb, Christopher, and Paul—decided what they would do with him, whether they would take him to the hospital or murder him. And can you imagine anyone laying, having to listen to your murder being planned like that? Believe me, I think about it. Anyway, they stabbed him either thirteen, my son, either thirteen or eighteen times. They took him up, the same place they had buried Damon. They buried him, but their hole that they buried him in wasn't big enough, so they jumped on his legs and broke his legs so he'd fit in their hole. They go home and wait for a while, the St. Pierres and Webb. So they decide that maybe with this bullet in John's head would identify them. So they go get an ax and go up there and cut my son's head off after he's been buried. They bring it down in Tacoma. They dropped it in a five-gallon bucket of cement, and dropped it off the bridge into the Puyallup River. I know Webb was involved in all that. Anyway, it took us two months to get part of my son buried. Just part of him. Took two more months for Tacoma Mountain Rescue to find John's head in the bay so we could get the other part of him buried. It took us four months getting him buried, and a lifetime that none of us will ever forget. I can't see Andrew Webb having any mercy because he was involved in John's death, and he did not mention that to anyone, not the governor or you."

When Opal Bitney left the hearing, Gail Webb followed her out. "I wanted to talk to her, tell her how sorry I was for what she went through. We had a short chat. She told me that during the trials she could see that my mom wanted to talk to her, but mom just couldn't bring herself to do it. Mrs. Bitney said that she would have welcomed it."

The last person offering an opinion to the clemency board was, once again, Pepper Black. In what was literally a last-minute appeal, she said that she had only recently found out about the murder and decapitation of John Achord.

"Andrew, just the last couple weeks, told me about the second murder that he was involved with indirectly. When Andrew wrote and said he was a part of the murder, Andrew felt that because, because this young man was still breathing and he didn't take [him] to the hospital, he felt like he contributed to the murder. Andrew did not stab him. Andrew was not there when they buried the young man. The St. Pierre boys had taken him up on the hill. Andrew had been stuck in a ditch and he was waiting for a tow truck at that time. He had no part in dismembering this young man, nor did he have any part in jumping on this man and breaking his limbs. That was completely the sole responsibility of Chris and Paul St. Pierre. Andrew was not there. And when he wrote that letter saying that he contributed to the murder, I want to make it very clear it was because he felt that because he was still—he was still breathing, that he felt that he should've done something else. I also would like to remind everyone that Andrew was a victim as well," she said, referring to the morning Andrew Webb was shot. "When Andrew walked in Paul's home, he was about ready to shoot another man. We've been trying to get hold of this man so that he could come and testify today. I have not been able to get hold of him. He's in the witness protection program, but Paul St. Pierre was going to kill him, and Andrew walked in and just said, 'Man, you've got to stop killing people. You just cannot go around shooting people.' And so Andrew stepped in and got in front of Paul St. Pierre, and this man ran from the home, and Paul St. Pierre then shot Andrew for intervening, shot Andrew to kill him. The only thing that saved Andrew's life was the fact that he was wearing tight pants." With that, Black sat down.

"I make a motion that we recommend to the governor that the petition be denied," announced a board member. The motion was seconded, the votes taken, and the motion carried. Andrew Webb would not receive clemency. He returned to his cell at the Washington State Prison. He will be eligible for a parole hearing in the year 2005.

𝕍 In retrospect, and despite his manipulations and duplicity, refusing to testify may have been Andrew Webb's one moment of loyalty—loyalty not to the St. Pierres, but loyalty to his father's unwavering standard of honesty. Lowell Webb hated liars. To him, a liar was the lowest life-form. To Andrew Webb, the next lowest creature was a snitch.

"Our sister once snitched on Andrew," recalled Gail. "She told on him to Dad about something. Because of that, Andrew did not speak to her for three years. The idea of him being a snitch was abhorrent. He knew he killed Damon Wells all by himself. He slit the kid's throat; he threw the knife into Wells's back. It was Andrew who did those things, not Paul or Chris St. Pierre. Sure, Andrew made that deal, or his lawyer did, with the prosecutor's office when Andrew was furious with Paul for shooting him, and mad as hell at Chris for rolling over and ratting out everything to the cops. But he could not, and would not, take the stand and be both a liar and a snitch. I think he figured that Paul St. Pierre would be put in a mental institution and that Chris would get some punishment for going along with everything. Andrew didn't keep his word to Griffies about testifying against the St. Pierres, and that self-justified violation may be his one selfless and ethical act of loyalty and honesty. Dad hates liars, and loyalty is a top priority for all us Webbs. Andrew ended that nice kid's life out of selfishness and fear—not fear of Paul St. Pierre, but fear of being locked up. Once being locked up was the reality, the only things he had to fall back on were family, faith, and the power of the Holy Spirit. Damned if he was going to add disloyalty and dishonesty to his list of grievous sins."

"Family loyalty? Honesty? Integrity? Who's this we're talking about? Andrew Webb, my ex-husband who talked to dead beavers, throttled his bride, shoved rifles in people's mouths, and slit an innocent boy's throat, is trying to get sole custody of our kids—and he's in prison! You know what he told the judge? He said that he was in prison for killing a burglar who broke into our home. Damon Wells wasn't a burglar, he never broke into our home, and I made damn sure that the judge knew exactly why Andrew was in prison."

Anne Webb devoted fifteen years of fidelity to Andrew Webb. In all that time, she said, there was no evidence whatsoever that her beloved husband experienced any alteration other than waist size or inseam.

"He's no different today than he was the night he forced his way through Nellie Sanford's back door," she insisted. "He's still out to get what he wants; he's still loaded with ammo. Instead of bullets, it's bullshit. He's got everything a convict needs—big black lies, little white lies, and a few lines from First Corinthians. A changed man? Let me tell you something, the man quoting Second Timothy is still the *first Andrew*. The only thing that's changed is that he's had more than fifteen years' experience as a convict. That's fifteen years to learn new ways to con people, and the new words, new justifications, and new tools to do it with.

Some people change for the better, some for the worse. No one ever said about Andrew Webb what they said about Christopher St. Pierre—no one ever said, 'I can't believe a nice kid like that would wind up in prison.' "

Mark Ericson, Christopher St. Pierre's former employer, could never comprehend his young friend's involvement in the Wells and Achord homicides. "I have a hard time reconciling the Chris I knew—a bright kid with a good future—with the man who stood there watching Damon Wells die," he said. "I just can't imagine anyone doing that stuff. I can't comprehend it."

Over the years, Christopher St. Pierre called Mark Ericson several times from the Corrections Center in Shelton, Washington. Ericson accepted the calls, and the two former friends shared superficial conversations. "Then one day Chris called," said Ericson, "and I just had to say what I had on my mind, ask what I needed to ask."

Ericson's revulsion for the deeds, the deaths, the decapitation, and the overwhelming horror of the crimes found expression, and he asked Christopher St. Pierre how he could live with himself, how he could sleep at night, knowing what he had done to those innocent victims. " 'Fuck them,' " snapped St. Pierre, according to Ericson, " 'fuck them both. They're dead. I'm alive, and I'm the victim here.'

"That was the last time I talked to Chris. He called again, but I never accepted the charges. He's not the same anymore. He sees himself as a victim, and in some ways, he is. Prison does that, I guess. It makes victims out of people either for real or in their own minds. Being in prison doesn't do nothin' much for those in there, maybe, except harden the heart."

Marc Ericson paused and looked off toward the open doorway through which Christopher St. Pierre walked for the last time on that sunny summer morning in 1984. Focused beyond the sunlit exit, past the rental house where Damon Wells was beaten, John Achord murdered, and a nameless girl with pink tennis shoes tearfully begged the boys to let her go home, Ericson's inner sight watched the intervening years pass over like a flight of birds. It was as if the unspeakable remained unspoken, the dreadful deeds undone; June 1984 best remembered as thirty temperate, uneventful days pleasantly spiced by honest work and casual conversations with a nice guy in white coveralls—a likable lad from a fine family "right here in the neighborhood."

"He was a good kid, Christopher St. Pierre . . ." Ericson said, but his comment's conclusion remained unspoken. The phone rang; a customer came in. Mark Ericson tugged on the battered brim of his baseball cap and got back to work. "Sometimes," he remarked a few minutes later as he wiped his hands, "well, sometimes there's just nothing more to say."

Afterword

Damon Wells and John Achord didn't lay down their lives protecting America's interests overseas, nor did they die on the battlefield defending the right to vote in a free democracy. Had they fallen on foreign soil as two servicemen sacrificed for an altruistic principle or popular political opinion, all America would mourn their loss.

Neither Damon nor John was of military fabric or of mettle suited for the armed forces, fire fighting, or law enforcement. Previous physical injuries precluded such careers. They wore no uniforms, carried no weapons, and had no enemies.

Achord loved driving fast cars, and driving cars fast. A traumatic brain injury suffered in an auto accident ended his days behind the wheel. Wells preferred the ocean to asphalt, imagining himself a nautical man. An injured spleen, also the result of an auto accident, confined Damon's world-embracing vision to the Port of Tacoma.

No gold watch awaited Wells or Achord for years of exemplary employment; no offsprings' accomplishments offered them old-age bragging rights. Damon's and John's worldly achievements—the ones of least lasting value—are contained within the phrase "the two innocent victims."

Life, including death, appears incomprehensibly unfair. Time heals all wounds except the fatal. Scars of the heart seldom fade, and comforting the bereaved is a temporary social obligation.

A natural desire for simplicity and certitude tempts us to sanctify the innocent and demonize the guilty, burying the depth of our pain in the shallow "It was God's will."

"What my Uncle Andrew did to Damon Wells was not God's will," insisted Travis Webb. "God's will is, simply put, the Golden Rule. Treat other people the way you would like to be treated. God's will is love and unity, not beatings, beheadings, and homicide. I can understand why people would want to just not think about why these things really happen, and we all want the easy explanation and the sound-bite solution."

There are no explanations for the inexplicable, reasons for the irrational, nor justifications for injustice. If an immediate answer is urgently imperative, fabrication is sufficient. Anne Webb, for example, needed to know why her husband strangled her. In response, her mother-in-law provided a quick, convenient, and entirely fictional answer validated by its immediacy alone. The truth, detained by time-consuming investigation, often arrives late, unwelcome, and rebuffed.

If we do not search out the truth, and strive to understand what made Andrew Webb a killer, we do disservice to Damon Wells's sacrifice. If we fail to consider the factors that contributed to the ghoulish treatment of John Achord, we make a mockery of his previous heroic recovery.

Jack Olsen, my friend and fellow author, once said, "Any true crime book that doesn't try to explain how and why the killer behaved the way he did is pornography." This book is not pornography.

Recent scientific research indicates that hypervigilant, overly suspicious, and anger-driven violence devoid of guilt or remorse—what experts define as psychopathic behavior—are primary symptoms of an incurable brain disorder. An individual is either born with this severe defect or it is acquired as the result of a serious head injury, especially when aggravated by sexual, emotional, or physical abuse.

Childhood beatings, for example, interfere with the proper development of the hypothalamus, which regulates the body's emotional and hormonal systems. An excess of the hormone noradrenaline or low levels of the brain chemical serotonin may cause violent responses to imaginary threats.

Physical damage to the brain may mark the difference between a person who occasionally turns his pent-up violence on family or friends, and someone, such as Andrew Webb, who turned his anger loose on strangers. The additional presence of intoxicants, narcotics, mood-altering drugs, and stressful interpersonal dynamics in the household increase the possibility of psychopathic behavior.

The foundation of all current knowledge on the topic of psychopaths and their behavior is based upon the extensive research—over thirty years—of Dr. Robert Hare, author of *Without Conscience*. It was he who first delineated the relationship between psychopathy and crime, and defined psychopathic behavior.

According to Dr. Hare, psychopaths are "social predators who use charm, manipulation, intimidation, and violence to satisfy their own needs. They are found in both sexes and in every society, race, culture, ethnic group, and socioeconomic level." Although small in number, their contribution to the seriousness of crime, violence, and social distress in every society is grossly out of proportion to their numbers.

Psychopaths can readily be identified by qualified clinicians utilizing the Hare Psychopathic Checklist. "Clinicians are not the only ones in the mental health and criminal justice systems who need to make critical judgments about patients, offenders, and suspects," said Hare. "Many others, including prosecutors, law enforcement officers, hostage negotiators, parole and probation officers, social workers, correctional officers, therapists, and case management personnel, routinely evaluate and deal with individuals with [the] potential of being psychopaths. In many cases, the accuracy of their evaluations and judgments will have serious consequences."

He and his colleagues have also addressed crucial questions regarding the defining features of the disorder. Among these are repetitive, casual, and seemingly thoughtless lying; apparent indifference to, or inability to understand, the feelings, expectations, or pain of others; defiance of rules; continually in trouble; persistent aggression, bullying, and fighting; a complete lack of conscience.

Just as the color blind cannot experience red, blue, green, or yellow, a person without conscience cannot experience empathy, sympathy, compassion, remorse, guilt, or shame. "Psychopaths," said Dr. Hare, "have no anxieties, doubts, or concerns about being humiliated, causing pain, sabotaging future plans, or having others be critical of their behavior."

Comte & Associates noted that Andrew Webb showed no emotional connection to his assaults, and that there might be something wrong with his brain. They also stated that Webb was unlikely to feel guilt or remorse for his deeds. Even though he knew the difference between right and wrong, legal and illegal, such knowledge did not deter Webb in the least. Andrew Webb showed no remorse or shame for killing Damon Wells; he only showed anger and resentment at Christopher and Paul St. Pierre.

The senses of guilt, shame, and remorse (penitence) are not the same. Guilt is feeling bad about what you have done. Shame is feeling bad about what you have not done—the actions not taken, the standard not attained. Remorse, or penitence, is a combination of emotions. Philosopher Adam Smith considered it the most dreadful of all sentiments. He described it as "made up of shame from the sense of the impropriety of past conduct; of grief for the effects of it; of pity for those who suffer by it; and of the dread and terror of punishment."

There is no "terror of punishment" for the psychopath—except perhaps an understandable aversion to the death penalty; reprimand is a waste of time; penitentiaries never teach them penitence. Incarcerated psychopaths reinforce each other's lack of remorse, virtually assuring that any expression of heartfelt shame and regret is more show than sincerity, more performance than penitence.

Fear of punishment is not the primary reason "normal" people don't commit horrid acts, such as the murder and decapitation of John Achord or the slaughter of Damon Wells. "Most important perhaps is the capacity for thinking about, and being moved by, the feelings, rights, and well-being of others," stated Dr. Hare. "There is also an appreciation of the need for harmony and social cooperation, and the ideas of right and wrong instilled in us since childhood."

Traditionally, it is religion that cultivates a conscious awareness of morality and ethics. The moral/ethical content of one's deeds is nurtured and reinforced by religion's morality-centered philosophy. In the Webb household, however, God was cast against type.

The nine Webb offspring would sing "Jesus loves the little children, all the children of the world" while having the unshakable conviction that God was hell-bent on sentencing those children to eternal damnation. Thus, the Webb children found themselves caught in the relentless grip of an all-loving God turned despotic dictator—a deity as irrational and jealous as Dolores Armstrong Webb's father. Sadly, this religiosity instilled more despair than dedication, more fear than faith.

Fear, according to human behavior specialist Dr. H.B. Danesh, is the primary component of all violence. Violent aggressors, he asserts, are afraid of everyone and everything, most especially themselves. Andrew Webb was constantly afraid that people were stealing from him, and Paul St. Pierre was continually paranoid. Irrational fears acted upon with anger and violence are, as previously noted, symptoms of both congenital and acquired psychopathy. Although there is no known cure, all cases of acquired psychopathic behavior are preventable.

Prevention of severe head injuries—the primary component of acquired psychopathy—is a primary objective of the Brain Injury Association (BIA). Founded in 1980, it is dedicated to creating a better future through brain injury prevention, research, education, and advocacy. This is done in part by providing information, support, and hope to family members, by increasing public awareness of brain injury, planning for the development of services for persons with brain injury, and developing programs aimed at its prevention.

The association's HeadSmart Schools Campaign, along with the Brain Building Basics and Changes, Choices, and Challenges programs, encompasses a

wide variety of activities, from elementary school cur-
ricula to antiviolence initiatives. BIA also reaches a
wide spectrum of professionals with its "education
first" mentality. Conferences and symposia designed
with the practical needs of attendees in mind take
place locally, nationally, and internationally. From physicians and rehabilitation specialists to trial lawyers,
educators, and pharmaceutical representatives, no
need or desire is overlooked. A variety of public figures frequently appear on BIA's behalf, including BIA
chairman and former presidential press secretary
James Brady; actors Beau Bridges, Cameron Bancroft,
Joan Collins, and Ben Vereen; sports heroes, such as
football legend Frank Gifford, former NHL player
Brett Lindros, and former Olympian Jim Beatty.

The Brain Injury Association's forty-seven state associations offer detailed information about a variety
of specialized resources within particular regions
across the country. The national toll-free Family Help
Lines that directs callers to appropriate and geo-
graphically accessible physicians, therapists, attorneys,
and other professionals, as well as peer and family support groups, is 1-800-444-6443.

Accidents involving motor vehicles, bicycles, motor-
cycles, and school sports were once the primary
sources of traumatic brain injury (TBI). Shifts in our
global American culture, however, are now presenting
us with a broader and more insidious primary cause
for brain injuries: violent behavior, including child
abuse, such as shaken infant syndrome and injuries
caused by domestic violence. Researchers have found
that the head is indeed a primary target in domestic
attacks against women and the effects of these batter-
ings can result in cumulative brain injuries. Women
who care for survivors of TBI are a high-risk group
for this kind of acquired brain injury due to sudden

outbursts of violent behavior by the person for whom they care.

Violence is a major cause of brain injuries in the United States. Brain injuries are a significant risk factor for the subsequent development of violent behavior. Prevention efforts must focus on the reduction of both violence and brain injuries.

Dr. H.B. Danesh, author of *A New Perspective on Violence,* asserts that nonpsychopathic violence is symptomatic of an underlying social disease—disunity. "Violence exists when unity is absent," says Danesh.

Noting a parallel between violence and illness, Dr. Danesh urges the adoption of the same preventative strategies against violence that one would utilize to acquire or maintain optimum health. Distrust, competition, self-centeredness, inequality, injustice, separation, and disunity are all, notes Danesh, "fertile grounds for the development of violence."

Lifestyles, families, and societies encouraging and demonstrating the exact opposite of these violence-fostering characteristics may be our most powerful weapon in reducing violence-induced head injuries—the number-one component of acquired psychopathy.

Reducing physical violence and encouraging greater safety precautions in sports, cycling, and motor vehicle operation do not address the other aggravating factors of psychopathic behavior. New brain-imaging techniques, such as MRI and PET scanning, have shown neuroscientists that adolescence is a period when the developing brain is vulnerable to traumatic experiences, drug abuse, and unhealthy influences.

In the scientific journal *NATURE,* researchers presented evidence that part of the reason teenagers aren't good at risk-taking is that the brain isn't fully developed. Risk-taking leads to accidents—the primary cause of death among adolescents—and nonfatal traumatic brain injury.

Craig Harris at the University of Massachusetts Medical Center in Worcester asserts that adolescent experiences can determine how people will behave for the rest of their lives. Bullies, for example, are easily created. According to Harris, if you place an adolescent hamster in a cage for one hour a day with an aggressive adult hamster, it will grow up to become a bully who picks on smaller hamsters; when faced with a hamster its own size, it will cower in fear. Once again, research confirms that fear is the underlying component of aggression. "All bullies are cowards" is simply another way of stating that all bullies are filled with fear, whether they be schoolyard bullies, political dictators, or violent sociopaths.

"If the environment provokes or encourages aberrant behaviors, those behaviors become the norm," said Jordan Grafman of the National Institute of Neurological Diseases and Stroke. We need only look at the inappropriate sexual norms experienced by Dolores Webb and the consequences of those experiences on her own children to validate Grafman's remark.

The massive amounts of alcohol consumed by Andrew Webb and Paul St. Pierre certainly did them no good. Research at the University of North Carolina recently tested the sensitivity of the adolescent brain to binge drinking. The results, published in the November 2000 issue of *Alcoholism: Clinical and Experimental Research,* advanced the hypothesis that this damage is a component of alcoholism.

So overwhelming is the task before us—preventing acquired psychopathic behavior—that it calls for nothing less than a turnaround at the deepest seat of our social consciousness, a new vision in which realization of our essential unity is absolute and unquestioned.

This is not a vague longing for the unattainable. Indeed, this very concept is regarded by an increasing number of thoughtful individuals as not only an approaching possibility but the necessary life-saving outcome of our current social situation.

Our world, contracted and transformed into a single highly complex organism by the marvelous progress achieved in the realm of physical science, by the worldwide expansion of commerce and industry, by the stunning advancements in lightning-speed communication, cries out for an end to fear-born violence.

One individual's efforts can influence the lives of thousands. For more information on preventing the characteristics of psychopathic behavior, or the alleviation of various aggravating factors, consult the following resources. All efforts are valuable. Perhaps someone reading this book will save a life, prevent an injury, cheer the downcast, free the captive, awaken the heedless, or bring new life to someone whose life seemed without hope or purpose. If so, Damon Wells and John Achord did not die in vain; rather, they sacrificed their lives for the future well-being of others.

Burl Barer
January 4, 2001

ACKNOWLEDGMENTS

This horrific story of homicide, lies, blame, betrayal, beatings, incest, molestation, and madness was adapted from three interrelated cases that implicated three perpetrators in two grisly murders. The criminal proceedings stretched over an entire year, generated over 700 pages of clerk's papers, over forty volumes of trial transcripts, and raised a significant issue concerning possible violation of the United States Constitution—an issue ultimately resolved by the Washington State Supreme Court.

Condensing such elaborate and complex events, issues, and interpersonal relationships into a comprehensible narrative would have been impossible were it not for the exemplary cooperation afforded the author by Detective Robert Yerbury of the Tacoma Police Department and others too numerous to mention individually, who appear within these pages. Suffice it to say, the help of the city of Tacoma, the Tacoma Police Department, Travis Webb, the Tacoma School District, the Pierce County Prosecutor's Office, the Washington State Supreme Court, the various defense attorneys who, at one time or another, represented the defendants, and the friends and relatives of primary characters is much appreciated. The history of the

Tacoma Police Department was provided by the city of Tacoma, and based upon original research by Officer Erik Timothy.

Conversations and statements recounted in this book are adaptations of such as recalled from memory. For purposes of clarity, concision, and continuity, statements, conversations, legal arguments, and certain testimonies necessitated condensation and emendation.

The families of Damon Wells and John Achord, for understandable reasons, decided not to participate in this project. The various siblings of Andrew Webb cooperated in varying degrees, the most forthcoming being Gail Webb. Her two former sisters-in-law Anne and Marty made significant contributions of their time, memories, and emotions. The author has made every effort to preserve accuracy of fact and portrayal. Any errors are unintentional. Karen Haas is the long-suffering editor who put up with my literary eccentricities, and did everything in her power to assure you a positive reading experience. Gratitude is also expressed to my kind, compassionate, and talented agent, the unflappable Charlotte Dial Breeze, and my entire extended family for their support and understanding.

UPDATE FOR 2012 EDITION

John Achord and Damon Wells are still mourned by those who knew and loved them, and Achord's relatives often send e-mails to me or post on my website.

In a heartfelt outpouring to me, Achord's niece, Angela, wrote:

> *Johnny Achord was my uncle. We used to have a lot of fun at family gatherings. I remember once we were all at uncle Dennis's house for a barbecue, and when it got dark, all us kids went outside in the front yard to play. It was okay because the fire department was next door, and the sky was full of stars. I asked what makes a star, and Johnny said, "That's for all you kids afraid of the dark. It is holes that are punched in the sky so it won't be so dark." I believed him.*
>
> *I remember the car accident where he was in the coma and woke up a different person. He loved his family again, and started going to church. Grandma Opal said she had her son back. I remember when he was still missing; my mom and grandma Opal hired a psychic to help find him. Mom told me the lady saw something in her vision but she didn't know what it meant: she saw a*

concrete wall with a red car parked next to it and some bucket next to the wall. This was before we knew about his head, or any bucket, or that he was dead.

Mom told me about how they got to go into the house on 43rd, and the carpet was pulled up and the hardwood floors had bloodstains on it, and all over the bathroom on the walls were tabs with writing on them. They were told there was more than just the two people's blood present. I have a box in my garage with the newspaper articles and his missing poster my mom sent to me during all this because I lived in California for a year while all this was happening.

I also remember my brother Mark was at that same Rush concert, and saw Johnny there after it was over. Mark asked him what he was doing afterward, and if he needed a ride home. He said that he was gonna go hang out with some people and he had a ride. I wish so much he had just taken the ride from Mark.

If John had taken the ride from Mark, Paul St. Pierre would have certainly killed someone else, instead. Out there, somewhere, is someone who, albeit indirectly, owes his or her life to John Achord.

Having served their sentences, Andrew Webb and Christopher St. Pierre attended their thirty-year high-school reunion. St. Pierre is now in a wheelchair; and the Andrew Webb of the twenty-first century is *not* the Andrew Webb who slashed Damon Wells's throat, helped bury John Achord, survived being shot by Paul St. Pierre, conned a prosecutor, and brought souls to Christ in Washington State Penitentiary.

Webb found Jesus in prison and that's exactly where

he left Him upon release. His commitment to Jesus lasted only as long as his incarceration. Andrew Webb abandoned Christianity and returned to his long-standing fascination with the gods of Norse legend. The post-prison Andrew Webb authored a well-reviewed and exceptionally scholarly book on North European native religion, and founded a nonprofit religious corporation to do "good works and community service."

"Andrew earned several college degrees while behind bars," his nephew, Travis, revealed. "He has degrees in anthropology, philosophy, religion, and business."

Once a recalcitrant troublemaker with a violent temper, Andrew Webb has conducted "Handling Hostility" seminars for numerous organizations, volunteered at homeless shelters, and counseled at-risk youth. All this is certainly preferable to home invasions and murder.

"Andrew is Andrew," Marty, his former sister-in-law, said. "He has always been an ace manipulator. Did you know that as soon as he was out of prison, his ex-wife started spending time with him and my ex? Maybe it's so his kids can have some sort of relationship with him, but as I don't want anything to do with Andrew or his brother, I don't see much of her anymore. That poor family is so screwed up. Hell, I was part of it. There were nine kids in the Webb family, and I don't think any of them could possibly have gone through what they went through without being damaged, to one extent or another. Some have owned their lives, and have reached out to others. One of them is just plain nuts, if you ask me. I could go down the list, but there is no sane reason to expect otherwise when you consider Mrs. Webb's upbringing and mental illness, and all the murders and madness that went on. That was so different from the St. Pierre family. Paul was never right in the head, and the booze and drugs made him worse, but Christopher was a real nice kid, who would never have gotten into any of that trouble were it not for his big brother."

Christopher St. Pierre, the sweet young boy with the promising future, the one who went to the police, the one who wanted nothing to do with the lifestyle of his deranged brother, spent the most time in prison. He is the one most fondly remembered by those who knew him in high school, and the author receives e-mails from those who, to this day, cannot believe that a good kid such as Christopher St. Pierre could have ever been involved with such heinous behavior.

Stacey Anderson, for example, remembers the St. Pierre brothers, and retains a marked affection for the younger Christopher. "I knew Chris St. Pierre, and fairly well," recalls Anderson. "I attended 6 years at Stewart Jr. High and Lincoln High Schools with him. It was at Stewart that we shared several classes and became buddies. Until reading this book, I had completely forgotten about his heart condition and surgery, and then as I read the memories came flooding back of that cute kid and him telling me about his heart and showing me his scars. And I also remember just loving his thick luxurious head of hair which at the base of his neck he had a small patch of blond, almost like a weird little hair birthmark, and couldn't resist playing with it and teasing him—he sat directly in front of me in Geography class. We had to be pulled in line quite often for talking in class. When they say this was a good kid—he was!"

According to Stacey Anderson, even as a 7th grader at the young age of 13, Christopher St. Pierre possessed a magnetic personality. "[Chris had] a dry, ironic wit that could send me into fits of laughter. And he remained to be just a sweetheart of a guy all through school to graduation . . . then, I lost contact with him. Then in June 1984, I will never forget my best girlfriend Kathy (who knew Chris from kindergarten on up, lived just up the street from the St. Pierres) calling me at about 11:30 a night with the shocking news on the front page of the Tribune. I remember literally having to stop her as she was reading and relaying the horrible details of what they had done so I could take a breath and try to absorb wha she was telling me. I remember saying, 'Stop it!! NC WAY!! How can this be??—NOT Chris!!' It was so mind boggling and heartbreaking for all of us who grew up with him to find out this was his fate. And the shocking nature of what they were involved in right at our back door was beyond comprehension."

Anderson lives only a few blocks away from the house on Pacific Avenue where much of the tragic story took place. "There is not a time we pass by Erickson's and tha house to this day that my mind does not go to the eerie and frightening visions of what went on there. It's never faded. Same thing when we have to go into Fife and pass over the Puyallup River Bridges that I don't think of wha happened to John Achord. As gruesome as it all is, ir the end it is just an absolutely tragic tale. And learning the slick moves made between the prosecutor and Andrew Webb is just revolting, making the story even more profound."

As for memories of Paul St. Pierre, he has taken or almost an iconic image of evil to kids from the old neighborhood. "There are tales told to this day," said Anderson, "of how screwed up Paul always seemed to be Tales of things he may have done or not have done . . Tales of how blood thirsty he seemed, and the joy he seemed to take in bragging about his guns and murder. One of our closest friends who was Paul's best friend during their Stewart Jr. High years was drinking with him one night at Ray & Gene's Tavern and then over at the house not long after the shooting at IGA, and he tells how Paul was just going on and on and on about it and couldn't let go of it, and it just freaked our friend out to no end. He says he made an excuse and a hasty exit and never went back. You can see the eeriness on him to this day when he recalls that night."

Detective Robert Yerbury's distinguished career with the Tacoma Police Department earned him a well-deserved national reputation as a living example of what it means to protect and to serve with honesty, integrity, and dedication. He found it of interest that Christopher St. Pierre was recently summoned to jury duty in Tacoma, and Yerbury still regards the Wells/Achord homicides as among the most disturbing and senseless killings he's encountered.

Prosecutor John Ladenburg, after a brutal sex crime occurred in Pierce County, created the nation's first "Sex Predator Notification Law," which was later approved by the U.S. Supreme Court. John was a major participant in the rewriting of Washington's sex predator laws. John's office wrote the nation's first sex predator "Civil Commitment" law.

Ladenburg was also one of the founding members of Safe Streets of Pierce County, a nationally recognized neighborhood watch program, where he served ten years on its board of directors. In an effort to treat addiction as a disease, he helped organize the first "Drug Court" in Washington State.

The Webb family fully cooperated in the preparation of *Head Shot,* and shared a lot of sensitive information, much of which was not used in the book because we saw no reason to bring up potentially embarrassing details of people's lives, especially when they were only linked to the story by virtue of birth. When recounting family stories, and the impact of various events, the family members didn't always agree, but there is nothing unusual about that. The degree of disunity and animosity manifested after the book came out is another matter. Some of them felt my portrayals were honest and accurate. Others found the honesty and accuracy humiliating.

I didn't create these lives, nor did I live them. None of us could take too much scrutiny, even though our worst indiscretions—short of murder—are worthy of no more than one night's dinner conversation in someone else's home. I write these books with the sincere hope that someone's life will be saved, or improved, or we will somehow learn more about how to keep people from manifesting sociopathic or psychopathic behavior.

Burl Barer
December 2011